always up to date

The law changes, but Nolo is on top of it! We offer several
ways to make sure you and your Nolo products are up to date:

1 **Nolo's Legal Updater**
We'll send you an email whenever a new edition of this book
is published! Sign up at **www.nolo.com/legalupdater**.

2 **Updates @ Nolo.com**
Check www.nolo.com/update to find recent changes
in the law that affect the current edition of your book.

3 **Nolo Customer Service**
To make sure that this edition of the book is the most
recent one, call us at **800-728-3555** and ask one of
our friendly customer service representatives.
Or find out at **www.nolo.com**.

please note

Table of Contents

Introduction

1 Choosing the Right Legal Structure for Your Business

The Different Ways of Doing Business 6

Comparing Business Entities at a Glance.. 23

2 How California Corporations Work

Types of California Corporations 30

Corporate Powers 34

Corporate People 35

How Many People May Organize the Corporation?........................... 42

Capitalization 43

Selling Stock 45

Paying Dividends 46

Dissolving a Corporation 47

Piercing the Corporate Veil 48

3 Issuing and Selling Stock

Securities Laws and Exemptions 52

The Limited Offering Exemption 53

Federal Securities Act.. 63

4 Corporate Taxation

California Taxes... 71

Federal Taxes... 72

S Corporation Tax Status.. 76

Corporate Accounting Periods and Tax Years..................................... 80

Tax Concerns When Stock Is Sold.. 81

Tax Treatment When an Existing Business Is Incorporated 83

Tax Treatment of Employee Compensation and Benefits................. 89

5 Steps to Form Your Corporation

Step 1. Choose a Corporate Name 93

Step 2. Prepare Your Articles of Incorporation 100

Step 3. Set Up a Corporate Records Book (Or Order a Corporate Kit) ... 107

Step 4. Prepare Your Bylaws 108

Step 5. Prepare Minutes of the First Meeting of the
Board of Directors 113

Step 6. Prepare Shareholder Representation Letters 129

Step 7. Prepare and File Notice of Stock Transaction Form 136

Step 8. Issue Shares of Stock 143

6 After You Incorporate

Postincorporation Paperwork and Tasks 161

Tax Forms—Federal 167

Tax Forms—State 170

Licenses and Permits 173

Workers' Compensation Insurance 173

Private Insurance Coverage 173

7 Lawyers and Accountants

Lawyers 176

Accountants and Tax Advisors 177

A Appendix A: How to Use the CD-ROM

Installing the Form Files Onto Your Computer 180

Using the Word Processing Files to Create Documents 181

Using California Secretary of State Forms 183

Files Included on the Forms CD 185

B Appendix B: Contact Information and Incorporation Forms

List of Forms

Name Availability Inquiry Letter

Name Reservation-Order Form

Articles of Incorporation

Cover Letter for Filing Articles

Bylaws

Waiver of Notice and Consent to Holding of First Meeting of Board of Directors

Minutes of First Meeting of the Board of Directors

Shareholder Representation Letter

Notice of Transaction Pursuant to Corporations Code Section 25102(f)

Bill of Sale for Assets of a Business

Receipt for Cash Payment

Form for Cancellation of Indebtedness

Bill of Sale for Items of Property

Receipt for Services Rendered

Share Register and Transfer Ledger

Stock Certificates

Index

Introduction

The start of the 21st century marks an exciting time for small business owners and other entrepreneurs. With the downsizing and privatizing of many of their larger, publicly held corporate counterparts, small businesses have an even more important role to play in revitalizing and expanding the U.S. economy and redefining the American workplace. Coupled with the fact that smart, hardworking small business owners often do extremely well financially, the trend toward small business formation continues to swell, as more and more escapees from the corporate treadmill step out on their own to form their own business.

Fortunately, it's not difficult to start a business in California, but you do need to make key decisions—one of which is to decide which legal structure your business will assume. One of the most popular choices is the small, privately held corporation. In large part, this is because the corporate form has a unique set of characteristics that can't be found all together in any of the other business forms.

One of the corporation's most appealing characteristics is the limited liability protection it provides to all business owners. The shareholders of a corporation are not personally liable for the debts or liabilities of the business—their personal assets are not at risk to satisfy business debts, losses, or legal liabilities, including lawsuits.

Limited liability protection is a tried-and-true feature of corporate law, well settled by years of court decisions. And the rare instances when a corporation may be denied limited liability are also clearly established. It usually happens when a small corporation owner commingles corporate and personal funds or otherwise blatantly disregards the fundamentals of doing business as a corporation.

A corporation is also a separate tax entity from its owners. In practice, this means you can often use your corporation to shelter business income instead of having to pay personal income taxes on all business profits each year (as you would with a sole proprietorship or partnership, where you and your business are treated as the same person for tax purposes). Of course, you have to pay corporate income taxes on money left in the corporation, but because initial corporate tax rates are lower than the marginal (top) tax rates most business owners pay, you often get an overall tax savings.

Organizing your business as a corporation is also a handy way to provide yourself and other employees with unique corporate perks such as stock options and stock bonuses. There is nothing more motivating to attract and keep talented corporate employees than sharing a piece of the corporate equity pie with them. For example, corporations often offer signing bonuses, consisting of shares of stock, to attract key people to work for them, and continue to offer stock option privileges to workers who are loyal over the long term.

Corporations are also a natural for raising private start-up and expansion capital from business associates, friends, and others. That's because the corporate form has a number of built-in activity layers—shareholders, directors, officers, and employees—that allow a number of people to easily and sensibly participate financially and managerially in its operations. Financial participation by others, which can take a variety of forms, is part and parcel of the corporate package. An investor can lend money to the corporation, or invest in its stock, and shares can be split into different classes and series to allow different types of investors to obtain different financial benefits and voices in corporate governance. For example, some investors may wish to purchase shares that give them preferential treatment in a distribution of corporate assets when the corporation is wound up; others may want first rights to the distribution of dividends when declared by the board. Still other investors can be granted special voting rights—for example, a right to appoint one of the members of the managing board of directors.

Another unique feature of the corporate form is its ability to help you raise capital and fund future growth by making a public stock offering of your shares. Yes, this is a big step and one that may be quite a way down the road for your business. It is nonetheless exciting to realize that as you move forward with your business, you may be able to set your corporate sights on a public offering of shares.

Of course, there are other considerations to weigh and balance when deciding whether to incorporate your small business. Certainly, one part of the process is to clearly understand the possible advantages of organizing your business in a different way. After study, you may even conclude that another business form, such as the limited liability company, is a better fit for your business. We explain and compare all business forms and the pros and cons associated with each in Chapter 1.

Who This Book Is For

This book provides the instructions and forms necessary to organize a privately held, profit-making (business) corporation in California. It also covers the legal, tax, and practical issues related to forming a corporation and can help you figure out whether incorporating is the best choice for your business.

You cannot use this book to form a California nonprofit or California professional corporation (one set up to practice law, medicine, accounting, and other special state-licensed professions). The special types of corporations needed for these purposes are summarized in Chapter 2.

RESOURCES

This book provides only a brief overview of ongoing corporate responsibilities and tasks. For more help with corporate formalities and paperwork, see *The Corporate Records Handbook,* by Anthony Mancuso (Nolo). It shows how to prepare standard minutes for director and shareholder meetings and includes sample resolutions for various legal, tax, financial, and business transactions that commonly occur during the life of a small, closely held corporation. If you want to incorporate in another state, see *Incorporate Your Business,* by Anthony Mancuso. This is Nolo's 50-state incorporation book.

Getting Professional Help

Lawyers can charge up to $2,000 (or more) to incorporate your business. To allow you to save money and spend it more usefully elsewhere, this book shows you how to prepare standardized incorporation forms. As you'll see, it's not hard and should require only a modest investment of time and energy. Beyond this, *How to Form Your Own California Corporation* is geared to help you ask and answer questions related to the specific needs of your corporate organization.

Even if you do most or all of the paperwork yourself, it often makes sense to consult an attorney to check over your incorporation papers. This is particularly true if you have special questions or needs—for example, you want to create a complicated stock structure. Or, you may have unanswered questions about the tax implications of operating your business as a corporation. You will want to discuss those questions with a tax advisor. To help you find the right person to answer legal and tax questions, we discuss how to locate a lawyer and tax advisor in Chapter 7.

How to Use This Book

Completing the articles of incorporation, bylaws, minutes, and other forms necessary to form a small California corporation isn't difficult. You will find the how-to-do-it material clearly set out in Chapter 5. But before you start filling in blanks, carefully read the material in the first four chapters.

This will give you background information about how corporations work and warns you about potential danger areas. Some of this information may be more technical than you need, especially if you are incorporating a small business. That's fine. You won't have lost much by reading it, and you will learn some things you need to know.

Finally, if you are confused by anything you read here, check with an expert. Remember, if you form your own corporation, the ultimate responsibility for making the right decisions is yours.

 RESOURCES

You can incorporate using a software program. *Incorporator Pro* (Nolo) is an interactive software program that lets you prepare, assemble, and print incorporation documents for any state on your computer. You can create your own articles, bylaws, organizational minutes, and other corporate documents easily and quickly.

CD-ROM For California Incorporators

Included at the back of this book is a CD-ROM containing files for the tear-out incorporation forms included in Appendix B. This CD-ROM can be used with both Windows and Macintosh computers. The files provided are in standard file formats that can be opened, completed, printed, and saved using a word processor. For details on how to use the CD and install the files, see the instructions in Appendix A.

Choosing the Right Legal Structure for Your Business

The Different Ways of Doing Business 6

    Sole Proprietorship 6

    Partnership 8

    The Limited Liability Company 12

    The Corporation 14

Comparing Business Entities at a Glance 23

To help you make sure that forming a California corporation is the best legal and tax choice for your business, this chapter compares the California corporation to other small business legal structures. Our discussion is based upon recent tax and legal rule changes, and—most significantly—the rise in use of the limited liability company. This relatively new business structure shares some of the traditional legal and tax qualities of the corporation, while at the same time offering some of the less formal attributes of a partnership. The corporation continues, however, to stand apart from all other business forms because of its built-in organizational structure and unique access to investment sources and capital markets. It also continues to uniquely answer to a need felt by many business owners for the formality of the corporate form, a quality not shared by the other business structures.

The Different Ways of Doing Business

There are several legal structures or forms you can use to operate a business, including a sole proprietorship, partnership, limited liability company, or corporation. Two of these structures have important variants: The partnership form has spawned the limited partnership and the registered limited liability partnership. And the corporation can be recognized, for tax purposes, as either the standard C corporation or an S corporation. In a standard C corporation, the corporation and its owners are treated as separate taxpaying entities, whereas in an S corporation, business income is passed through the corporate entity and the owners are taxed on their individual tax returns.

Often, business owners start with the simplest legal form, the sole proprietorship, then move on to a more complicated business structure as their business grows. Other businesspeople pick the legal structure they like best from the start, and let their business grow into it. Either way, choosing the legal structure for your business is an important decision you must make when starting a business. The analysis that follows, which includes examples of businesses that might sensibly choose each type of business structure, should help you make a good decision.

RESOURCES

For an expanded analysis and comparison of the different limited liability business forms, see *LLC or Corporation?* **by Anthony Mancuso (Nolo).**

Sole Proprietorship

A sole proprietorship is the legal name for a one-owner business.

Spousal Business. When a husband and wife carry on a business together and share in the profits and losses, generally they are considered co-owners of a partnership, not a sole proprietorship. There is an exception, however. A husband and wife who own an unincorporated business as community property in the community property states of Arizona, California, Idaho, Louisiana, Nevada, New Mexico, Texas, Washington, and Wisconsin, can choose to treat the business as a sole proprietorship. They do this by filing an IRS Form 1040, Schedule C, for the business, listing one of the spouses as the owner. Only the listed spouse pays income and self-employment taxes on the reported Schedule C net profits. Presumably, only the listed Schedule C owner-spouse will receive Social Security account earning credits for the Form SE taxes paid with the Form 1040 return. For this reason, some eligible spouses will decide not to make this Schedule C filing and will continue to file partnership tax returns for their jointly owned business. The IRS treats the filing of a Schedule C for a jointly owned spousal business as the conversion of a partnership to a sole proprietorship, which can have significant tax consequences. For more information, see "Forming a Partnership" in IRS Publication 541, and be sure to check with your tax advisor before deciding on the best way to own a business with your spouse.

Ease of Formation. The sole proprietorship is the easiest to establish legally. Just hang out your shingle or "Open for Business" sign, and you have established a sole proprietorship. Sure, there are other legal steps you may wish to take—such as registering a fictitious business name different from your own individual name by filing a "dba statement" with the county clerk—but these steps are not necessary to establish your business legally.

Personal Liability for Business Debts, Liabilities, and Taxes. In this simplest form of small business legal structures, the owner, who usually runs the business, is personally liable for its debts, taxes, and other liabilities. Also, if the owner hires employees, he or she is personally responsible for claims made against these employees acting within the course and scope of their employment.

Simple Tax Treatment. All business profits (and losses) are reported on the owner's personal income tax return each year (using Schedule C, *Profit or Loss From Business,* filed with the owner's 1040 federal income tax return). And this remains true even if a portion of this money is invested back in the business—that is, even if the owner doesn't pocket business profits for personal use.

Legal Life Same as Owner's. On the death of its owner, a sole proprietorship simply ends. The assets of the business normally pass under the terms of the deceased owner's will or trust, or by intestate succession (under the state's inheritance statutes) if there is no formal estate plan.

> **WARNING**
>
> **Don't let business assets get stuck in probate.** The court process necessary to probate a will can take more than a year. In the meantime, it may be difficult for the inheritors to operate or sell the business or its assets. Often, the best way to avoid having a probate court involved in business operations is for the owner to transfer the assets of the business into a living trust during his or her lifetime; this permits business assets to be transferred to inheritors promptly on the death of the business owner, free of probate. For detailed information on estate planning, including whether or not it makes sense to create a living trust, see *Plan Your Estate,* by Denis Clifford and Cora Jordan (Nolo).

Sole Proprietorships in Action. Many one-owner or spouse-owned businesses start small with very little advance planning or procedural red tape. Celia Wong is a good example—Celia is a graphic artist with a full-time salaried job for a local book publishing company. In her spare time she takes on extra work using her home computer to produce audio cassette and CD jacket cover art for musicians. These jobs are usually commissioned on a handshake or phone call. Without thinking much about it, Celia has started her own sole proprietorship business. Celia should include a Schedule C in her yearly federal 1040 individual tax return, showing the net profits (profits minus expenses) or losses of her sole proprietorship. Celia is responsible for paying income taxes on profits, plus self-employment (Social Security) taxes based on her sole proprietorship income (IRS Form SE is used to compute self-employment taxes; Celia attaches it to her 1040 income tax return).

If Celia has any business debts (she usually owes on a charge account at a local art supply house), or a disgruntled client successfully sues her in small claims court for failing to deliver prepaid art work, Celia is personally liable to pay this money. In other words, she can't simply fold up Wong Designs and walk away from her debts claiming that they are the legal responsibility of her business only.

> ⚠️ **WARNING**
>
> **Put some profits aside to buy business insurance.** Once Celia begins to make enough money, she should consider taking out a commercial liability insurance policy to cover legal claims against her business. While insurance normally won't protect you from business mistakes (like performing incomplete or late work or failing to pay bills), it can cover many risks including slip-and-fall lawsuits, damage to your or a client's property, or fire, theft, and other casualties that might occur in a home-based business.

Running the business as an informal sole proprietorship serves Celia's needs for the present. Assuming her small business succeeds, she will eventually need to put it on a more formal footing by establishing a separate business checking account, possibly coming up with a fancier name and registering it as a dba with the county clerk. If she hires employees, she will need to obtain a federal Employer Identification Number (EIN) from the IRS. She may also feel ready to renovate her house to separate her office space from her living quarters (this can also help make the portion of the mortgage or rent paid for the office deductible as a business expense on her Schedule C).

Celia can do all of this and still keep her sole proprietorship legal status. Unless her business grows significantly or she takes on work that puts her at a much higher risk of being sued—and therefore being held personally liable for business debts—it makes sense for her to continue to operate her business as a sole proprietorship.

> **RESOURCES**
>
> **A great source of practical information on how to start and operate a small sole proprietorship is *Small Time Operator*, by Bernard Kamoroff (Bell Springs Press).** Also, see *Tax Savvy for Small Business*, by Frederick W. Daily (Nolo), a small business guide to taxes, which includes a full discussion of setting up and deducting the expenses of a home-based business.

Partnership

A partnership is simply an enterprise in which two or more co-owners agree to share in the profits of a business activity. No written partnership agreement is necessary. If two people go into business together, and do not incorporate or form a limited liability company, they automatically establish a legal partnership. Partnerships are governed by each state's partnership law. But since all states have adopted a version of the Uniform Partnership Act, laws are very similar throughout the U.S. Mostly, these laws contain basic rules that provide for an equal division of profits and losses among partners and establish the partners' legal relationship with one another. These rules are not mandatory in most cases, and you can (and should) spell out your own rules for dividing profits and losses and operating your partnership in a written partnership agreement. If you don't prepare your own partnership agreement, all provisions of California's partnership law apply to your partnership.

California Limited Partnerships

Most smaller partnerships are general partnerships—this means that all owners agree to manage the partnership together, and each partner is personally liable for debts of the partnership. However, there are two other fairly common types of partnerships: limited partnerships and registered limited liability partnerships (RLLPs). Each of these is quite different from a general partnership.

The Limited Partnership. The limited partnership structure is used when one or more of the partners are passive investors (called "limited partners") and another partner (called a "general partner") runs the partnership. A certificate of limited partnership is filed with the secretary of state to form a limited partnership, and a filing fee must be paid. The advantage of a limited partnership is that, unlike a general partnership where all partners are personally liable for business debts and liabilities, a limited partner is allowed to invest in a partnership without the risk of incurring personal liability for the debts of the business. If the business fails, all that the limited partner can lose is his or her capital investment—the amount of money or the property paid for an interest in the business. However, in exchange for this big advantage, the limited partner normally is not allowed to participate in the management or control of the partnership. To do so means losing limited liability status and being held personally liable for partnership debts, claims, and other obligations.

Typically, a limited partnership has a number of limited partner investors and one general partner (there can be more, but there must be at least one) who is responsible for partnership management and is personally liable for its debts and other liabilities.

The Registered Limited Liability Partnership. The registered limited liability partnership (RLLP) is a special legal structure designed for persons who form a partnership in California to perform the licensed professional services of attorneys, accountants, or architects. Architects can form a California RLLP only until January 1, 2012. An RLLP is formed by filing a registration of limited liability partnership form with the California Secretary of State.

The point of an RLLP is to relieve professional partners from personal liability for debts, contracts, and claims against the partnership, including claims against a nonparticipating partner for professional malpractice by another partner. However, a professional in an RLLP remains personally liable for his or her own professional malpractice.

EXAMPLE: Martha and Veronica have a two-person accounting partnership, registered as an RLLP. Each has her own clients. If Martha loses a malpractice lawsuit, and Veronica did not participate in providing services to that client, Veronica should not be held personally liable for the judgment. If Martha's malpractice insurance and partnership assets are not sufficient to pay the judgment, Martha's personal assets, but not Veronica's, are subject to seizure to satisfy the unrecovered judgment. If they had an accounting general partnership practice that was not registered as an RLLP, both Martha and Veronica could be held personally liable for either CPA's individual malpractice.

Many professionals cannot form an LLC in California. They can obtain similar legal liability protection by forming a California professional corporation. Ask your state licensing board for additional information.

A general partnership has the following characteristics:

Each partner has personal liability. Like the owner of a sole proprietorship, each partner is personally liable for the debts and taxes of the partnership. In other words, if the partnership assets and insurance are insufficient to satisfy a creditor's claim or legal judgment, the partners' personal assets can be attached and sold to pay the debt.

The act or signature of each partner can bind the partnership. Each partner is an agent for the partnership and can individually hire employees, borrow money, sign contracts, and perform any act necessary to the operation of the business. All partners are personally liable for these debts and obligations. This rule makes it essential that the partners trust each other to act in the best interests of the partnership and each of the other partners.

Partners report and pay individual income taxes on profits. A partnership files a yearly IRS Form 1065, *U.S. Partnership Return of Income*, which includes a schedule showing the allocation of profits, losses, and other tax items to all partners (Schedule K). The partnership must mail individual schedules (Schedule K-1s) to each partner at the end of each year, showing the items of income, loss, credits, and deductions allocated to each partner. When a partner files an individual income tax return, she reports her allocated share of partnership profits (taken from the partner's Schedule K-1), and pays individual income taxes on these profits. As with the sole proprietorship, partners owe tax on business profits even if they are plowed back into the business.

Partnership dissolves when a partner leaves. Legally, when a partner ceases to be associated with carrying on the business of the partnership (when he or she withdraws or dies), the partnership is dissolved. However, a properly written partnership agreement provides in

---

Partnerships Can Choose To Be Taxed as Corporations

Unincorporated co-owned businesses, including partnerships and limited liability companies (discussed below), can choose to be taxed as corporations by filing IRS Form 8832, *Entity Classification Election*. Most smaller partnerships will not wish to make this election, preferring instead to have profits divided among the partners and then taxed on their individual tax returns. But this is not always true. For example, some partnerships—especially those that want to reinvest profits in expanding the business—may prefer to keep profits in the business, and have them taxed to the business at the lower initial corporate tax rates. Your tax advisor can tell you if this tax strategy makes sense for your business. (See Chapter 7.)

---

advance for these eventualities, and allows for the continuation of the partnership by permitting the remaining partners to buy out the interest of the departing or deceased partner. Of course, if one person in a two-partner business leaves or dies, the partnership is legally dissolved—you need at least two people to have a partnership.

WARNING

Watch out for a partnership tax termination. A partnership terminates for tax purposes if 50% or more of the interest in the partnership's capital and profits are sold or exchanged within a 12-month period. Under these circumstances, the partnership might continue legally under the terms of the partnership agreement, but would terminate for tax purposes. Upon the deemed termination of partnership, each partner could owe significant income taxes. (I.R.C. § 708(b).)

Why You Need a Written Partnership Agreement

Although it's possible to start a partnership with a verbal agreement—or even with no stated agreement at all—there are drawbacks to taking this casual approach. The most obvious problem is that a verbal agreement can be remembered and interpreted differently by different partners. And having no stated agreement at all almost always means trouble. Also, if you don't write out how you want your partnership to be operated, you lose a great deal of flexibility. Instead of being able to make your own rules in a number of key areas—for example, how partnership profits and losses are divided among the partners—California state partnership law will automatically come into play. These state-based rules may not be to your liking (for example, state law generally calls for an equal division of profits and losses regardless of partners' capital contributions).

Another reason why you should prepare and sign a written partnership agreement is to avoid disputes over what happens when a partner wants to leave the business. Here are just a few of the difficult questions that can arise if a partner wants to leave the partnership:

- If the remaining partners want to buy the departing partner out, how will the interest be valued?

- If you agree on value, how will the departing partner be paid—in a lump sum or installments? If in installments, how big will the down payment be; how many years will it take for the balance to be paid; and how much interest will be charged?

- What happens if none of the remaining partners wants to buy the departing partner's interest? Will your partnership dissolve? If so, can some of the partners form a new partnership to continue the partnership business? Who gets to use the dissolved partnership's name and client or customer list?

California law does not necessarily provide helpful answers to these questions, which means that if you don't have a written partnership agreement, you may face a long legal battle with a partner who decides to call it quits. To avoid these and other problems, a basic partnership agreement should, at a minimum, spell out how much interest each partner has in the partnership, how profits and losses will be split up between or among the partners, and how any buyout or transfer of a partner's interest will be valued and handled. The aftermath of the dissolution of the partnership also should be considered, and rules set out for a continuance of the partnership's business by ex-partners if desired.

RESOURCES

For a much more thorough look at the legal and tax characteristics of partnerships, and for a clause-by-clause approach to preparing a partnership agreement, see *The Partnership Book*, by Denis Clifford and Ralph Warner (Nolo).

Partnerships in action. George and Tamatha are good friends who have been working together in a rented warehouse space where they share a kiln used to make blown glass pieces. They recently collaborated on the design and production of a batch of hand-blown halogen light fixtures, which immediately become popular with local lighting vendors. Believing that they can streamline the production of these custom pieces, they plan to solicit and fill larger orders with retailers, and look into wholesale distribution. They shake hands on their new venture, which they name "Halo Light Sculptures." Although they obtain a business license and file a dba statement with the county clerk showing that they are working together as "Halo Light Sculptures," they don't bother to write up a partnership agreement. Their only agreement is a verbal one to equally share in the work of making the glass pieces and splitting expenses and any profits that result.

This type of informal arrangement can make sense for the very early days of a co-owned business, where the owners, like George and Tamatha, wish to split work, expenses, profits, and losses equally. However, for the reasons mentioned earlier, from the moment the business looks like it has long-term potential, the partners should prepare and sign a written partnership agreement. Furthermore, if either partner is worried about personal liability for business debts or the possibility of lawsuits by purchasers of the fixtures, then forming a limited liability company or a corporation probably would be a better business choice.

The Limited Liability Company

The limited liability company (LLC) is the new kid on the block of business organizations. It has become popular with many small business owners, in part because it was custom-designed by state legislatures to overcome particular limitations of each of the other business forms, including the corporation. Essentially, the LLC is a legal ownership structure that allows owners to pay business taxes on their individual income tax returns like partners (or, for a one-person LLC, like a sole proprietorship), but also gives the owners the legal protection of personal limited liability for business debts and judgments as if they had formed a corporation. Or, put another way, with an LLC you can simultaneously achieve the twin goals of one-level taxation of business profits and limited personal liability for business debts.

 WARNING

Licensed professionals can't form an LLC in California. Only businesses that render services under nonprofessional, occupational licenses can form an LLC in California. Professionals who must form a professional corporation if they incorporate (doctors, architects, lawyers, pharmacists, and so on) are the same group of professionals who can't form an LLC in the state. There may be others, however, who fall into this group. If you provide any type of licensed service that might be considered a professional service, contact your state licensing board and ask if you are allowed to form an LLC in California before getting started on the process.

Here are some of the most important LLC characteristics:

Limited liability. The owners (members) of an LLC are not personally responsible for the LLC's debts and other liabilities. Specifically, members are not personally liable for any debt, obligation, or liability of the LLC, whether that liability or obligation comes from a contract dispute, tort (injury to other persons or damage to their property), or any other type of claim. This type of sweeping personal legal liability protection is the same as that enjoyed by shareholders of a California corporation. In short, the LLC and the corporation offer the same level of limited personal liability protection.

Pass-through taxation. Federal tax law normally treats an LLC like a partnership, unless the LLC elects to be taxed as a corporation (by filing IRS Form 8832). The California Franchise Tax Board treats a California LLC for state income tax purposes as it is treated for federal income tax purposes. An LLC with an annual gross income of $250,000 or more must pay an additional annual fee, based upon a graduated fee schedule that is subject to adjustment from year to year.

If an LLC is treated as a partnership at the federal and state levels, it files a standard partnership tax return (IRS Form 1065, Schedules K and K-1) with the IRS (and Form 568 with the state). The LLC members (owners) pay taxes on their share of LLC profits on their individual federal and state income tax returns. An LLC that elects corporate tax treatment files federal and state corporate income tax returns.

Ownership requirements. You can form an LLC with only one owner (member). Members need not be residents of California, or even the U.S. for that matter. Other business entities, such as a corporation or another LLC, can be LLC owners.

Management flexibility. LLCs are normally managed by all the owners (members)—this is known as member-management. But state law also allows for management by one or more specially appointed managers (who may be members or nonmembers). Not surprisingly, this arrangement is known as manager-management. In other words, an LLC can appoint one or more of its members, one of its CEOs, or even a person contracted from outside the LLC, to manage its affairs. This setup makes sense if one person wishes to assume full-time control of the LLC while the other owners act as passive investors in the enterprise.

Formation requirements. Like a corporation, LLCs require paperwork to get going. Articles of organization must be filed with the California Secretary of State. And if the LLC is to maintain a business presence in another state, such as a branch office, it also must file registration or qualification papers with the other state's secretary of state or department of state. California's LLC formation fee is $70.

California LLCs, like California corporations and limited partnerships, must pay an annual minimum $800 tax to the Franchise Tax Board. There is an additional LLC annual fee, with a tiered rate structure, for LLCs with annual gross incomes of $250,000 or more. The additional fee may be anywhere from $900 to $11,790.

WARNING

Add in the cost of goods sold when computing annual gross income. A California LLC engaged in an active trade or business must include its cost of goods sold. (Typically, the cost of goods sold is subtracted from gross income.) This means that even unprofitable LLCs can be subject to the annual LLC fee. Ask your tax advisor for more information.

Like a partnership, an LLC should prepare an operating agreement to spell out how the LLC will be owned, how profits and losses will be divided, how departing or deceased members will be bought out, and other essential ownership details. However, preparation of an LLC operating agreement is not legally required. If it is not prepared, the default provisions of California's LLC Act will apply to the operation of the LLC. Because LLC owners will want to control exactly how profits and losses are apportioned among the members rather than following the default rules set out in the LLC Act, preparing an LLC operating agreement is a practical necessity.

RESOURCES

See *Form Your Own Limited Liability Company*, by Anthony Mancuso (Nolo). It contains instructions on how to form a California LLC, prepare an operating agreement (member- and manager-managed agreements are included), and handle all other LLC formation formalities.

LLCs in action. Under the name "Aunt Jessica's Floral Arrangements," Barry and Sam jointly own and run a flower shop that specializes in unique flower arrangements (the name stems from the fact that Barry used to work for his aunt Jessica, who taught him the ropes of floral bouquet design). Lately, business has been particularly rosy, and the two men plan to sign a long-term contract with a flower importer to supply them with larger quantities of seasonal flowers. Once they receive the additional flowers, they will be able to create more floral pieces and wholesale them to a wider market. Both men are aware that they will encounter more risks as their business grows. Accordingly, they decide to protect their personal assets from business risks by converting their partnership to an LLC. They could accomplish the same result by incorporating, but they prefer the simplicity of paying taxes on their business income on their individual income tax returns (rather than reporting profits and paying business taxes on a separate corporate income tax return). They also realize that they can convert their LLC to a corporation later to obtain the advantage of lower corporate tax rates on money kept in the flower business or, even more simply, make an IRS election to have their LLC taxed as a corporation without changing its legal structure.

The Corporation

Now let's look at the basic attributes of the corporation, the type of business organization this book shows you how to organize.

A corporation is a statutory creature, created and regulated by state law. In short, if you want the privilege—as the courts call it—of turning your business enterprise into a California corporation, you must follow the requirements of the California Corporations Code.

What sets the corporation apart from all other types of businesses is that it is a legal entity separate from any of the people who own, control, manage, or operate it. The state corporation and federal and state tax laws view the corporation as a legal person—it can enter into contracts, incur debts, and pay taxes separately from its owners.

Limited Personal Liability

Like the owners (members) of an LLC, the owners (shareholders) of a corporation are not personally liable for the corporation's business debts, claims, or other liabilities. This means that a person who invests in a corporation (a shareholder) normally only stands to lose the amount of money or the value of the property which he or she has paid for its stock. As a result, if the corporation does not succeed and cannot pay its debts or other financial obligations, creditors cannot seize or sell the corporate investor's home, car, or other personal assets.

EXAMPLE:

Rackafrax Dry Cleaners, Inc., a California corporation, has several bad years in a row. When it finally files for bankruptcy it owes $50,000 to a number of suppliers and $80,000 as a result of a lawsuit for uninsured losses stemming from a fire. Stock in Rackafrax is owned by Harry Rack, Edith Frax, and John Quincy Taft. Their personal assets cannot be taken to pay the money Rackafrax owes.

Exceptions to the Rule of Personal Limited Liability Protection

In some situations, corporate directors, officers, and shareholders of a corporation can be held responsible for debts owed by their corporation. Here are a few of the most common exceptions to the rule of limited personal liability (these exceptions also apply to other limited liability business structures, such as the LLC):

Personal guarantees. When a bank or other lender makes a loan to a small corporation, particularly a newly formed one, it often requires that the people who own the corporation agree to repay it from their personal assets should the corporation default on the loan. Shareholders may even have to pledge equity in a house or other personal assets as security for repayment of the debt. Of course, shareholders can just say no—but if they do, their corporation may not qualify for the loan.

Federal and state taxes. If a corporation fails to pay income, payroll, or other taxes, the IRS and the California Franchise Tax Board are likely to attempt to recover the unpaid taxes from responsible employees—a category that often includes the principal directors, officers, and shareholders of a small corporation.

Unlawful or unauthorized transactions. If you use the corporation as a device to defraud third parties, or if you deliberately make a decision (or fail to make one) that results in physical harm to others or their property (such as failing to maintain premises or a work site properly, manufacturing unsafe products, or causing environmental pollution), a court may pierce the corporate veil and hold the shareholders of a small corporation individually liable for damages (monetary losses) caused to others.

Fortunately, most of the problem areas where you might be held personally liable for corporate obligations can be avoided by following a few commonsense rules (rules you'll probably adhere to anyway). First, don't do anything that is dishonest or illegal. Second, make sure your corporation does the same, by having it obtain necessary permits, licenses, or clearances for its business operations. Third, pay employee wages and withhold and pay corporate income and payroll taxes on time. Fourth, don't personally obligate yourself to repay corporate debts or obligations unless you fully understand and accept the consequences.

Corporate Tax Treatment

Let's now look at a few of the most important tax characteristics of the corporation. We'll start with the dual level of taxation built into the corporate business structure.

Dual Taxation and Income Splitting

The corporation is a taxpayer, with its own income tax rates and tax returns separate from the tax rates and tax returns of its owners. This separate layer of taxation allows corporate profits to be kept in the business and taxed at the initial corporate tax rates, which are generally lower than the marginal (top) tax rates of the corporation's owners. The result of this type of business income splitting between the corporation and its owners can result in an overall tax savings for the owners (compared to pass-through taxation of all business profits to the owners, which is the standard tax treatment of sole proprietorships, partnerships, and LLCs).

EXAMPLE:

Jeff and Sally own and work for their own two-person corporation, Hair Looms, Inc., a mail order synthetic wig supply business that is starting to enjoy popularity with overseas purchasers. To keep pace with the surge in orders, they need to expand by reinvesting a portion of their profits back in the business. Since Hair Looms is incorporated, only the portion of the profits paid to Jeff and Sally as salary is reported and taxed to them on their individual tax returns—let's assume their marginal (top) tax rate is over 30%. By contrast, the first $50,000 in profits left in the business for expansion is reported on Hair Looms' corporate income tax return and taxed at the lowest corporate tax rate of only 15%. The next $25,000 is taxed at 25%.

TIP

Corporate tax rates max out at 34% for most corporations. Even though corporate tax rates can go up to 39%, all corporate net income below $10 million is subject to an effective flat tax rate of 34%. (See Chapter 4.)

TIP

LLCs and partnerships can elect corporate tax treatment. Dual taxation and income splitting are no longer unique to corporations. Partnerships and LLCs can elect to be taxed as corporations if they wish to keep money in the business and have it taxed at corporate rates. (See "Partnerships Can Choose to Be Taxed As Corporations," above.)

Corporations Can Elect Pass-Through Taxation of Profits

Just as partnerships and LLCs have the ability to request corporate tax treatment, corporations can change their tax treatment to the type of pass-through taxation that normally applies to partnerships and LLCs. A corporation accomplishes this by making an S corporation tax election with the IRS.

TIP

When just starting out, form an LLC instead. An LLC, like an S corporation, gives its owners pass-through taxation of business profits plus limited personal liability for business debts. It also is more flexible than an S corporation for technical reasons (see "LLCs and Partnerships Have Technical Tax Advantages Over S Corporations," below). Therefore, it usually makes more sense to form an LLC when you are just starting to organize your business.

How Small Corporations Avoid Double Taxation of Corporate Profits

What about the old bugaboo of corporate double taxation? Most people have heard that corporate income is taxed twice: once at the corporate level and again when it is paid out to shareholders in the form of dividends. In theory, the Internal Revenue Code says that most corporations are treated this way (except S corporations, whose profits automatically pass to shareholders each year—see below). In practice, however, double taxation seldom occurs in the context of the small business corporation. The reason is simple: Employee-owners don't pay themselves dividends, which are taxed at the corporate rate when earned and at the shareholder level when paid to them. Instead, the shareholders, who usually work for their corporation, pay themselves salaries and bonuses, which are deducted from the profits of the corporate business as ordinary and necessary business expenses. The result is that profits paid out in salary and other forms of employee compensation to the owner-employees of a small corporation are taxed only once, at the individual level. In other words, as long as you work for your corporation, even in a part-time or consulting capacity, you can pay out business profits to yourself as reasonable compensation. Your corporation won't have to pay taxes on these profits.

Furthermore, because most individuals now pay a 15% tax rate on dividends, the double tax associated with dividends is not as severe as it once was. And, dividends are not subject to Social Security tax, so business owners may realize a small tax savings by choosing to have part of their corporate salaries paid out to them as dividends.

If you are already doing business as a corporation, switching over to S corporation tax status—by making an S corporation tax election—makes sense if you wish to keep your corporation intact but want pass-through treatment of profits and losses to save tax dollars. This might be true, for example, for a corporation that no longer wishes to keep profits in the business, but can't pay all of them out to shareholders as salaries (if some shareholders don't work for the corporation or if the payout of all profits as salaries would render them excessive and subject to IRS attack, for example). It also may be true if a corporation begins to lose money and the owners want to deduct these losses on their individual income tax returns to offset other income (a number of technical hurdles must be overcome for this pass-through of losses in an S corporation to work—see "LLCs and Partnerships Have Technical Tax Advantages Over S Corporations," below, for more information).

The only other way an existing corporation can get the limited liability protection and pass-through tax treatment of the S corporation is to dissolve, then reorganize as an LLC. This can be costly from a legal and tax perspective and a lot more trouble than simply electing S corporation tax status.

U.S. corporations with 100 or fewer shareholders who are U.S. citizens or residents can elect federal S corporation tax treatment by filing IRS Form 2553. Once an S corporation election is made with the IRS, the corporation is automatically treated as a California S corporation. It can opt out of S corporation treatment by filing FTB Form 3560 with the California Franchise Tax Board. An S corporation has all its profits, losses, credits, and deductions passed through to its shareholders, who report these items on their individual tax returns. In effect, this allows

LLCs and Partnerships Have Technical Tax Advantages Over S Corporations

LLC owners and partners can split profits disproportionately to their ownership interests in the business (these are called special allocations of profits and losses under the tax code); S corporation shareholders can't. Also, the amount of corporate losses that may be passed through to S corporation shareholders is limited to the total of each shareholder's basis in his or her stock, plus amounts loaned personally by each shareholder to the corporation. (The basis is the amount paid for stock plus and minus adjustments during the life of the corporation.) Losses allocated to a shareholder that exceed these limits can be carried forward and deducted in future tax years if the shareholder then qualifies to deduct the losses. In contrast, LLC owners and partners may be able to personally deduct more business losses on their tax returns in a given year than S corporation shareholders. The reason is that both LLC members and partners get to count their pro-rata share of all money borrowed by the business, not just loans personally made by the member or partner, in computing how much of any loss allocated to them by the business they can deduct in a given year on their individual income tax returns. Ask your tax advisor for more information.

the corporation to sidestep federal corporate income taxes on business profits, passing the profits (and the taxes that go with them) along to the shareholders. Each S corporation shareholder is allocated a portion of the corporation's profits and losses according to her percentage of stock ownership in the corporation (a 50% shareholder reports and pays individual income taxes on 50% of the corporation's annual profits, for example).

These profits are allocated to the shareholders whether the profits are actually paid to them or kept in the corporation.

EXAMPLE:

Fred's Furniture and Appliance was incorporated during a period of fast business growth, when Fred brought in two relatives as investors and moved his business to a larger storefront in an upscale neighborhood. He chose the corporate form to limit his and the investors' personal liability and to accommodate his investors by issuing them shares in his business. With the business growing fast, the investors wanted to see some return of profits. Fred elects S corporation tax treatment. Net profits of the business pass through to the S shareholders directly and are taxed on their individual income tax returns. This meets the investors' needs and avoids the double tax that would have been paid if profits were distributed to the investors as dividends. This also helps Fred, since he can keep his corporate salary reasonably low and still get money out of his corporation. Also, S corporation profits allocated to shareholders, unlike salaries, are not subject to self-employment taxes. (See Chapter 4.) This means Fred ends up with more after-tax money in his pocket.

Tax Consequences of Corporate Dissolution

You should consider an additional tax aspect of forming a corporation before deciding to incorporate—the tax consequences of ending the corporation when it is dissolved or sold. The general rule is that when a corporation is sold or dissolved, both the corporation and its shareholders have to pay tax on appreciated corporate assets. However, there are ways to minimize this double tax, if you plan in advance. The primary strategy is to arrange for a sale of stock (not assets) when the corporation is sold. (Best of all is a tax-free sale of stock/assets as part of a tax-free reorganization that is a merger with an acquiring corporation.) Check with your tax advisor on the eventual tax ramifications of dissolving your corporation right from the start. One of the most important pre-incorporation services your tax advisor can provide is to make sure that the future dissolution or sale of your corporation will not result in an unexpectedly hefty tax bill for your corporation and its owners.

Owners Who Work in the Business Are Treated as Employees

A potential benefit of the corporate structure is that business owners who also work in the business become employees. This means that you, in your role as an employee, become eligible for tax-deductible corporate fringe benefits, some of which you would not qualify for as a sole proprietor, partner, or an LLC member.

For example, Henry incorporates his California sole proprietorship, "Big Sur Shoes, Inc." He now works as a full-time corporate employee and is entitled to tax-deductible corporate perks, such as reimbursement for medical expenses and $50,000 worth of group term life insurance paid for by his business. If he gave himself these perks in his unincorporated business, his business could deduct them as ordinary and necessary business expenses, but he would have to report them as income and pay income taxes on them. Corporation employees also receive special tax benefits if they are issued qualified incentive stock options, restricted stock, and other forms of equity-sharing participation interests unique to corporations. (See Chapter 4 for more on corporate fringe and equity benefits.)

Built-In Organizational Structure

Perhaps the most unique benefit of forming a corporation is the ability to divide management, executive decision making, and ownership into separate areas of corporate activity. This separation is achieved automatically because of the separate legal roles which reside in the corporate form: the roles of directors (managers), executives (officers), and owners (shareholders). Unlike partnerships and LLCs, the corporate structure comes ready-made with a built-in separation of these three roles, each with its own legal authority, rules, and ability to participate in corporate income and profits.

EXAMPLE 1:

Myra, Danielle, and Rocco form their own three-person corporation, Skate City, Incorporated, a skate and bike shop in Venice Beach, Los Angeles. Storefront access to the Venice Beach rollerblade, skating, and bike path makes it popular with local rollerbladers and bicyclists. Needing more cash, the three approach relatives for investment capital. Rocco's brother, Tony, and Danielle's sister, Collette, chip in $10,000 each in return for shares in the business. Myra's Aunt Kate lends the corporation $25,000 in return for an interest-only promissory note, with the principal amount to be repaid at the end of five years. Here's how the management, executive, and financial structure of the corporation breaks down:

Board of Directors. The management team, which meets once each quarter to analyze and project financial performance and review store operations, consists of the three founders, Myra, Danielle, and Rocco, and one of the other three investors. The investor board position is a one-year rotating seat. This year Tony has the investor board seat; next year, Collette; the third year, Aunt Kate. This pattern repeats every three years. Directors have one vote apiece, regardless of share ownership—this means the founders can always outvote the investor vote on the board, but this also guarantees that each of the investors will have an opportunity to hear board discussions and give input on major management decisions.

Executive Team. The officers or executive team charged with overseeing day-to-day business; supervising employees; keeping track of ordering, inventory, and sales activities; and generally putting into practice the goals set by the board are Myra (president) and Danielle (vice president). Rocco fills the remaining officer positions of secretary/treasurer of the corporation, but this is a part-time administrative task only. Rocco's real vocation—or avocation—is blading along the beach and training to be a professional, touring rollerblader with his own corporate sponsor (maybe Skate City if profits continue to roll in).

Participation in Profits. Corporate net profits are used to stock inventory, pay rent on the West End storefront, and pay all the other usual and customary expenses of doing business. The two full-time executives, Myra and Danielle, get a corporate salary, plus a year-end bonus when profits are good. Rocco gets a small stipend (hourly pay) for his part-time work. Otherwise, he and the two investor shareholders are simply sitting on their shares. Skate City is not in a position yet to pay dividends—all excess profits of the corporation are used to continue expanding the store's product lines and add a new service facility at the back of the store. Even if dividends are never paid, all three know that their stock will be worth a good deal if the business is successful. They can cash in their shares when the business sells or when they decide to sell their shares back to the corporation (or, who knows, if Skate City goes public someday). Aunt Kate, the most conservative of the investment group, will look to ongoing interest payments as her share in corporate profits, getting her capital back when the principal amount of her loan is repaid.

As you can see from this example, the mechanisms to put this custom-tailored management, executive, and investment structure into place are built into the Skate City corporation. To erect it, all that is needed is to fill in a few blanks on standard incorporation forms, including stock certificates, and prepare a standard promissory note. To duplicate this structure as a partnership or LLC would require a specially drafted partnership or LLC operating agreement with custom language and plenty of review by the founders and investment group (and, no doubt, their lawyers). The corporate form is designed to handle this division of management, day-to-day responsibilities, and investment with little extra time, trouble, or expense.

There is a flip side to this division of corporate positions and participation in profits. Some business people—particularly those who run a business by themselves or who prefer to run a co-owned business informally—feel that the extra levels of corporate operation and paperwork are a nuisance. That's why incorporating may be a bit of an overload for small start-up companies—they may be better and more comfortably served by the less formal business structures of the sole proprietorship or partnership, or, if limited legal liability is an overriding concern, by the LLC legal structure.

But for many business owners, the ability to separate out corporate management and oversight from day-to-day executive decisions, plus the ability to treat people who invest in the business strictly in their capacities as co-owners

and not as active day-to-day participants, makes the corporate model extremely attractive. The fact that there are legal differences among directors, officers, and shareholders becomes particularly attractive as a business grows and people from outside the initial circle of incorporators become involved in the business (as investors, lenders, or even public shareholders).

EXAMPLE 2:

Leila runs a lunch counter business that provides her both a decent income and an escape from the cubicled office environment in which she was once unhappily ensconced. Business has been slow, but Leila has a new idea to give the business more appeal, as well as make it more fun for her. She changes the decor to reflect a tropical motif, installs a salt water aquarium facing the lunch counter, adds coral reef (metal halide) lighting and light-reflective wall paneling, and renames the business the "The Tide Pool." The standard lunch counter fare is augmented with a special bouillabaisse soup entrée and a selection of organic salads and fruit juice drinks, and a seafood and sushi dinner menu is added to cater to the after-work crowd. Leila has her hands full, doing most of the remodeling work herself and preparing the expanded menu each day.

The new operation enjoys great success, and a newspaper in the nearby capital city features the Tide Pool in an article on trendy eating spots, giving it a rave review. Patronage increases and Leila hires a cook and three waiters to help her.

A local entrepreneur, Sally, who represents an investment group, asks Leila if she would be interested in franchising other Tide Pools throughout the country. Sally says an investment group would help develop a franchise plan, plus fund the new operation.

Leila would be asked to travel to help set up franchise operations for the first year, and would have a managerial role and substantial stake in the new venture.

Leila likes the idea—sure, she'll have to get back into the working world, but on her own terms, and as a consultant and business owner. Besides, she's feeling overworked running the Tide Pool by herself, and it would be a relief to have the new venture take over the business. The investment group wants a managerial role in the franchise operation, plus a comprehensive set of financial controls. Leila and the investment group agree to incorporate the new venture as "Tide Pool Franchising, Inc." The corporate business structure is a good fit. Leila will assume a managerial role as a director of the new company, along with Sally and a member of the venture capital firm. The new firm hires two seasoned small business people, one as president and one as treasurer, to run the new franchise operation. Business begins with the original Tide Pool as the first franchise, and Leila gets started working for a good salary, plus commission, setting up other franchise locations.

If the new venture makes a go of it, Leila and the investment group can either sell their shares back to the corporation at a healthy profit or, if growth is substantial and consistent, take the company public in a few years, selling their stock in the corporation at a sizable profit once a market has been established for the corporation's publicly held shares.

Raising Money—Corporate Access to Private, Venture, and Public Capital

Corporations offer a terrific structure for raising money from friends, family, and business associates. There is something special about stock ownership, even in a small business, that attracts others. The corporate structure is designed to accommodate various capital interests—for example, you can issue common voting shares to the initial owner-employees, set up a special nonvoting class of shares to distribute to key employees as an incentive to remain loyal to the business, and issue yet another preferred class of stock (one that gives investors a preference if dividends are declared or the corporation is sold) to venture capitalists willing to help fund future expansion of your corporation.

Incorporated businesses also have an easier time obtaining loans from banks and other capital investment firms (assuming a corporation's balance sheet and cash flow statements look good). That's partially due to the increased structural formality of the corporation (discussed above). In addition, loans can be made part of a package where the bank or investment company obtains special rights to choose one or more board members, or has special voting prerogatives in matters of corporate governance or finance. For example, a lender may require veto power over expenditures exceeding a specified amount. The range of capital arrangements possible, even for a small corporation, is almost limitless, which helps the corporation attract outside investment.

 TIP

Employees often prefer to work for corporations. Key employees are more likely to work for a business that offers them a chance to profit if future growth is strong through the issuance of stock options and stock bonuses—financial incentives that only the corporate form can provide.

Perpetual Existence

A corporation is, in some senses, immortal. Unlike a sole proprietorship, partnership, or an LLC, which can terminate upon the death or withdrawal of the owner or owners, a corporation has an independent legal existence that continues despite changeovers in management or ownership. Of course, like any business, a corporation can be terminated by the mutual consent of the owners for personal or economic reasons and, in some cases, involuntarily, as in corporate bankruptcy proceedings. Nonetheless, the fact that a corporation does not depend for its legal existence on the life or continual ownership interest of a particular individual does influence creditors, employees, and others to participate in the operations of the business. This is particularly true as the business grows.

Downsides of Incorporating

Just about everything, including the advantage of incorporating, comes at a price. And, of course, the answer to the question "How much does it cost?" is an important factor to weigh when considering whether to incorporate your business. For starters, a corporation, unlike a sole proprietorship or general partnership, requires the filing of formation papers—articles of incorporation—with the California Secretary of State. The filing cost is $100. Corporations must pay an annual franchise tax (as explained in Chapter 4). Ongoing paperwork is generally not burdensome, but you will have to hold and document annual meetings of shareholders and directors and keep minutes of important corporate meetings. Creating this paper trail is a good way to show the IRS, in case of an audit (or the courts, in case of a lawsuit which tries to hold shareholders personally liable), that you have, in fact, respected the corporate form and are entitled to claim (hide behind) its insulating layer of limited personal liability.

RESOURCES
You can take care of ongoing corporate paperwork at minimal expense by using *The Corporate Records Handbook,* by Anthony Mancuso (Nolo). This book contains minute forms to hold corporate meetings and helps corporations cope with the tax, business, legal, and financial decisions and transactions that commonly arise during the life of the business.

The other main disadvantage of incorporating has traditionally been the $1,000 to $2,000 (or more) you could expect to pay an attorney for creating the initial paperwork. This book, together with a little effort on your part, should significantly reduce, if not eliminate, this cost.

Corporations in action. Sal Sr. and his son, Sal Jr., co-own and run Sal's Mimeo and Copy Center, a family business run for over 30 years as a partnership with a minimum of legal paperwork. In fact, before Sal Jr. joined the partnership firm, Sal Sr. ran the business as a sole proprietorship. Sal Sr. is retiring, letting Sal Jr., a business school grad, take over operational control.

Sal Jr. plans to expand the business by bringing in two business school friends, Ellen and Wilbur, as investors. Sal Jr. will contribute the business and its assets (including a long-term commercial lease to its storefront location and goodwill), to the new operation. Ellen and Wilbur will invest cash in two ways: Each will pay cash in return for shares, and each will also lend money to the business in exchange for promissory notes, which will be repaid by the firm. Interest only will be paid by the business on the notes over a five-year period, with repayment of the principal amount at the end of loan term. Ellen and Wilbur hope that in five to seven years they can sell their shares back to Sal Jr. at an increased price per share, or to another company wishing to buy into Sal's business. In the meantime, they are content to look to the interest payments on their notes as an adequate return on their investment in the business.

Sal Jr. will work as full-time manager of the business, which will continue to offer traditional copying services. In addition, the new capital will be used to expand into desktop publishing aimed at both the small business and the student markets.

Sal Jr., seeing that a change in business structure is needed to give Ellen and Wilbur a stake in the business, decides to incorporate. The investors like the corporate form because it limits their personal liability for its debts and other liabilities. Incorporating also should give the business a lift in its lending status at the local bank, which likes the fact that Sal Jr. is formalizing and expanding his business operations. Sal Jr. also realizes that forming a corporation will have tax advantages since it is one good way to split business income between the business entity, the investors, and himself. Specifically, the corporate form allows Sal to leave profits in the business, part of which will be used to pay back and retire Ellen's and Wilbur's promissory notes. Of course, the corporation will get to deduct Sal's salary and fringe benefits (as well as those of his employees) as well as the interest paid on the investors' notes. In short, the corporate form, with its built-in limited liability legal status, income- and tax-splitting capability and stock ownership structure, suits Sal's new business needs to a T.

Comparing Business Entities at a Glance

In the tables that follow, we highlight and compare general and specific legal and tax traits of each type of business entity. We include a few technical issues in our chart to tweak your interest. Should any of the additional points of comparison seem relevant to your particular business operation, we encourage you to talk them over with a legal or tax professional.

RESOURCES

For an in-depth legal and tax comparison of limited liability entities, see *LLC or Corporation?* by Anthony Mancuso (Nolo).

Does It Make Sense to Incorporate Out of State?

You have no doubt heard about the possibility of incorporating in another state, most likely Delaware, where initial and ongoing fees are lower and regulations may be less restrictive than in California. Does this make sense? For large, publicly held corporations looking for the most lenient statutes and courts to help them fend off corporate raiders, perhaps yes. But for a small, privately held corporation pursuing an active California business, our answer is generally no—it is usually a very poor idea to incorporate out of state.

The big reason is that you probably will have to qualify to do business in California even if you don't incorporate here, and this process takes about as much time and costs as much money as filing incorporation papers in California in the first place. You'll also need to appoint a corporate agent to receive official corporate notices in the state where you incorporate—another expensive pain in the neck.

Incorporating in another state with a lower corporate income tax isn't likely to save you any money. If your business makes money from operations in California, even if it is incorporated in another state, you still must pay California taxes on this income.

EXAMPLE: Best Greeting Card, Inc., plans to open a Jenner, California, facility to design and market holiday greeting cards throughout the country. If it incorporates in Delaware, it must qualify to do business in California and pay California corporate income tax on its California operations. It also must hire a registered agent to act on its behalf in Delaware. It decides to incorporate in California instead.

Unless you plan to open up a business with offices and operations in more than one state and, therefore, have a real reason to shop for the best corporate domiciles, you generally should incorporate in your home state—California.

Business Entity Comparison Tables—Legal, Financial, and Tax Characteristics

	Sole Proprietorship	General Partnership	Limited Partnership	C Corporation	S Corporation	LLC
Who owns business?	sole proprietor	general partners	general and limited partners	shareholders	same as C corporation	members
Personal liability for business debts	sole proprietor personally liable	general partners personally liable	only general partner(s) personally liable	no personal liability of shareholders	same as C corporation	no personal liability of members
Restrictions on kind of business	may engage in any lawful business	may engage in any lawful business	same as general partnership	can't be formed for banking or trust business and other special businesses	same as C corporation —but has shareholder restrictions	same as C corporation; in California, many licensed professionals cannot form an LLC (lawyers, accountants, and architects—until 1/1/2007 for architects—can form RLLP instead)
Restrictions on number of owners	only one sole proprietor	minimum two general partners	minimum one general partner and one limited partner	one-person corporations allowed	same as C corporation, but no more than 100 shareholders allowed (who must be US citizens or residents)	one-member LLCs allowed
Who makes management decisions?	sole proprietor	general partners	general partner(s) only (not limited partners)	board of directors; number of board members, if less than 3, must at least be equal to number of shareholders	same as C corporation	ordinarily members; or managers if manager-managed LLC
Who may legally obligate business?	sole proprietor	any general partner	general partner(s) only (not limited partners)	officers	same as C corporation	ordinarily any member; or any manager if manager-managed LLC
Effect on business if an owner dies or departs	dissolves automatically	dissolves automatically unless otherwise stated in partnership agreement	same as general partnership	no effect	same as C corporation	most LLC agreements say that LLC continues after a member leaves

Business Entity Comparison Tables—Legal, Financial, and Tax Characteristics (cont'd.)

	Sole Proprietorship	General Partnership	Limited Partnership	C Corporation	S Corporation	LLC
Limits on transfer of ownership interests	free transferability	consent of all general partners usually required under partnership agreement	same as general partnership	transfer of stock may be limited under securities laws or restrictions in articles of incorporation or bylaws	same as C corporation —but transfers should be limited to persons and entities that qualify as S corporation shareholders	most LLC agreements require membership consent to admit new member
Amount of organizational paperwork and ongoing legal formalities	minimal	partnership agreement recommended	startup filing required; partnership agreement recommended	startup filing required; bylaws recommended; annual meeting of shareholders required	same as C corporation	startup filing required; operating agreement recommended; meetings not normally required
Source of start-up funds	sole proprietor	general partners	general and limited partners	initial shareholders (in California, cannot invest with promise to perform services or to pay later (unless note is adequately secured)	same as C corporation —but cannot issue different classes of stock with different financial provisions	in California, members can invest by promising to perform services or contribute cash later
How business usually obtains capital, if needed	sole proprietor's contributions; working capital loans backed by personal assets of sole proprietor	capital contributions from general partners; business loans from banks backed by partnership and personal assets	investment capital from limited partners' bank loans backed by general partners' personal assets	flexible; outside investors (may be issued various classes of shares); bank loans backed by shareholders' personal assets (if corporation has insufficient credit history); venture capital	generally same as C Corporation—but can't have foreign partnership or corporate shareholders; must limit number of shareholders to 100; can't offer different classes of stock to investors except for share with different or no voting rights, hence venture capital opportunities are limited	capital contributions from members; bank loans backed by members' personal assets (if LLC has insufficient credit history)

Business Entity Comparison Tables—Legal, Financial, and Tax Characteristics (cont'd.)

	Sole Proprietorship	General Partnership	Limited Partnership	C Corporation	S Corporation	LLC
Ease of conversion to another business form	may change form at will; legal paperwork involved	may change to limited partnership, corporation, or LLC; legal paperwork involved	may change to corporation or LLC; legal paperwork involved	may change to S corporation by filing simple tax election; change to LLC can involve tax cost and legal complexity	generally same as C corporation—may terminate S tax status to become C corporation but cannot reelect S status for five years after	may change to general or limited partnership or corporation; legal paper involved
Is establishment or sale of ownership interests subject to federal and state securities laws?	generally not	generally not	issuance or transfer of limited partnership interests is subject to state and federal laws	issuance or transfer of stock subject to state and federal securities laws	same as C corporation	generally not, if all members are active in the business
Who generally finds this the best way to do business?	owner who wants legal and managerial autonomy	joint owners who are not concerned with personal liability for business debts	joint owners who want partnership tax treatment and some nonmanaging investors; general partners must be willing to assume personal liability for business debts	owners who want limited liability, the built-in formality and capital incentives of the corporate form, and the ability to split business income to lower overall taxes	owners who want limited liability, the built-in formality of the corporate form with the pass-through of corporate profits to individual owners	owners who want limited liability, a less formal legal structure, and automatic pass-through of profit
How business profits are taxed	individual tax rates of sole proprietor	individual tax rates of general partners, unless partners file IRS Form 8832 to elect corporate tax treatment	individual tax rates of general and limited partners, unless partners file IRS Form 8832 to elect corporate tax treatment	split up and taxed at corporate rates and individual tax rates of shareholders; $800 minimum state tax for second and subsequent tax years	individual tax rates of shareholders; $800 minimum tax for second and subsequent tax years	individual tax rates of members, unless LLC files IRS Form 8832 and elects corporate taxation; $800 minimum tax each year plus additional fees if gross income is $250,000 or more

Business Entity Comparison Tables—Legal, Financial, and Tax Characteristics (cont'd.)

	Sole Proprietorship	General Partnership	Limited Partnership	C Corporation	S Corporation	LLC
Tax-deductible fringe benefits available to owners who work in business	sole proprietor may set up IRA or Keogh retirement plan	general partners and other employees may set up IRA or Keogh plans; can make corporate tax election to obtain corporate benefits	same as general partnership	employee-shareholders eligible for medical reimbursement, term life insurance, and equity-sharing plans	employee-shareholders owning 2% or more of stock are restricted to partnership rules	can get benefits associated with sole proprietorship, partnership, or corporation, depending on tax treatment of LLC
Automatic tax status		yes	yes, upon filing certificate of limited partnership with state filing office	yes, upon filing certificate of limited partnership with state filing office	no; must meet requirements and file tax election form with IRS; revoked or terminated tax status cannot be re-elected for five years	yes, one-owner LLC treated as sole proprietorship; co-owned LLC treated as partnership; one-owner and co-owned LLCs can elect corporate tax treatment
Deductibility of business losses	owner may use losses to deduct other income on individual tax returns (subject to active-passive investment loss rules that apply to all businesses)	partners may use losses to deduct other income on individual tax returns if at risk for loss or debt	same as general partnership, but limited partners may only deduct nonrecourse debts (for which general partners are not specifically liable)	corporation may deduct business losses (shareholders may not deduct losses)	shareholders may deduct share of corporate losses on individual tax returns, but must comply with special limitations	follows sole proprietorship, partnership, or corporate tax rules depending on tax status of LLC
Tax level when business is sold	personal tax level of owner	personal tax level of individual general partners	personal tax level of individual general and limited partners	two levels: shareholders and corporation are subject to tax on liquidation	normally taxed at personal tax levels of individual shareholders, but corporate level tax sometimes due if S corporation was formerly a C corporation	follows sole proprietorship, partnership or corporate tax rules depending on tax status of LLC

How California Corporations Work

Types of California Corporations 30

    The Privately Held California Profit Corporation 30

    Nonprofit Corporations 31

    Professional Corporations 31

    The Close Corporation 32

Corporate Powers 34

Corporate People 35

    Incorporators 35

    Directors 36

    Officers 40

    Shareholders 41

How Many People May Organize the Corporation? 42

Capitalization 43

Selling Stock 45

Paying Dividends 46

Dissolving a Corporation 47

Piercing the Corporate Veil 48

This chapter gives you detailed information on the legal, financial, and practical considerations relevant to California corporations. Much of the information discussed here will help you decide whether to incorporate. Some information relates to the day-to-day operations of the corporation.

WEBSITE

California corporations code is online. If you want to browse the California Corporations Code, go to www.leginfo.ca.gov, click "California Law," then select "Corporations Code" and click on "Search." The General Corporation law, which applies to California business corporations, is contained in Title 1, Division 1.

Types of California Corporations

California classifies corporations in several, sometimes overlapping, ways. The first classification is domestic versus foreign. A domestic corporation is one that is formed under the laws of California by filing articles of incorporation with the California Secretary of State. If you form a corporation in another state, even if the corporation does business in California, it is a foreign corporation. We've already taken a look at the relative advantages and disadvantages of setting up a foreign corporation in Chapter 1.

Corporations can also be classified as profit or nonprofit. The California Corporations Code does not contain any precise definition of these terms, but does refer to regular profit corporations as business corporations to distinguish them from nonprofit corporations. We will refer to regular business corporations as profit corporations. A nonprofit corporation is one that is set up under the special provisions of the California Nonprofit Corporation Law.

Another corporate category is the professional corporation. This type of corporation is regulated by special statutes and, as its name implies, is a separate type of corporation formed for the purpose of engaging in the practice of certain professions.

Finally, the Corporations Code contains provisions for setting up a unique —and rarely used—type of profit corporation, the close corporation. A close corporation is one with a limited number of shareholders, who can enter into a shareholders' agreement that waives or alters many of the provisions of the Corporations Code.

Now let's briefly look at each of these types of corporations, starting with the privately held California profit corporation—the type of corporation we expect our readers to be interested in.

The Privately Held California Profit Corporation

This book shows you how to form a privately held profit corporation. The forms and information we provide will enable you to form a regular profit corporation that is eligible to issue its initial shares under the limited offering exemption contained in the Corporate Securities Law of California. Essentially, this means that your corporation can offer and issue its shares of stock privately, without public solicitation or advertisement. (The limited offering exemption is explained in detail in Chapter 3.) The remainder of this book explains the rules and procedures you will have to follow to organize and operate your corporation—and shows you, step by step, how to incorporate.

We occasionally use the term "closely held corporation." The Internal Revenue Code defines this term as a corporation in which five or fewer people own more than 50% of the value of the corporation's stock during the last half of the corporation's tax year. However, when we use this term outside of its technical tax context, all we mean is that the corporation is formed and operated by a small number of people who will be active in the affairs of the corporation, and that it will not rely on the resources and capital of outside investors or public subscribers to its shares. This is the type of corporation most readers will wish to set up.

Nonprofit Corporations

A nonprofit corporation is a corporation formed by one or more persons, for the benefit of the public, the mutual benefit of its members, or religious purposes. California public benefit nonprofit corporations are usually formed for tax-exempt purposes under Section 501(c)(3) of the Internal Revenue Code for religious, charitable, literary, scientific, or educational purposes. For example, child care centers, shelters for the homeless, community health care clinics, museums, hospitals, churches, schools, and performing arts groups normally incorporate as nonprofits.

With the exception of mutual benefit nonprofit corporations, nonprofit corporations cannot distribute profits to their members. When they dissolve, most nonprofit corporations dedicate all corporate assets to another nonprofit corporation to comply with state and federal tax laws and to avoid paying corporate income tax (the main reason for organizing a nonprofit corporation). For example, if you establish a nonprofit corporation to educate the public about the need to preserve wetlands for birds, you might state that upon dissolution all remaining money will go to the Audubon Society.

Nonprofit corporations, like regular profit corporations, have directors who manage the business of the corporation. The nonprofit can collect enrollment fees, dues, or similar amounts from members. Like regular corporations, a nonprofit corporation may sue or be sued, pay salaries and provide fringe benefits, incur debts and obligations, acquire and hold property, and engage in any lawful activity not inconsistent with its purposes and its nonprofit status. It also provides its directors and members with limited liability for the debts and liabilities of the corporation and continues perpetually unless steps are taken to terminate it. If you are interested in forming a California nonprofit, see *How to Form a Nonprofit Corporation in California,* by Anthony Mancuso (Nolo). To form a nonprofit corporation in another state, see *How to Form a Nonprofit Corporation,* by Anthony Mancuso (Nolo), a 50-state guide.

Professional Corporations

Certain specified groups of professionals must form professional corporations when incorporating their practices in California. There are special rules that govern how professional corporations must operate. In some cases, the professionals must obtain a certificate of registration from the governmental agency that regulates the profession (such as the State Bar for lawyers). Everyone who provides professional services through a professional corporation must be licensed to practice the particular profession in which the corporation is engaged. Only persons who hold such a California license in the primary (or a related) profession can own shares in the professional corporation. The corporation is subject to the rules, regulations, and disciplinary powers of the agency that regulates the particular profession. Special forms and procedures must be used to incorporate a professional corporation—we don't cover that process here.

TIP

Most professionals don't have to form a professional corporation. Only a few professions have to incorporate their practices as professional corporations. For example, engineers, computer scientists, real estate brokers, financial advisors, and most professions outside the areas of law, health care, and accountancy can incorporate as regular profit corporations (the type of corporation formed by using this book).

Only the following professionals must incorporate as professional corporations (professions marked with an asterisk may incorporate either as a regular business corporation or as a professional corporation):

- accountant
- acupuncturist
- architect
- attorney
- chiropractor
- clinical social worker
- dentist
- doctor (medical doctors including surgeons)
- marriage and family therapists
- naturopathic doctor
- nurse
- optometrist
- osteopath (physician or surgeon)
- pharmacist
- physical therapist
- physician's assistant
- podiatrist
- psychologist
- shorthand and court reporter
- speech-language pathologist and audiologist
- veterinarian.

Architects and veterinarians have the option to incorporate as a professional corporation or as a regular profit corporation. (California attorneys, accountants, and architects—until January 1, 2012, for architects—can also organize their practices as RLLPs.) If you decide to use this book to form your architecture or veterinary corporation, check with your state board to make sure that you have the option to form a regular profit corporation instead of a professional corporation.

WARNING

A flat corporate income tax rate applies for certain professionals. Professionals who work in the fields of health, law, engineering, architecture, accounting, actuarial science, or consulting will be subject to the maximum 35% federal corporate tax rate if substantially all the stock of the corporation is owned by the employees who perform professional services for the corporation (see "Federal Corporate Income Tax" in Chapter 4). It doesn't matter whether the corporation is a professional corporation or regular profit corporation. The 35% rate applies to all taxable income left in the corporation at the end of the tax year (and not paid out as salary, fringe benefits, or otherwise).

The Close Corporation

A California profit corporation with 35 or fewer shareholders may, by including special close corporation provisions in its articles of incorporation and on its stock certificates, elect to be organized as a California close corporation. Technically, California close corporations are referred to as statutory close corporations, because they are set up and operated under special California statutes, which allow them to establish their own operating procedures according to the terms of a close corporation shareholders' agreement. We usually refer to this type of corporation simply as a close corporation.

Registered Limited Liability Partnerships

Lawyers and accountants and—until January 1, 2012—architects can form a special type of partnership, the registered limited liability partnership. This relatively new business entity gives the professional partners in an RLLP immunity from personal liability for the malpractice of other partners in the firm. (Normally, all partners are personally liable for their own and other partners' negligence in a professional partnership.) The only other way to achieve this type of personal protection in a business that is taxed as a partnership is to form a limited liability company. However, California licensed professionals are prohibited from forming an LLC (see "The Limited Liability Company" in Chapter 1).

Those California statutes are different from similar laws in other states (all states have adopted RLLP statutes) in that:

- California RLLP professionals are also personally protected against business debts, contracts, and other claims against the RLLP firm.

- California RLLP professionals are not personally liable for the negligence of people they supervise.

- Only three of California's 60+ licensed professions are allowed to form RLLPs.

If you are an accountant or lawyer, or, until January 1, 2012, an architect, you may want to consider forming an RLLP. Check with your state board and your legal and tax advisors. If you practice in another profession, then you may decide to incorporate to obtain limited liability protection.

The primary reason for electing close corporation status is to operate the corporation under the terms of a close corporation shareholders' agreement, which can provide for informal management of the corporation and allow the corporate entity to operate under partnership-type rules. Through a shareholders' agreement, the close corporation can dispense with the need for annual director or shareholder meetings, corporate officers, or even the board of directors itself, and instead allow shareholders to manage and carry out the business of the corporation directly. As with a partnership, profits can be distributed without regard to capital contributions (stock ownership); thus a 10% shareholder could, for example, receive 25% of the profits (dividends). In effect, a close corporation can waive many of the statutory rules that apply to regular California profit corporations and establish its own operating procedures according to the terms of a close corporation shareholders' agreement.

EXAMPLE:

Kelley Greene, a successful junior tennis champion, together with her financial backer, forms her own California close corporation, What a Racquet, Ltd., a California limited partnership consisting of a general partner and ten limited-partner investors. In the close corporation shareholders' agreement, the limited partnership is given complete managerial control of the corporation and the limited partner investors are provided with a participation in 80% of the profits and liquidation proceeds of the corporation, while Kelley is assured an annual salary and a 20% share in corporate profits and liquidation proceeds.

Complex investment arrangements of this sort are the primary use of the close corporation. Most incorporators will not wish to organize their corporation as a close corporation. Indeed, fewer than 2% of all California profit corporations are formed in this manner.

There are a number of reasons for the lack of popularity of the close corporation. To begin with, most people do not need, or wish, to operate their corporation under informal or nonstandard close corporation shareholder agreement rules and procedures. In fact, many incorporators form a corporation in order to rely on the traditional corporation and tax statutes that apply to regular profit corporations. Second, shares of stock in a close corporation contain built-in (automatic) restrictions on transferability, and most incorporators do not want their shares to be subject to these transfer restrictions. Third, there are a number of potential problems related to the use of a close corporation shareholders' agreement, which make it inadvisable unless you first consult with an attorney and an accountant. If you are interested in forming a close corporation, you should see a lawyer.

Corporate Powers

Profit corporations have carte blanche to engage in any lawful business activity in California. Lawful doesn't just mean not criminal; it means not otherwise prohibited by law. Generally, this means that a corporation can do anything that a natural person can do. By way of illustration, the California Corporations Code lists the following corporate powers:

- to adopt, use, and alter a corporate seal
- to adopt, amend, and repeal bylaws
- to qualify to do business in any other state, territory, dependency, or foreign country

- subject to certain restrictions, to issue, purchase, redeem, receive, acquire, own, hold, sell, lend, exchange, transfer, dispose of, pledge, use, and otherwise deal in and with its own shares, bonds, debentures, and other securities
- to make donations, regardless of specific corporate benefit, for the public welfare or for community fund, hospital, charitable, educational, scientific, or civic or similar purposes
- to pay pensions and establish and carry out pension, profit-sharing, stock bonus, share pension, share option, savings, thrift, and other retirement, incentive, and benefit plans, trusts, and provisions for any or all of the directors, officers, and employees of the corporation or any of its subsidiary or affiliated corporations and to indemnify and purchase and maintain insurance on behalf of any fiduciary of such plans, trusts, or provisions
- except with respect to certain restrictions as to loans to directors and officers which we discuss later, to assume obligations, enter into contracts (including contracts of guaranty or suretyship), incur liabilities, borrow and lend money, or otherwise use its credit and secure any of its obligations, contracts, or liabilities by mortgage, pledge, or other encumbrance of all or any part of its property, franchises, and income
- to participate with others in any partnership, joint venture, or other association, transaction, or arrangement of any kind, whether or not such participation involves the sharing or delegation of control with, or to, others.

Corporate People

While a corporation is considered a legal person capable of making contracts, paying taxes, and so on, it needs real people to carry out its business. The law classifies corporate people in the following ways:

- incorporators
- directors
- officers, and
- shareholders.

These corporate people have varying powers and responsibilities which we discuss below.

In a Small Corporation, One Person Often Fills Several Roles

Distinctions between the different roles of corporate personnel often become blurred in a small corporation because one person may simultaneously serve in more than one, or all, of these capacities. For example, if you form your own one-person California corporation, you will be your corporation's only incorporator, director, officer, and shareholder.

Incorporators

Your incorporator is the person who signs the articles of incorporation and files them with the secretary of state to form the corporation. In a practical sense, incorporators are the key people who make the business happen. Typically, they are the entrepreneurs who arrange to get the money, property, people, and whatever else the corporation will need to make a go of it.

An incorporator (sometimes called a corporate promoter) is considered by law to be a fiduciary of the corporation. This means that he or she has a duty to make full disclosure to the corporation of any personal interest in, and potential benefit from, any of the business he or she transacts for the corporation. For example, if the incorporator arranges for the corporation to buy property in which he has an ownership interest, he must disclose his ownership interest and any personal benefit he plans to realize from the sale.

Incorporators May Be Liable for Contracts Signed Prior to Incorporation

The corporation is not bound by contracts the incorporator enters into with third persons before the corporation is formed, unless these contracts are later ratified by the board of directors or the corporation accepts the benefits of the contract (for example, it uses office space available through a lease the incorporator signed). On the other hand, the incorporator may be personally liable on these preincorporation contracts unless he or she signs the contract in the name of the corporation only and clearly informs the third party that the corporation does not yet exist, may never come into existence, and, even if it does, may not ratify the contract.

If you want to arrange for office space, hire employees, or borrow money before the corporation is formed, state clearly that you are acting on the corporation's behalf, and that your contracts are subject to ratification by the corporation when, and if, it comes into existence. The other party may refuse to do business with you under these conditions and tell you to come back after the corporation is formed. This is usually the best approach to preincorporation business anyway—namely, to postpone it until you file your articles.

Directors

Directors have the authority and responsibility for managing the corporation. The directors meet and make decisions collectively as the board of directors. For the board to take action, a majority of a quorum vote is usually necessary. However, the board may pass a resolution delegating most of the management of the corporation to an executive committee consisting of two or more directors. This arrangement is often used when one or more directors are unable or unwilling to assume an active voice in corporate affairs. The board of directors may also delegate management of the day-to-day operations of the corporation to a management company or others, as long as these people remain under the ultimate control of the board.

Directors normally serve without compensation. After all, they are intimately involved in the business and will gain financially if it does well by paying themselves a better salary and/or eventually selling the business. The corporation may pay its directors reasonable compensation, however, if it is for services they actually perform for the corporation. A director may also receive an advance or reimbursement for reasonable out-of-pocket expenses (for example, travel costs) incurred in the performance of corporate duties. Any compensation, advancement, or reimbursement paid to a director should be authorized before the payments are made.

Directors' Duties and Conflicts of Interest

Directors, like promoters, are fiduciaries of the corporation. This means they must act in the corporation's best interests and exercise care in making management decisions. In an effort to flesh out these responsibilities, the law says a director must act "in good faith, in a manner [which the] … director believes to be in the best interests of the corporation and its shareholders and with such care, including reasonable inquiry, as an ordinarily prudent person in a like position would use under similar conditions." This vague standard effectively leaves it up to the courts to define the duty of good faith a director owes the corporation. Courts, in turn, usually decide cases on an individual basis.

Broadly speaking, however, honest errors in business judgment are usually allowed, while fraudulent or grossly negligent behavior isn't. A director is allowed to rely on the apparently accurate reports of attorneys, accountants, and corporate officers in arriving at decisions, unless there was some indication that the director needed to look into the matter further. (Below, we discuss special provisions of California law that allow you to insulate your directors in many cases from personal liability for breach of their duty to the corporation or shareholders.)

The director also has a duty of loyalty to the corporation. This means, among other things, that a director usually must give the corporation a right of first refusal as to business opportunities he becomes aware of in his capacity as corporate director. If the corporation fails to take advantage of the opportunity after full disclosure or clearly would not be interested in it, the director can go ahead for himself.

The board of directors may vote on a matter in which one or more of the directors has a personal interest (the Corporations Code uses the term "material financial interest"), but only if:

- the director's interest in the transaction is fully disclosed or known to the board, and
- there are sufficient votes to pass the resolution without counting the vote of the interested director.

Alternatively, the board can approve such a contract if the contract or transaction is just and reasonable as to the corporation. (There are additional procedures for validating actions that benefit directors—see Cal. Corp. Code § 310.)

Subject to some exceptions, if the corporation lends money or property to, or guarantees the obligations of, directors, the shareholders must approve these transactions, either by a unanimous vote or by a majority vote of the shares not counting those held by benefited directors. Of course, the shareholders are entitled to full disclosure of the nature and extent of the benefit to the directors before votes are cast.

If a director violates one of the above rules, by grossly mismanaging or taking advantage of the corporation, receiving unauthorized or unwarranted compensation, or participating in unauthorized or unfair transactions, he or she can be subject to personal financial liability for any loss to the corporation, its shareholders, and its creditors. In addition to actual damages, the director can also be subject to monetary penalties (punitive damages), be temporarily or permanently ousted from directorship, and, in certain cases, face criminal penalties.

Of course, if you are forming a small corporation with, let's say, just you and a friend acting as the corporation's only directors, shareholders, and officers, much of this discussion will not apply to you. You will not have to worry about unfairly taking advantage of your own corporation or its shareholders because you cannot defraud or take advantage of yourselves—nor would you want to. When you and your closely held corporation have an identity of interest, it's not as important that you deal with the corporation at arm's length. However, if even a few others invest in your corporation, all the rules and legal principles regarding fair dealing discussed above apply.

Director Immunity and Indemnification Rules

California corporations can add provisions to their articles of incorporation that, in many cases, eliminate their directors' personal liability for monetary damages. They can also add provisions that allow the corporation to indemnify their directors (pay them back) for expenses, settlements, fines, judgments, and other costs associated with lawsuits brought against the directors beyond the indemnification limits provided by law. We discuss each of these optional provisions below.

Director immunity. California corporations can include language in their articles limiting or eliminating the personal liability of their directors for monetary damages, in suits brought by or on behalf of the corporation for breach of a director's duties to the corporation and its shareholders. (See Cal. Corp. Code §§ 204(a)(10) and 204.5.) You must include this language in your articles of incorporation for your corporation to qualify for this higher level of director protection. The articles of incorporation included in this book contain this director immunity language.

These provisions do not insulate directors from lawsuits brought by third parties (for example, a lawsuit for damages to an outsider caused by the act or omission of a director). They can be used, however, to protect directors from personal liability in shareholder derivative suits in many situations where the director is acting in good faith and according to law. A shareholder derivative suit arises when a shareholder sues the directors in the name of the corporation for damages caused to the corporation or its shareholders.

For example, if your board of directors makes what turns out to be a poor management decision that results in a monetary loss to the corporation (and a corresponding reduction in the value of the shareholders' stock), a shareholder—perhaps one who has been at odds with the directors for years—may decide to sue the directors personally in a shareholder's derivative action to allow the corporation to recoup this loss from the directors. In this situation, including a director immunity provision in your articles would protect your directors from liability. Of course, if a shareholder is injured personally (for example, by slipping and falling in the corporation's office), the shareholder could not bring a shareholder derivative suit on behalf of the corporation. Instead, the shareholder would have to sue the directors (and the corporation) in a regular third-party lawsuit—and the director immunity rules would not protect the directors from liability.

Even in shareholder derivative suits, there are some situations in which a director will be personally liable, regardless of the language in your articles. These exceptions, which generally involve illegal or unethical director conduct, are discussed below.

Indemnification. Although the director immunity rules may relieve a director of personal liability in certain types of lawsuits, there are many other costs that a director might incur in the course of defending or disposing of a lawsuit, such as settlement amounts, attorney fees, court costs, and other litigation-related expenses, which are not covered by the director immunity rules. Generally, California's indemnification rules allow the corporation to indemnify (pay back) a director (and officers, employees, and other corporate agents) for some or all of these additional types of lawsuit-related payments, if certain requirements are met. With the high incidence of out-of-court settlements (regardless of the actual merits of the case) and the mammoth costs of preparing for and defending

even the most frivolous lawsuit, indemnifying your directors is essential.

Corporations can (and, in some cases, must) indemnify a director, officer, employee, or other corporate agent for expenses incurred in defending a shareholder's derivative suit, and for expenses, judgments, fines, and settlements incurred in third-party actions. Specific requirements must be met in all cases to fall within the indemnification provisions. These indemnification provisions used to be exclusive—that is, corporations could not indemnify directors and officers for circumstances and amounts not specifically allowed under the indemnification provisions set forth in Section 317 of the California Corporations Code.

However, this exclusivity rule has changed. Now, a California corporation can include language in its articles authorizing the indemnification of corporate agents beyond what is expressly permitted by Section 317. Under these new rules, the corporation can provide additional indemnification for directors and officers for breaching a duty to the corporation or its shareholders (shareholder derivative suits) and for acts or omissions affecting others (third-party liability suits). (See Cal. Corp. Code § 204(a)(11).) However, a corporation cannot indemnify corporate agents if they engage in certain types of wrongdoing— see "Exceptions to Special Director Immunity and Indemnification Rules," below.

In the articles of incorporation provided in this book, we include language which authorizes indemnification *to the fullest extent permissible under California law*. This language allows the corporation to indemnify directors and officers both for shareholder derivative suits and third-party liability suits. Article VII of the bylaws contains a general statement requiring indemnification of directors and officers in all cases not prohibited by the Corporations Code. This language should suffice for most small California corporations, but check this conclusion with your small business lawyer if indemnification is important to you. If you wish to provide your own language for director and officer indemnification, see Sections 317 and 204(a)(11) of the Corporations Code and refer to the discussion and suggestions in Chapter 5, Step 4.

Exceptions to Special Director Immunity and Indemnification Rules

You cannot protect your directors from personal liability (or provide additional indemnification for corporate agents) for:

- acts or omissions that involve intentional misconduct or a knowing and culpable violation of law

- acts or omissions that the director believes to be contrary to the best interests of the corporation or its shareholders, or that the director takes in bad faith

- any transaction from which the director derived an improper personal benefit

- acts or omissions that show a reckless disregard for the director's duty to the corporation or its shareholders in circumstances in which the director was aware, or should have been aware, in the ordinary course of performing a director's duties, of a risk of serious injury to the corporation or its shareholders

- acts or omissions that constitute an unexcused pattern of inattention that amounts to an abdication of the director's duty to the corporation or its shareholders

- liability arising under Section 310 (for certain unauthorized transactions between the corporation and a director of a corporation in which the director has a material financial interest) and Section 316 (for certain unauthorized distributions, loans, or guarantees made by directors) of the California Corporations Code

- liability for acts occurring prior to the effective date of the immunity or indemnification provisions in the articles (before your articles are filed), and

- liability for acts while acting as an officer of the corporation. You cannot limit or eliminate an officer's liability under these special rules, even if the officer is also a director or the directors have ratified the officer's actions.

Officers

Officers (president, vice president, secretary, and chief financial officer) are in charge of supervising or actually carrying out the day-to-day business of the corporation. For example, in smaller corporations, the president will often actively run the business and the chief financial officer (treasurer) will sign checks, make deposits, prepare invoices and receipts, and so on. In larger corporations, the officers will oversee various corporate departments or regular corporate personnel who will perform these day-to-day activities. The powers, duties, and responsibilities of the officers are set by the articles, bylaws, or board of directors.

Like directors, officers owe a fiduciary duty to the corporation and are subject to the same requirement of acting in good faith and in the best interests of the corporation. Although not specified by statute, the day-to-day authority of officers should not include authority to enter into certain major business transactions that are generally understood to remain within the sole province of the board of directors (for example, the mortgage or resale of corporate property). The board will have to delegate special authority to the officers if it wants them to handle major transactions.

In smaller corporations, the board of directors and the officers will often be the same people. However, the directors should still meet as a board to approve major corporate transactions, so that courts and the IRS recognize the business as a true corporate entity.

Officers are considered agents of the corporation. This means that the corporation can be held liable for their negligent or intentional acts, if they are committed within the course and scope of their employment. The corporation, moreover, is bound by the contracts and obligations entered into or incurred by the corporate officers, as long as they had legal authority to transact the business. This authority can be actual authority (a bylaw provision or resolution by the board of directors), implied authority (a necessary but unspecified part of duties set out in the bylaws or a board resolution), or apparent authority (where a third party reasonably believes that the officer has authority).

Apparent authority is a tricky concept. Basically, any third party can rely on the signature of the president or chairman of the board, vice president, secretary, assistant secretary, chief financial officer, or assistant treasurer, whether or not this officer has any actual or implied authority to sign for the corporation, as long as the third party did not actually know that the corporate officer didn't have the authority to sign.

Furthermore, one signature on a corporate instrument is sufficient to bind the corporation if the person holds both of the required positions (for example, if he or she is both the president and secretary of a one-person California corporation).

Any act performed by an officer without legal authority can still bind the corporation if the corporation accepts the benefits of the transaction or if the board of directors ratifies it after the fact.

Corporate officers are normally compensated for their services to the corporation, either as officers or simply as employees of the corporation. The compensation should be reasonable and should be paid only for services actually performed for the corporation.

EXAMPLE:

Jason Horner and Elmore Johnson form their own publishing company. Jason is the president and Elmore is the treasurer of the corporation. Jason is paid a salary for acting as the publisher (not for serving as

> **WARNING**
>
> **Keep loan transactions reasonable.** If shareholders lend money to the corporation, it's best not to overdo it—some tax advisors think it's dicey to have a debt-to-equity ratio that exceeds 3 to 1, while others are more aggressive and balk only if the ratio gets close to 10 to 1. Ask your tax advisor for specific advice.

There are several reasons for caution with shareholder loans. First, the IRS may become suspicious of a corporation that has a high ratio of debt to equity or very loose shareholder loan arrangements. For instance, if a disproportionate amount of money is "loaned" to a closely held corporation rather than paid in for stock, and the repayment terms are unduly permissive or generous, the IRS or a court may find that the contribution was, in essence, an equity transaction contrived as debt to obtain favorable tax treatment (deduction by the corporation of interest payments on the debt). In this situation, the interest payments on the loan can be treated as dividends, which means the corporation cannot deduct these payments as a business expense and the lender-shareholder has to report repayment of the principal of the loan as dividend income rather than a return of capital.

Another practical reason for watching your debt-to-equity ratio is that banks are unlikely to lend money to your corporation if this ratio is particularly lopsided (too much debt/not enough equity).

Your debt arrangement is most likely to survive scrutiny if the debt instrument is drawn up as a regular promissory note with a fixed maturity date and a specified rate of interest, and the corporation has the right to enforce the terms of the note. The corporation should not arbitrarily grant the person making the loan any special preferences over other lenders or allow this person to postpone payments on the note. If the corporation has a high ratio of debt to equity, can obtain loan funds from outside lenders, or uses the loan proceeds to acquire capital assets, the loan is more likely to be disallowed and treated as an equity contribution.

Loans Are Securities

Notes issued by a corporation to lenders (shareholders, investors, and so on) are considered securities and must be qualified by the Commissioner of Corporations—usually by a somewhat complicated and costly procedure requiring the assistance of an attorney—unless the notes are exempt from qualification under a special rule. As you'll see in Chapter 3, we assume all the initial securities issued by your corporation to your shareholders (including shareholder loans) will be exempt from qualification under the California limited offering exemption. Many small corporations do not substantially capitalize their corporation with loans. Even if they do, their loan transactions should be exempt from qualification under the California limited offering discussed in the next chapter. Nonetheless, because of the technicalities involved with this area of law, you should consult with a lawyer if you capitalize your corporation with loan proceeds.

Selling Stock

Corporate stock may be sold for:

- money
- labor done
- services actually rendered to or for the benefit of the corporation in its formation or reorganization
- cancelled debts, and

- tangible or intangible property actually received by the corporation.

If shares are sold for something other than money, the board of directors must state, by resolution, the fair value to the corporation in monetary terms (that is, they must state a dollar amount which represents the fair market value) of the services, property, or other form of payment given for the shares.

In California, shares cannot be sold in return for promissory notes of the purchaser (shareholder) unless secured by collateral other than the shares themselves, nor can they be sold in return for the performance of future services (unless as part of an employee or director stock purchase or option plan).

EXAMPLE:

Thomas and Richard, after a bit of brainstorming, decide to form a Beverly Hills hang gliding tour service called "Two Sheets in the Wind, Inc." Unfortunately, they know only one person who would be willing to actually strap himself in as their tour guide—a fellow flying enthusiast, Harold. Harold sees the unique possibilities associated with this enterprise and insists on owning shares in the corporation rather than being a mere employee. Everyone agrees that not just any Tom, Dick, or Harry would be willing to assume this position, so they agree to give Harold one-third of the corporation's shares in exchange for his agreement to enter into an employment contract with the corporation. Although this arrangement may seem fair to all the parties involved, it isn't allowed because shares cannot be issued in return for future services. Harold suggests that the corporation instead issue shares to him in return for an unsecured long-term note (he'll pay for them after he's survived a few tours). This also won't work because

shares cannot normally be issued in return for a promissory note. Harold decides to pay cash (or borrow enough cash) to purchase his shares outright.

Paying Dividends

There are restriction on a corporation's right to declare dividends. Before dividends can be paid to shareholders, certain legal and financial tests must be met. For the most part, the law applies generally accepted accounting procedures to determine the validity of dividend payments (or distributions to shareholders).

A dividend cannot be paid unless:

- The amount of retained earnings of the corporation, immediately prior to the payment of the dividend, equals or exceeds the amount of the proposed dividend, or
- Immediately after the dividend is issued:
  - corporate assets (not including goodwill and certain other assets) would at least equal 1¼ times the liabilities of the corporation (not including certain deferred items); and
  - subject to certain exceptions, the current assets of the corporation would be at least equal to its current liabilities or, in some cases, at least equal to 1¼ times its current liabilities.

In addition, no dividend can be paid if the corporation is, or as a result of the payment of a dividend would be, likely to be unable to meet its liabilities as they become due. Certain other tests apply for payment of a dividend to certain classes of stock if the corporation has more than a one-class stock structure.

The rules for determining the validity of distributions to shareholders apply technical accounting standards, and you should consult an accountant or a lawyer before declaring and paying a dividend. If a dividend is paid and does not meet the appropriate tests, the directors of the corporation may be held personally liable to the creditors and shareholders of the corporation for the amount of the illegal dividend.

Dissolving a Corporation

We're sure the dissolution of your corporation is the last thing on your mind at this point. Nevertheless, it might be comforting to know that you can wind up the affairs and business of your corporation with a minimum of legal formality. Here is a quick look at the basic rules that apply when voluntarily dissolving a California corporation.

Any California corporation may, on its own motion and out of court, elect to voluntarily wind up and dissolve for any reason. This act requires the vote of at least 50% of the voting power of the shareholders.

In addition, the board of directors may elect to dissolve the corporation without shareholder approval if any of the following conditions apply:

- The corporation has not issued any shares.
- An order for relief has been entered under Chapter 7 of the federal bankruptcy law for the corporation.
- The corporation has disposed of all its assets and hasn't conducted any business for the past five years.

Upon the request of the corporation, three or more creditors, or other interested parties, a corporation's voluntary dissolution may be subject to court supervision.

In any dissolution, whether voluntary or involuntary, the corporation must stop transacting business except to the extent necessary to wind up its affairs and, if desired, to preserve the goodwill or going-concern value of the corporation pending a sale of its assets. All shareholders and creditors on the books of the corporation must be notified of the dissolution. All debts and liabilities, to the extent of corporate assets, must be paid or otherwise provided for, with any remaining assets distributed to shareholders in proportion to their stockholdings and any special stock preferences. A certificate of dissolution must be filed with the secretary of state.

Corporate dissolutions subject to superior court supervision must publish a notice to creditors at least once a week for three successive weeks in the county in which the court is located. Creditors who don't file claims within a specified period are barred from participating in any distribution of the general assets of the corporation.

RESOURCES

What about involuntary dissolutions? The rules in this section deal with a voluntary dissolution of the corporation (where a majority of your shareholders mutually agree to dissolve the corporation). There are also involuntary dissolution procedures. In an involuntary dissolution, the court is petitioned by dissatisfied or deadlocked shareholders, directors, or the attorney general to force the dissolution of a corporation. (If you're interested in these special rules, see the Corporations Code, starting with Section 1800.)

Voluntary Dissolution—How to Do It

The dissolution of a small corporation is usually a relatively simple procedure. You must prepare and file two forms with the California Secretary of State. First, you file a certificate of election to wind up and dissolve. Then, after the creditors have been paid and any remaining assets have been distributed to the shareholders, you file a certificate of dissolution. You don't have to file a certificate of election if the election to dissolve was approved by all outstanding shares, and you note this fact on your certificate of dissolution. The certificate of dissolution or a separate statement attached to it must indicate that the corporation or an individual agrees to assume any taxes that are owed or may be assessed against the corporation. The secretary of state will wait to get a tax clearance for the corporation from the Franchise Tax Board before filing the certificate and dissolving the corporation. These formalities are simple, and there is no fee for filing these forms. For further information on the voluntary dissolution of a California corporation, together with sample forms and instructions, go to the California Department of Corporations website, at www.corp.ca.gov.

Piercing the Corporate Veil

After you've set up a corporation, you must act like one if you want to qualify for the legal protections and tax advantages the corporate form offers. Filing your articles of incorporation with the secretary of state brings the corporation into existence and transforms it into a legal entity. However, this is not enough to ensure that a court or the IRS will treat you as a corporation.

Courts occasionally scrutinize the organization and operations of corporations, particularly closely held corporations where the shareholders also manage, supervise, and work for the corporation as directors, officers, and employees. If a corporation is inadequately capitalized, doesn't issue stock, diverts funds for the personal use of the shareholders, doesn't keep adequate corporate records (for example, minutes of annual or special meetings), or, generally, doesn't pay much attention to the theory and practice of corporate life, a court may decide that your corporation is a bogus legal entity you are using to avoid liability. If this happens, the court can disregard the corporate entity and hold the shareholders liable for the debts of the corporation. Using the same criteria, the IRS has been known to treat corporate profits as the individual income of the shareholders. This is called piercing the corporate veil.

Piercing the corporate veil is the exception, not the rule. However, to avoid problems, your corporation should be adequately capitalized; issue its stock; keep accurate records of who owns its shares; keep corporate funds separate from the personal funds of the shareholders, officers, and directors; and keep accurate records of all votes and decisions that occur at formal meetings of the board of directors and the shareholders. These formal meetings should be held at least annually and whenever you wish to document a change in the legal or tax affairs of your corporation (such as an amendment of your bylaws or board approval of an important tax election) or an important business transaction (like the purchase of corporate real estate or authorization of a bank loan).

For one-person or other small corporations, your formal meetings will often be held on paper, not in person, to document corporate actions or formalities that have already been agreed to ahead of time by all the parties.

RESOURCES

For help with ongoing corporate formalities, see *The Corporate Records Handbook,* **by Anthony Mancuso (Nolo).** This book shows you how to hold and document ongoing corporate meetings of your board and shareholders. It also contains corporate resolutions to insert in your minutes to handle common legal, tax, and business transactions that occur after incorporating.

Issuing and Selling Stock

Securities Laws and Exemptions..52

The Limited Offering Exemption 53
    General Rules of the Limited Offering Exemption...54
    Special Shareholder Suitability Rules 56
    Special 35-Shareholder Rule..60
    Applying the Limited Offering Exemption 60

Federal Securities Act...63

This chapter will explain how to offer and sell your stock shares without running afoul of California and federal securities laws. In California, most small private corporations qualify for the limited offering exemption, which allows you to make an initial private stock offering without getting a permit from the state commissioner of corporations. If you don't fall within this exemption, you'll have to submit lots of complicated paperwork to get your permit—this book doesn't cover that process, because most readers will qualify for the exemption.

Because all stock transactions are also subject to the federal securities laws, we provide information on exemptions under the federal Securities Act and its regulations.

On first impression, some of the information in this chapter may seem complicated. If so, don't despair—it will make sense when you actually go through the steps in Chapter 5 to prepare the documentation necessary to issue your initial shares under the limited offering exemption. So for now, relax, read this information carefully, and, if it still seems muddy, read it again when you go through Steps 7 and 8 of Chapter 5.

WARNING

You must qualify for the limited offering exemption to use this book. If you conclude, after reading this chapter, that you are not eligible to form a California corporation using the limited offering exemption, or if you have any questions, see a lawyer.

Securities Laws and Exemptions

One of the most important steps in forming your corporation is the issuance of your initial shares of stock. You are responsible for making sure that your shares are offered and sold in strict compliance with the securities laws of California and the federal Securities Act. Federal securities law is intended to ensure that corporations fully disclose all relevant facts to all prospective purchasers of shares. California law goes a step beyond this: Its purpose is to make sure that the stock issuance transaction is fair, just, and equitable to all offerees and purchasers of stock (that is, your shareholders). The California system is therefore referred to as a merit system (as opposed to the federal disclosure system), and is considered by many securities specialists to be the most rigorous in the nation.

WARNING

Selling shares outside of California will subject you to other states' laws. The securities laws of another state may also apply to your stock issuance transaction if you offer to sell your shares outside of California or your offer to sell shares is directed to people in another state. Many states provide exemptions similar to California's limited offering exemption for shares privately offered and sold to a limited number of people within the state. However, we don't cover those laws here. If you plan to offer or sell shares in another state, see a lawyer. Remember, technical violations of the securities laws (even though no one is defrauded or unfairly treated) can come back to haunt you later on—this is particularly true if you decide to have distant (out-of-state) investors in your corporation.

In California, your stock issuance must be qualified (approved) by the commissioner of corporations, usually by means of obtaining a permit for the issuance of shares, unless you fall within an exemption. Under federal law, you must register your stock issuance with the Securities and Exchange Commission (SEC) unless a federal exemption is available. Qualifying or registering a stock issuance requires the preparation and submission of complex legal and financial statements, takes time, and can be expensive due to accountant, attorney, and filing fees.

Fortunately, stock issuance exemptions exist in California and at the federal level that allow most small, closely held corporations to privately offer and sell their initial shares of stock without having to obtain a permit from the department of corporations or register with the SEC. Most small, closely held corporations should be able to qualify for the California limited offering exemption. As you'll see, one-person corporations, small family corporations, and preexisting businesses that are incorporating their current operations should find it particularly easy to meet the requirements of this exemption.

TIP

There are other simplified California public offering exemptions. The exemption we discuss in this chapter is for a privately held corporation. California also has exemptions for corporations whose owners wish to make small offerings of shares to the public.

The first is a simplified securities permit procedure that allows a corporation to raise up to $1 million in a small public offering. The corporation must file a relatively simple question-and-answer form, Form U-7, commonly referred to as a Small Corporate Offering Registration or SCOR form. A fee of $2,500 is charged, plus up to $1,000 more based upon the Department of Corporations' average cost of

processing the form for all SCOR applicants. A number of other states recognize Form U-7; it may soon be the best way to obtain moderate amounts of equity capital from investors under state securities registration laws. Certain restrictions apply—for example, your stock price must be at least $5. If you are interested in raising capital through a small stock promotion, you may wish to check out this simplified permit procedure with a lawyer or order a SCOR form (Form U-7) from the nearest office of the California Department of Corporations.

A second exemption allows issuers—corporations —to make a general announcement of the sale of shares to the public. The announcement must contain certain information and meet conditions related to its dissemination to the public. You must file two notice forms; the first one requires a filing fee of $600. Unlike the limited offering exemption, we believe you always need a lawyer to rely on this exemption. For more information, call the nearest Department of Corporations office and ask for the 25102(n) packet.

The Limited Offering Exemption

The limited offering stock issuance exemption is available if you will be issuing shares privately to your shareholders without advertisements or public solicitation for your shares. There are other rules and requirements related to your stock issuance that you must meet that we discuss below. Most small, closely held corporations should not have any trouble meeting these rules, since they reflect the way most small corporations actually sell their shares.

RESOURCES

Where to get more information on the limited offering exemption. You can find the limited offering exemption at Section 25102(f) of the Corporations Code. The regulations that interpret the statute are contained in Title 10 of the California Code of Regulations, §§ 260.102.12 through 260.102.14.

Additionally, your shareholders must meet certain requirements, which we discuss below. Finally, we give you a series of down-to-earth examples to put this rather technical information in a more practical context.

> **WARNING**
>
> **This book doesn't cover future stock issuances.** The limited offering exemption contains technical rules relating to future stock issuances, which we do not cover here. If you issue shares again after your initial stock issuance, make sure this future stock offering meets the requirements of the securities laws. Otherwise, you could jeopardize your initial stock issuance.

General Rules of the Limited Offering Exemption

Here, we discuss the general requirements of the limited offering exemption. Most small corporations planning a limited, private offering and sale of their initial shares should not have a problem meeting these basic requirements.

The Investment Representation Rule

All purchasers of shares issued under the limited offering exemption are required to state, in writing, that they are purchasing their shares for their own account and not to resell to others. Shareholders in small, closely held corporations should not have any problem making this representation.

> **CROSS-REFERENCE**
>
> **This investment representation is included in the tear-out shareholder representation letter contained in Appendix B.**

The California Small Offering Exemption

If your proposed stock issuance does not qualify under the California limited offering exemption discussed in this chapter, you may be able to rely on another California stock issuance exemption—the small offering exemption. In practice, this exemption may serve as a useful alternative if you will be issuing stock to all your shareholders for cash only. The other situations covered by the small offering exemption are also covered by the limited offering exemption, although in broader terms.

Under the small offering exemption, a lawyer is required to sign an opinion of counsel statement on a notice form stating that in the lawyer's opinion, the stock offering and issuance meets the requirements of the small offering exemption. You file this with the Department of Corporations.

Because the small offering exemption is truly limited in scope and requires a lawyer's opinion, this book does not include the small offering exemption notice form or discuss its various requirements. However, if you experience any difficulty in understanding or meeting the (sometimes subjective) requirements of the limited offering exemption, we urge you to discuss this alternative with a lawyer.

> **TIP**
>
> The forms contained in Appendix B of this book, such as the articles of incorporation, bylaws, and most of the resolutions in the minutes of your first meeting, will work fine if you utilize the small offering exemption instead of the limited offering exemption.

The No-Advertising Rule

Your offer or sale of shares must not be accompanied by the publication of any advertisement. Advertisement is defined as any written or printed communication, recorded telephone messages, or radio, television, or similar communication, published in connection with the offer or sale of stock. Publish means to publicly issue or circulate by newspaper, mail, radio, or television, or otherwise to disseminate to the public. A public advertisement also includes sales pitches at seminars or meetings to which attendees have been invited by general advertising or solicitation. Although these terms cover a lot of ground, they do not prohibit circulation of disclosure materials to offerees, as long as these materials are not disseminated to the public.

If you disclose material about your stock issuance only to people reasonably believed to be interested in purchasing the shares or to persons whom the corporation reasonably believes may meet the qualifications required of purchasers under this exemption, you should not run afoul of these rules (as long as neither the corporation nor an agent acting on its behalf offers or sells shares through general solicitation or general advertising). Use common sense in communicating the fact that you are setting up a corporation and will be issuing your initial shares. Obviously, you should keep these types of discussions with potential investors on a private level and not disclose the availability of your shares publicly.

For example, you won't want to advertise your new corporation in the business opportunities section of the classifieds or use mailing lists as a means of targeting potential shareholders. Perhaps less obviously, you shouldn't invite the public to a seminar or a meeting where you plan to make even a soft pitch for your shares.

Most incorporators of small, closely held corporations will naturally limit any overtures to invest in the corporation to close friends, relatives, or business associates who are considered suitable purchasers under this exemption (that is, purchasers who fit within one of the specific limited offering categories as explained in "Special 35-Shareholder Rule," below). This will usually be done in the context of a one-to-one conversation. If you do this, you should not have a problem complying with this no-advertising rule.

The Consideration for Shares Rule

You may only issue shares in exchange for something of value (consideration). The consideration you may receive for stock includes money paid, tangible or intangible property received by the corporation, labor done for or services rendered to the corporation, or the cancellation of debts owed by the corporation to the person receiving the shares. Shares cannot be issued under California law in return for future services or promissory notes (unless the notes are adequately secured by collateral other than the shares themselves). This means, for example, that you shouldn't issue shares to a key employee in return for her entering into an employment contract with the corporation—this is really issuing shares in return for the performance of future services. Similarly, you can't normally issue shares in return for the promissory note of a shareholder who promises to pay for the shares over time or at some later date. (For further details on how to issue shares in return for different types of consideration, see Chapter 5, Step 8.)

The Notice of Transaction Rule

Your corporation must file a notice of transaction form with the Department of Corporations within 15 calendar days after the first sale of a security in this state.

CROSS-REFERENCE

You will prepare this notice form as part of Step 7 of Chapter 5. As you'll see, you will prepare and file this notice just before the actual issuance (sale) of your shares to stay on the safe side of this deadline date.

The Disclosure of All Material Facts Rule

Although the limited offering exemption does not contain any specific requirements relating to the disclosure of specific facts to shareholders, it is illegal "to offer or sell a security in this state or buy or offer to buy a security in this state by means of any written or oral communication which includes an untrue statement of a material fact or omits to state a material fact necessary in order to make the statements made, in light of the circumstances under which they were made, not misleading." (Cal. Corp. Code § 25401.)

Since you will undoubtedly be making at least oral communications in issuing your shares, you must make sure you are completely honest in your dealings with potential shareholders and that you disclose all material facts concerning your incorporation and share issuance to them.

Special Shareholder Suitability Rules

The limited offering exemption requires you to make sure that each of your shareholders qualifies to be issued shares under the limited offering exemption. Specifically, each purchaser must fit within one of six categories (although the statute includes only three categories, we've divided them into six to make them easier to understand). The basic purpose of these suitability categories is to ensure that each of your shareholders is able to protect him- or herself when purchasing shares in your corporation.

Our discussion of suitable shareholders looks only at types of shareholders who are most relevant to small corporations issuing shares to individual shareholders. We have excluded rules relating to affiliates and other types of shareholders that are unlikely to apply to you.

TIP

Most shareholders fit into Categories 1 and 6. Most incorporators will not need to get bogged down in the more technical categories discussed below. In the usual case, all your shareholders will fit nicely into Category 1 (inside shareholders such as directors or officers) and Category 6 (spouses or relatives of another suitable shareholder). Because each shareholder only need fit within one suitability category, most readers will be able to review these two categories and then skip ahead to the next section of this chapter.

Category 1. Inside Shareholders

The most common types of suitable shareholders under the limited offering exemption are those with a close relationship to the corporation, whom we refer to as inside shareholders. Many small corporations will find that most, if not all, of their shareholders will fall into one of the inside shareholder definitions discussed here.

These shareholders (sometimes referred to as uncounted shareholders by lawyers) are automatically suitable under the limited offering exemption—this means that they do not have to meet one of the subjective suitability standards discussed in Categories 2 and 3 of this section. Here's a list of the different types of shareholders who fit within this inside shareholder category:

- **Directors or officers of the corporation.** Because many small corporations will only issue shares to directors or officers, all of their shareholders will be suitable practical matter, it is unlikely that all of these people will be able to meet this test. Some, if not most, will have to designate and seek the advice of a professional advisor under Category 5 if the shares are to be issued under the limited offering exemption.

The alternative to the limited offering exemption in this type of situation is, as we've said, to have the corporation's initial stock offering and issuance qualified by obtaining a permit from the Department of Corporations (or issue shares for cash under the California small offering exemption—see "The California Small Offering Exemption," above). Because Bob is dealing with so many outsiders, it may be best to hire a lawyer to obtain a permit for his stock issuance rather than to try to qualify each one of these people as suitable purchasers.

The point of these last two examples is that you should be careful about considering relatives, friends, neighbors, business associates—and particularly casual acquaintances, customers, or clients of your business—as meeting the suitability standards of this exemption. They may not have a close enough personal or business relationship with one of the corporation's directors or officers or may not have sufficient personal business or financial experience to enable them to make an informed investment decision and protect their own interests. When making distinctions of this type, use your common sense, be a bit conservative, and, if you have any doubts about the suitability of a prospective purchaser, make sure that their interests are protected by a qualified professional advisor (Category 5).

Federal Securities Act

The federal Securities Act also applies to the offering of shares by a corporation. You must register your initial offering of stock with the federal Securities and Exchange Commission (SEC) unless you qualify for an exemption. There are several exemptions available—most small, closely held California corporations eligible for the California limited offering exemption should qualify under at least one of them.

Traditionally, most small, closely held corporations wishing to privately issue their initial shares to a limited number of people have been able to rely on the federal private offering exemption. Readers using this book (who will be eligible for the California limited offering) will probably also qualify for this federal exemption—as you'll see, the basic requirements of the two exemptions are similar.

The federal private offering exemption is a one-line exemption contained in Section 4(2) of the Securities Act for "transactions by an issuer [corporation] not involving any public offering." The courts have discussed the basic elements that should be present when relying on this exemption (a leading case on this exemption is *SEC v. Ralston Purina Co.,* 346 U.S. 119 (1953)):

- The offerees (people to whom shares are offered) and purchasers are able to fend for themselves due to their previous financial or business experience, relationship to the issuer (the corporation, its directors, or officers), and/or significant personal net worth.

- The transaction is truly a nonpublic offering involving no general advertising or solicitation.

- The shares are purchased by the shareholders for their own account and not for resale.
- The offerees and purchasers are limited in number.
- The offerees and purchasers have access to or are given information relevant to the stock transaction in order to evaluate the pros and cons of the investment—for example, financial statements or a business plan.

In order to better explain the factors which should, and should not, be present when relying on this exemption, the SEC has issued Release No. 33-4552. This release includes several statements and examples regarding the private offering exemption—please see "SEC Release 33-4552," below, for a summary.

The guidelines contained in this release and the language of the court decisions are very general but, as you can see, they are similar to the general requirements of the California limited offering exemption. In order to make things a little clearer, the SEC has issued Rule 506 (this rule is part of a series of provisions referred to as Regulation D), which provides a safe harbor set of rules and procedures under Section 4(2) of the federal Securities Act, intended to show you a safe way to issue shares to others in a qualified private offering.

Here are some of the requirements of Rule 506 (although you don't have to follow these rules, we suggest you do to increase the likelihood that you will qualify under this exemption):

- There can be no more than 35 purchasers of shares. However, certain purchasers of shares are not counted, including certain accredited investors and the spouses, relatives, and relatives of spouses of another purchaser, if they share the same principal residence as the other purchaser. Accredited investors include directors and executive officers of the corporation and individuals with a net worth of more than $1 million or with two years' prior individual income in excess of $200,000 (or joint income with a spouse in excess of $300,000). These categories of uncounted purchasers under the federal rule are similar to, but narrower than, Categories 1, 4, and 6 under the California limited offering exemption.
- The shares cannot be offered or sold by any form of general solicitation or advertising. The rules restricting the manner of offering and selling the shares are similar to those which apply under the limited offering exemption. (See "The No-Advertising Rule," above.)
- The corporation must reasonably believe that each purchaser who is not an accredited investor (either alone or together with his or her purchaser representative) has such knowledge and experience in financial matters that he or she is capable of evaluating the merits and risks of the prospective investment. This requirement resembles the sophisticated investor test under the limited offering exemption Category 3. This rule allows a purchaser to rely on the experience of his or her purchaser representative, a concept similar to that of reliance on the financial or business experience of a professional advisor under the limited offering exemption Category 5. As with the limited offering exemption, this purchaser representative must be designated by the purchaser in writing.
- The corporation must furnish specific types of information (financial statements, written disclosure of resale restrictions, and so on) to nonaccredited investors within a reasonable time prior to sale of the shares. To be safe, the regulation suggests that this information be disclosed to accredited investors as well.

SEC Release 33-4552

The SEC issued this release to explain the scope of the federal private offering exemption. Here are some of the key factors it covers:

- Whether a transaction is truly private is essentially a question of fact. The SEC will consider all surrounding circumstances, including such factors as the relationship between the offerees and the issuer (corporation) and the nature, scope, size, type, and manner of the offering.

- The number of persons to whom shares are offered doesn't determine whether this exemption is available. What's important is whether these people have sufficient association with and knowledge of the issuer so as to make the exemption available.

- If you talk to, negotiate with, or solicit an unrestricted and unrelated group of prospective purchasers to figure out who would be willing to buy stock, the transaction is a public offering—even if only a few knowledgeable purchasers ultimately buy the shares.

- Offering shares only to key employees may not be sufficient to qualify for this exemption. However, an offering made to executive personnel who, because of their position, have access to the same kind of information that the Act would make available in the form of a registration statement (financial statements and so on) may qualify for the exemption.

- The sale of stock to promoters who take the initiative in founding or organizing the business falls within this exemption.

- If the amount of the stock offering is large, it may be considered a public offering not eligible for the exemption.

- If the purchasers acquire shares with the intent to resell them, the exemption may not apply—and the corporation may be liable for civil penalties.

- The corporation should consider the nature of the purchaser's past investment and trading practices or the character and scope of his or her business to make sure the shares won't be purchased for resale. In particular, purchases by individuals engaged in the business of buying and selling securities require careful scrutiny.

- The issuer can help control the resale of the securities and thereby make reliance on this exemption a little safer. For example, the corporation may secure a representation from the initial purchasers that they are acquiring the securities only for investment and place a legend to this effect on the stock certificates.

- What may appear to be a separate offering to a properly limited group will not be considered exempt if it is one of a related series of offerings (if, for example, you offer and sell shares after your initial stock offering, this future issuance, if similar in structure, purpose, and scope, may be considered part of your initial stock issuance and may jeopardize your initial exemption).

- Regardless of whether an exemption is available for your stock offering, you cannot engage in any fraudulent activity (and should disclose all material facts to all potential shareholders) to avoid civil penalties.

- The corporation must give each purchaser the opportunity to ask questions and receive answers about the terms and conditions of the offering and to obtain any additional information which the corporation possesses, or can acquire without unreasonable effort or expense, that is necessary to verify the accuracy of information already furnished to the purchaser. The rule also indicates that the antifraud provisions always apply to any offer or sale of securities, and that the corporation must, generally, provide all material information to ensure that purchasers are not misled.

- The corporation must make a reasonable inquiry to determine whether the purchaser is acquiring the securities for him- or herself (and not for resale to other persons). Actions the corporation should take include: (1) making a written disclosure to each purchaser, prior to the sale, that the securities have not been registered under the Act and cannot be resold unless they are registered or are exempt from registration; and (2) placing a legend on the share certificates indicating that the securities have not been registered and referring to these restrictions on the transferability and sale of the shares.

- A Notice of Sales of Securities form (Form D) must be filed with the SEC.

It is not coincidental that Rule 506 so closely resembles the California limited offering exemption. Both were passed at approximately the same time, and were drafted and amended so as to achieve uniformity between federal and state security law exemptions. Perhaps the most significant procedural differences between the California limited offering exemption and Rule 506 is that the latter requires you to furnish specific information to certain purchasers of shares, including the disclosure of transfer restrictions on these shares to purchasers and the placement of a legend to that effect on the share certificates.

As mentioned above, we assume that you should be able to meet most of the general guidelines to the federal private offering exemption under Section 4(2) of the federal Securities Act when issuing your initial shares under the California limited offering exemption, and you should also be able to simultaneously meet most of the safe harbor provisions of Rule 506 just discussed.

TIP

Our documents contain some of the Rule 506 language. To help conform your limited offering stock issuance to some of the additional required and suggested procedures of Rule 506, we have: (1) included a statement of the restrictions on transfer of shares in the shareholder representation letters prepared in Step 6 of Chapter 5; and (2) placed a nonregistration legend on the share certificates contained in Appendix B of this book.

We have provided a practical and traditional method of issuing your shares under the general guidelines of the federal private offering exemption promulgated under Section 4(2) of the federal Securities Act and under some of the provisions of Rule 506. However, we can't anticipate the particular facts and circumstances surrounding your incorporation, and, of course, we can't guarantee that the federal private offering exemption will apply to you. Technical provisions of law (particularly of the securities laws) can be analyzed ad infinitum, and entire volumes, indeed libraries, have been devoted to the task. What we can do is provide you with (hopefully) helpful information, and repeat the reminder that you are ultimately responsible for making sure that you comply with the securities laws. We recommend you also ask an experienced business lawyer to review your proposed stock issuance to ensure compliance with federal and state securities laws.

Finally, one other point bears repeating: Remember to disclose, disclose, disclose all material information to every investor in your new corporation. This makes good business sense—and can help you steer clear of the SEC's antifraud rules.

Other Regulation D Exemptions

Federal Regulation D contains two other stock offering exemptions, which you may wish to discuss with a small business lawyer:

- Rule 504 exempts limited offerings up to $1 million. Although this rule does not limit the number of purchasers, it does prohibit general advertising, and no more than $500,000 of the stock can be sold without registering the sale with the state.

- Rule 505 exempts limited offerings up to $5 million. Generally no more than 35 nonaccredited investors are allowed, no general advertising is permitted, and specific information must be disclosed if any nonaccredited investors are included in the offering.

RESOURCES

For more information on SEC small business securities law exemptions, go to www.sec.gov/info/smallbus.shtml.

Corporate Taxation

California Taxes.. 70

    California Corporate Franchise Tax.. 70

    California Personal Income Tax... 70

    California S Corporation Tax Treatment.. 71

Federal Taxes.. 71

    Federal Corporate Income Tax.. 72

    Federal Individual Income Tax... 73

    Comparing Individual and Corporate Tax Rates and Payments

        for Owners of Smaller Corporations... 75

S Corporation Tax Status.. 75

    Federal S Corporation Tax Election Requirements... 76

    Advantages and Disadvantages of S Corporation Tax Treatment.................... 77

    S Corporation Tax Election for State Income Tax Purposes............................. 79

Corporate Accounting Periods and Tax Years.. 79

Tax Concerns When Stock Is Sold.. 80

    Section 1244 Tax Treatment for Stock Losses.. 80

    Section 1202 Capital Gains Tax Exclusion.. 81

Tax Treatment When an Existing Business Is Incorporated.............................. 82

    Tax-Free Exchanges Under Section 351... 82

    Potential Problems With Section 351 Tax-Free Exchanges.............................. 84

    Is a Section 351 Tax-Free Exchange Desirable?.. 85

    Additional Tax Considerations When Incorporating an Existing Business......... 86

    Liability for the Debts of the Unincorporated Business 87

Tax Treatment of Employee Compensation and Benefits.................................. 88

    Salaries 88

    Pension and Profit-Sharing Plans.. 88

    Medical Benefits... 89

    Life Insurance 89

    Disability Insurance.. 89

Most profit corporations, like individuals, must pay state and federal income taxes. (S corporations, discussed below, are exceptions.) In this chapter, we discuss the principal tax consequences of starting and operating a corporation and review special tax elections many small corporations will want to make. This information is meant to introduce you to the most important areas of corporate taxation and to provide you with enough background information to discuss them in greater depth with a tax expert.

RESOURCES

Keep up with changing tax rules. Tax laws and regulations are constantly changing. To keep up to date, see the most recent IRS and California tax publications. (See the tax publications listed in "Tax Forms–Federal" in Chapter 6.) For information on deductible business and home office expenses, see *Deduct It!* by Stephen Fishman (Nolo) and *Tax Savvy for Small Business,* by Frederick W. Daily (Nolo). Also, consult a tax advisor with small business experience on a regular basis to make sure you understand how all the latest tax wrinkles apply to your business.

California Taxes

Let's start by looking at the taxes and tax elections built into the California corporate tax scheme.

California Corporate Franchise Tax

California profit corporations must pay an annual corporate franchise tax—a fee you pay to the state for the privilege of doing business as a corporation. The tax is computed each year on the basis of the net income your corporation earned in the previous year from business activity in California (and, sometimes, outside California). The California franchise tax rate is 8.84% of the corporation's taxable income, with a minimum yearly payment of $800 regardless of the amount of annual income or profits. If you incorporate on or after January 1, 2000 you don't have to pay the minimum franchise tax for your first tax year, but you must estimate and pay any actual franchise taxes owed.

Corporations must estimate and pay franchise taxes during the year. (See "Corporate Estimated Tax Return" in Chapter 6.)

You must take your responsibility to estimate and pay corporate taxes seriously. If you fail to file state corporate tax returns or pay state corporate income taxes on time, your corporate privileges can be taken away. (You'll find a more detailed discussion of other taxes for which your corporation may be liable in Chapter 6.)

California Personal Income Tax

Corporate employees must report salaries and bonuses on their personal income tax returns, and pay tax on them at their personal state income tax rates. The fact that a corporate employee is also a corporate shareholder does not affect how income tax is calculated. As long as salaries and bonuses are reasonable (most are), the corporation can deduct these amounts as an ordinary and necessary business expense. This means that only the individual employee-shareholder pays income tax on corporate earnings paid out as salaries—the corporation does not.

In contrast, corporate profits paid to shareholders in the form of dividends are taxed twice. First, the corporation pays taxes at the corporate level, then the shareholders pay taxes on the individual distribution. Unlike salaries, the corporation cannot deduct dividend payouts to shareholders as a business expense on its income tax return. As a practical matter, however, double taxation is rare. Small corporations usually don't have to pay out

Comparing Individual and Corporate Tax Rates and Payments for Owners of Smaller Corporations

Incorporating and paying taxes as a corporate entity can result in business owners paying less tax on business income than they would pay as an individual. This is because income retained in a corporation may be taxed at the 15% and 25% corporate tax rates, instead of the higher marginal tax rates of the corporate owners, which can be as high as 35%

EXAMPLE:

Sally and Randolph run their own incorporated lumber supply company (S & R Wood, Inc.). With the boom in home renovations, their sales increase. After the close of the third quarter, S & R's accountant reports that they are on course to make $100,000 in taxable profits, even after dipping into the increased earnings to pay deductible bonuses and other operating expenses. Sally and Randy already receive a generous salary from their corporation, so they decide to keep the profits in the business to fund expansion in the following tax year. If S & R was taxed as a pass-through entity (a regular LLC or a general partnership), rather than as a corporation, the $100,000 would pass through the business and be taxed at Sally's and Randy's marginal (top) individual income tax rate of 35%. Instead, by retaining the money in the business, S & R Woods will pay corporate taxes at a rate of 15% and 25% for the first $75,000 of retained taxes, thus saving overall taxes for an effective tax rate of about 22%— a tax savings of $16,350 over what they would have had to pay at their individual tax rates (35% times $100,000, or $35,000).

TIP

Even corporations with sales of $1 million often benefit from the lower corporate tax rate. Why? Because after the corporation pays deductible salaries, bonuses, and corporate fringe benefits to the owner-employees of the corporation (and to other corporate personnel), and deducts other corporate business expenses, actual profits will be substantially reduced—often below the $75,000 threshold, where only the 15% and 25% corporate tax rates apply

WARNING

Don't forget to factor in other income earned by individual taxpayers. Individual taxpayers need to consider the money they are already earning—as salary and bonuses from their corporation and/or outside income—before comparing corporate versus individual tax rates. Many individuals will be paying taxes in one of the top individual tax brackets (33% or 35%) on individual income (this is their marginal tax bracket), and this is the rate that will apply to any additional income they earn. If income is not retained in the corporation, it will be taxed to them at this marginal rate—a rate that normally is higher than the 15% or 25% lowest corporate tax rates. For this reason, keeping money in a corporation often creates overall tax savings.

S Corporation Tax Status

This section covers a once highly popular tax election that still makes sense for some small corporations—the S corporation tax election. As noted above, if you elect S corporation tax status, all profits pass through the corporation and are taxed, one time only, on the individual income tax returns of the corporate shareholders.

TIP

Consider forming an LLC instead of an S corporation. The S corporation tax election is no longer the only way to simultaneously achieve limited personal liability for business debts and pass-through taxation of business profits. If you have not already incorporated (and most readers of this book probably haven't), you may be better off forming a limited liability company, especially if you do not need to raise money by giving equity investors a stake in your business.

Federal S Corporation Tax Election Requirements

To qualify for S corporation tax status with the IRS, a corporation must fall within the definition of a small business corporation under Subchapter S of the Internal Revenue Code. Only a corporation that meets these requirements qualifies:

- It must be a U.S. corporation, and its shareholders must be U.S. citizens or residents.

- There must be only one class of stock (all shares have equal rights, such as dividend and liquidation rights). However, differences as to voting rights are permitted.

- All shareholders must be individuals, estates, certain qualified trusts, or a tax-exempt organization (including tax-exempt charities and pension funds).

- There must be no more than 100 shareholders. Shares that are jointly owned by members of the same family (as defined in the Internal Revenue Code) are considered owned by one person.

A corporation that meets these requirements can elect S corporation tax treatment by filing IRS Form 2553 with the IRS, which must be signed by all current shareholders and by anyone else who owned shares during the preceding corporate tax year. The election must be made on or before the 15th day of the third month of the corporation's tax year for which the S status is to be effective, or any time during the preceding tax year. A new corporation that wishes to start off as an S corporation must make the election before the 15th day of the third month after the date the corporation's first tax year begins. The corporation's first tax year begins, under the S corporation election rules, when it issues stock to shareholders, acquires assets, or begins doing business, whichever occurs first. Generally, your first tax year will begin on the date you file your articles of incorporation. Check with your tax advisor to ensure that you fully understand these election rules and make your election on time—if you miss the deadline, your election won't be valid. (See "S Corporation Tax Election" in Chapter 6.)

Once a corporation elects to become an S corporation, it will be treated as one until the status is revoked or terminated. To revoke S corporation status, you must file shareholder consents to the revocation. You must have the consent of shareholders who collectively own at least a majority of the stock in the corporation to make the revocation effective.

S corporation status can also be automatically terminated, if the corporation doesn't continue to meet all of the requirements listed above, and therefore no longer qualifies as a small business corporation. For example, if the corporation issues a second class of shares or issues shares to a noneligible individual, or partnership, corporate, or LLC shareholders, it will lose S corporation status. Such a termination will be effective as of the date on which the terminating event occurs (not retroactively to the beginning of the tax year).

your individual tax return. And, of course, your corporation can deduct rent payments made under the lease (a rent comparable to the top amounts that similar commercial space rents for in your geographical area should pass IRS muster).

Finally, don't forget that if property is transferred to your corporation and it later appreciates, both your corporation and its shareholders may have to pay tax on the appreciation. Incorporators may decide not to transfer real property to their corporation to avoid this double tax—ask your tax advisor for more information.

Retaining Some of the Liabilities of the Prior Business

You may not wish to transfer—that is, have your corporation assume—all of the liabilities of the existing business. Here are two reasons why this might make sense:

- Assuming the liabilities of the prior business sometimes results in the assessment of tax (the amount by which the liabilities exceed the basis of the transferred assets—see "Potential Problems With Section 351 Tax-Free Exchanges," above).

- Payment of expenses by the prior business owners, rather than by the corporation, allows the owners to deduct these expenses on their individual tax returns, which reduces their individual taxable incomes.

Liability for the Debts of the Unincorporated Business

Another consideration when incorporating an existing business is whether the owners of the unincorporated business remain personally liable for its debts after it is incorporated. These rules have little practical significance for many incorporators who, as a matter of course and good-faith business practice, will wish to promptly pay all the debts and liabilities passed on to the new corporation. But, in case a debt is contested or for some other reason you wish to extend the time for payment, here are the legal basics:

- Whether or not the corporation assumes the debts and liabilities of the prior business, the prior owners remain personally liable for these debts and liabilities.

- The new corporation is not liable for the debts and liabilities of the prior business unless it specifically agrees to assume them. If it does not assume them, the prior owners remain personally liable.

- If the transfer is fraudulent or done with the intent to frustrate or deceive creditors, the creditors of the prior business can file legal papers to seize the transferred business assets. Similarly, if the corporation does not, in fact, pay the assumed liabilities of the prior business, the creditors of the prior business may be allowed to seize the transferred assets.

- If transferred assets are subject to recorded liens (for example, a mortgage on real estate), these liens will survive the transfer and the assets will continue to be subject to them.

- The former business owners can be personally liable for *postincorporation* debts if credit is extended to the corporation by a creditor who thinks that he or she is still dealing with the prior business (for example, a creditor who has not been notified of the incorporation). (See "Notify Creditors and Others of Dissolution of Prior Business" in Chapter 6 for the steps to take to notify creditors when you incorporate.)

- The corporation may be liable for delinquent sales, employment, or other taxes owed by the unincorporated business.

A corporation that specifically assumes all of the debts and liabilities of the unincorporated business is exempt from most of the provisions of the California bulk sales law. This results in a reduction in incorporation paperwork. (See Chapter 5, Step 8.)

Tax Treatment of Employee Compensation and Benefits

This section provides an overview of the tax treatment of corporate salaries and fringe benefits. This is a very general discussion—ask your tax advisor for the most current information.

Salaries

A regular or C corporation may deduct amounts paid to employees as salaries (including bonuses) for corporate income tax purposes. To be deductible, salaries and bonuses must be reasonable and must be paid for services actually performed by the employees. Huge salary increases or large discretionary lump-sum bonuses paid to shareholder-employees of closely held corporations may be scrutinized by the IRS, since they can be, and sometimes are, used as a means of paying disguised dividends to the shareholders.

But don't worry too much about the IRS claiming that your corporation's salaries or bonuses are too high. In an age when top execs of publicly held corporations are notoriously overpaid, and entertainment and sports figures who only make $1,000,000 often feel miserably underpaid, higher levels of compensation can be considered reasonable. You may be able to successfully argue that the salary, bonuses, and benefits you receive as compensation from your corporation are reasonable given the amount earned by executives in similar businesses. In

a sense, your argument boils down to this: If you are good enough to produce profits large enough to pay a huge salary, you reasonably deserve it.

In the unusual event that the IRS claims a salary is unreasonable, it will treat the excess amount as a dividend. This will not have an adverse effect on the shareholder-employee's tax liability, because the payment must be included on his or her individual tax return either way. In fact, dividends are taxed at 15% or less, which typically is less than the tax rate applied to other types of individual income. However, it will prevent the corporation from deducting the disallowed portion of compensation as an ordinary and necessary business expense. So the corporation will have to pay corporate taxes on the dividends amount too.

 TIP

Ask your board of directors to state how valuable you are. If you are nervous about paying yourself a large salary and a generous fringe benefit package, especially if you only work for your corporation part-time, ask your board to adopt a resolution detailing your abilities, qualifications, and responsibilities, showing why you are entitled to the wages and benefits your corporation is paying you. You can find such a resolution in *The Corporate Records Handbook*, by Anthony Mancuso (Nolo).

Pension and Profit-Sharing Plans

Corporations may deduct payments made on behalf of employees to qualified pension or profit-sharing plans. Contributions and accumulated earnings under such plans are not taxed until they are distributed to the employee. This is advantageous because employees generally will be in a lower tax bracket at retirement age, and the funds, while they are held in trust, can be invested and allowed to accumulate with no tax due on investment income or gains prior to their distribution.

Generally speaking, there are two basic types of pension plans: defined-contribution and defined-benefit plans (there are some hybrid types as well). A defined-contribution plan guarantees a specified yearly contribution of no more than 25% of an employee's annual salary to each employee. A defined-benefit plan guarantees a specified benefit upon retirement, which can be as large as 100% of an employee's annual pay during his or her highest-paid years. These contribution ceilings are subject to maximum yearly contribution limits, dollar amounts that are tied to the federal cost of living index. Your contributions cannot exceed these limits, even if an employee's yearly pay otherwise justifies a large pension contribution.

For detailed information on employee pension plan contribution and benefit rules, see *Tax Savvy for Small Business,* by Frederick W. Daily (Nolo). Also see the following IRS publications (available from the IRS website at www.irs.gov):

> 334: *Tax Guide For Small Business*
>
> 560: *Self-Employed Retirement Plans*
>
> 575: *Pension and Annuity Income*
>
> 590: *Individual Retirement Arrangements*
>
> 1048: *Filing Requirements for Employee Benefit Plans.*

Medical Benefits

Tax-favored corporate medical benefits include deductible direct reimbursement plans, term life insurance, and other benefits. Let's look at each.

Medical Expense Reimbursement

Amounts paid by a corporation as part of a medical expense reimbursement plan to repay the medical expenses of employees, their spouses, and dependents, are deductible by the corporation and are not included in the employee's income for tax purposes.

Accident and Health Insurance

A corporation may deduct premiums paid by the corporation for accident and health insurance coverage for employees, their spouses, and dependents. The premiums paid by the corporation are not included in the employee's income for tax purposes. In addition, insurance proceeds and benefits are not normally taxable. Coverage need not be part of a group plan, such as Blue Cross. If you prefer, the employee may pick her own policy, pay for it, and obtain reimbursement from the corporation.

Unincorporated business owners (and S corporation shareholder-employees) also are allowed to deduct the premiums paid for themselves and their spouses for health insurance.

Life Insurance

A corporation can deduct premiums paid on behalf of employees for group term life insurance, as long as the corporation is not the beneficiary. This tax break is available only if the plan does not discriminate in favor of key employees. An employee covered by a qualified group term insurance plan is not taxed on premium payments by the corporation for up to $50,000 worth of insurance coverage. Death proceeds under such insurance are also generally not included in the employee's income for tax purposes.

Disability Insurance

Premiums paid by a corporation for disability insurance coverage for its employees are deductible by the corporation. Benefits paid under a disability insurance policy are generally taxable to the employee unless the employee paid the premiums or suffers a permanent injury.

Fill In Your Articles

Instructions

❶ Type the name of the corporation in the blank in Article One. If you have reserved a corporate name, the name you specify here must exactly match your reserved name. If you have decided not to use your reserved corporate name, that's fine—just make sure to check the availability of the new name before you type it in here.

❷ Insert the name and business or residence address of the corporation's initial agent for service of process. This address must be within California. The initial agent for service of process is the person whom you wish to authorize to receive legal documents for the corporation. Most incorporators will give the name of one of the directors and the principal office of the corporation here as the name and address of the corporation's initial agent. Do not use a post office box address in this response.

❸ Indicate the number of authorized shares of the corporation. The traditional longhand method is to first spell out the number, then indicate the figure in parentheses; for example, "TWO HUNDRED THOUSAND (200,000)." There's no longer a sensible reason for this convention (it made sense in the days of the quill pen), so you can either spell out the number or type in a figure in this blank.

> **WARNING**
> **This articles form authorizes only one class of shares.** This article authorizes the corporation to issue one class of common shares, with each share having equal voting, liquidation, dividend, and other rights. If you want to authorize more than one class of shares, you will need to see a lawyer.

Authorized shares are shares of stock that the corporation can later sell to shareholders, at which time they are referred to as issued shares. There is no magic formula for computing the exact number of authorized shares you should specify—you can authorize as many or as few shares as you wish. However, the number of authorized shares you specify must, of course, be large enough to cover your initial stock issuance. You may wish to skip ahead to the instructions for preparing the "Issuance of Shares" resolution in your minutes in Step 5 of this chapter. After determining how many shares you will issue and adding a little extra to allow for the future issuance of additional shares (for example, if 1,000 shares will actually be issued, it is sensible to authorize at least 2,000 shares in your articles), type the final number you come up with here.

> **TIP**
> **You may want to authorize extra shares.** Authorizing additional shares beyond the actual amount you plan to issue can be helpful if you want to implement a stock bonus or option plan in the future. If you don't authorize additional shares now and decide later to increase the authorized number of shares stated in your articles, you will have to prepare a special amendment to your articles of incorporation and file it with the secretary of state.

❹ Type the full names and business or residence addresses of your initial director(s). Remember, a California corporation must generally have at least three directors. However, if you will have only two shareholders, you may have only two directors; if you will have only one shareholder, you can have only one director. Of course, you can provide for additional directors above these minimum limits if you wish (see "How Many People May Organize the Corporation?" in Chapter 2 for further information).

❺ Article Six uses the language contained in Section 204.5 of the Corporations Code to eliminate the personal liability of directors for monetary damages to the fullest extent permissible under California law. However, this provision applies only to shareholder derivative suits (suits brought by, or in the right of, the corporation for breach of a director's duty of care to the corporation or stockholders). It does not apply to third-party lawsuits (suits brought by individual shareholders or outsiders for individual wrongs).

Article Seven uses language contained in Section 317(g) of the Corporations Code to allow the corporation to provide indemnification for the directors and officers beyond the limits expressly permitted by other subsections of Section 317. This article authorizes the corporation to provide for additional indemnification elsewhere (for example, in the corporation's bylaws or in agreements entered into by the corporation and its directors and officers). We have included broad indemnification rights for directors and officers in Article VII of the bylaws (see Step 4, below).

❻ You have to fill out two sets of date and signature lines at the bottom of your articles. Although somewhat redundant, this is a requirement of California law if you want to name directors in your articles. We use this procedure because it eliminates the need to formally appoint initial directors later. Have all of the persons named as initial directors in Article Five date and sign the articles in both places shown. Make sure that their signed and typed names correspond exactly to their names as given in Article Five. Use a black-ink pen when signing your articles—the secretary of state must be able to photocopy them.

Prepare Your Cover Letter

A cover letter for your articles is included in Appendix B and on the CD-ROM. If you plan to file your articles in person at one of the offices of the secretary of state (in Fresno, Los Angeles, Sacramento, San Diego, or San Francisco), you do not need to prepare this letter. However, most incorporators will wish to use this letter to file their articles by mail with the Sacramento office of the secretary of state.

Below is a sample of the cover letter for your articles of incorporation.

❶ If you have reserved a corporate name (see Step 1, above), include this optional bracketed sentence from the sample cover letter, specifying your corporate name reservation number in the blank. (We've left space in the tear-out letter for you to type in this optional sentence).

❷ The fee you must pay to file your articles is $100. (Check that the fee hasn't changed.) Include a check with your cover letter, payable to the "California Secretary of State," for this amount.

The secretary will certify two copies of the articles for free (this is why the letter states that you are including two copies in addition to the original articles). If you include more than two copies, they will be certified at an extra cost of $8 each. Make sure to change the number of copies stated in the first paragraph of the letter, and add the certification fees to your total fees.

California corporations continue to increase. A side effect of this glut of corporate formations is that you can expect to wait longer for your articles to be filed and returned to you. Currently, you can expect to wait up to one month before your articles are filed by mail and returned to you. To eliminate this delay, you may want to trek over to the nearest local office of the secretary of state to file your articles in person.

The secretary of state offers expedited filing services for a fee. Filing can be accomplished within 24 hours of receipt of the document (delivered in person to the Sacramento office of the secretary of state) for an extra $350 fee. Class A, four-hour service requires a pre-clearance of your articles and costs even more. These are whopping fees compared to the more modest expedited filing fees typically charged by other states ($25 to $50 seems to be the average). To find out more about these services (the secretary may suspend the service occasionally if the filing volume is too high), go to the secretary of state's website at www.ss.ca.gov.

❸ One of your initial directors should sign here. If you have reserved your corporate name, the person who submitted your corporate name reservation letter should also sign this cover letter.

Delaying the Filing of Your Articles. You may be able to incorporate on a specific date (to establish a particular tax year). California law allows you to request a delayed filing date for your articles as long as this date is no more than 90 days from the date of receipt of your articles. If you wish to do this, add a conspicuous sentence to your cover letter asking that your articles be filed on a specific future date (the delayed date may be a weekend day or a holiday, but your articles must be received at least one business day before the requested future filing date).

Make Copies of Your Articles

After completing your articles of incorporation, make three copies. The original will be filed with the secretary of state's office; two copies will be sent to the secretary of state's office with the original form to be certified for free and returned to you; the other copy is your file copy (keep it until you receive the certified copies back from the secretary's office). Make one copy of the completed cover letter to keep for your records. You will mail the original cover letter with your articles of incorporation to the Sacramento office of the secretary of state.

Staple the pages of each copy of your articles together (use one staple in the upper left corner of each copy).

All copies of your articles should be legible, with good contrast.

If you retype your articles of incorporation, please be aware that articles of incorporation must be typed on one side of a standard 8½" x 11" (letter-sized) page.

COVER LETTER FOR FILING ARTICLES

(name of incorporator)

(address)

(telephone number)

Secretary of State
Business Programs Division
1500 11th Street
Sacramento, CA 95814
Attention: Document Filing Support Unit

Re: ___ _(name of corporation)_ _____

Dear Secretary of State:

I enclose an original and two copies of the proposed Articles
of Incorporation of ___ _(name of corporation)_ _____.
["This corporate name was reserved with your office pursuant to
Certificate of Reservation #(_____)." ❶]

Also enclosed is a check/money order in payment of the
following fees:

Filing Articles of Incorporation $100❷

Please file the original Articles and return the certified
copies to me at the above address.

Very truly yours,

(signature of incorporator)   ❸
_____
(typed name) , Incorporator

File Your Articles of Incorporation

Filing your articles is a formality. The secretary of state will file your papers if they conform to law and the proper fees are paid. The articles are the only formal organizational document that you must file with the secretary of state (the only other incorporation filing is your Notice of Stock Transaction with the department of corporations—see Step 7). You do not file your bylaws, minutes of your first meeting, or any of the other incorporation forms or documentation contained in this book with any state agency.

To file your articles, mail the original and two copies, the cover letter, and a check or money order for the total fees payable to the "California Secretary of State." *To expedite processing, also enclose a stamped, self-addressed envelope.* Send these papers to the Sacramento office of the secretary of state shown in the heading of the tear-out cover letter.

It normally takes two to four weeks for your articles to be filed and returned to you by mail (it can take longer during busy filing periods, so you may need to be patient).

Filing Your Articles in Person. You may also file your articles in person at any office of the secretary of state—the secretary of state's office addresses and telephone numbers are listed at the beginning of Appendix B.

There is an additional $15 special handling fee, however, for filing your articles in person. You must write a separate check for this amount; it will not be refunded if your over-the-counter articles are not acceptable for filing. Also, you must provide the Fresno, Los Angeles, San Diego, or San Francisco office of the secretary of state with an extra signed copy of your articles (this copy is in addition to the two copies indicated above). This additional copy will be forwarded by the local office to the Sacramento office of the secretary of state.

Step 3. Set Up a Corporate Records Book (Or Order a Corporate Kit)

Creating a corporate records book is an essential part of setting up a corporation. Your records book will help you keep important corporate papers in good order.

Set Up a Corporate Records Book

You will need a corporate records book to keep all your documents in an orderly fashion, including your articles, bylaws, minutes of your first board meeting and ongoing director and shareholder meetings, stock certificates, and stubs. Setting up and maintaining a neat, well-organized records book is one of your most important tasks—it will serve as a repository for corporate documents and as a formal paper trail documenting organizational and ongoing corporate formalities. You should keep your corporate records book at the principal office of your corporation.

To set up a corporate records book, you can simply place all your incorporation documents in a three-ring binder. If you prefer, however, you can order a corporate records kit through a legal stationery store.

A corporate kit typically includes:

- a three-ring binder corporate records book with the corporate name engraved on the book
- lithographed stock certificates with the name and state of formation of the corporation printed on the face of each certificate
- share register and transfer ledger pages, and
- a metal corporate seal to emboss your corporate name and year of incorporation on corporate documents.

The standard corporate kits sold by legal stationers and suppliers also contain bylaws, minutes of the first meeting, and printed stock certificates. These forms contain blanks that you must type in yourself. The bylaws and minutes contained in these other kits are often generic or minimal in nature and will not correspond to our forms or the specific instructions contained in this book.

Corporate Seals

A corporation is not legally required to have or use a corporate seal, but many find it handy to do so. A corporate seal is a formal way of indicating that a given document is the duly authorized act of the corporation. It is not normally used on everyday business papers (invoices, purchase orders, and the like) but is commonly employed for more formal documents such as leases, stock certificates, deeds of trust, and certifications of board resolutions. Most seals are circular in form and contain the name of the corporation, the state, and the year of incorporation. Embossed and stamped seals are also available separately through legal stationers.

Stock Certificates

This book contains black-and-white stock certificates intended for use by corporations issuing shares under the California limited offering exemption.

The book certificates contain a special legend noting that the shares have not been registered under state or federal securities laws (as discussed in Chapter 3). This legend is not legally required under the California limited offering exemption, however.

WARNING

You can't use the stock certificates in this book if you form a close corporation or don't use the limited offering exemption. In the unusual event that you have decided to set up your corporation as a close corporation, or if you will not be relying on the California limited offering exemption when offering and issuing your shares, you cannot use the stock certificates contained in this book. In either of these special situations, you will need to order special certificates with different stock certificate legends printed on their face. Ask the lawyer who helps you in these situations to order the proper certificates for you.

TIP

Wait before ordering stock certificates or a seal. We suggest you wait until you have received the certified copies of your filed articles back from the secretary of state's office before you order a corporate kit, printed certificates, or a seal. This way, you'll be sure that you really have set up a corporation before you pay for these materials. However, if you are committed to forming your corporation and you have reserved your proposed corporate name for your use, then it's probably safe to order these corporate materials ahead of time.

Step 4. Prepare Your Bylaws

Your next step is to prepare the corporate bylaws included with this book. Bylaws are an internal corporate document that set out the basic ground rules for operating your corporation. They are not filed with the state.

The Bylaws Form

After you have received the certified copies of your articles from the secretary of state (and ordered a corporate kit if you decide to do so),

STOCK CERTIFICATE

The secretary then presented to the meeting for adoption a proposed form of stock certificate for the corporation. Upon motion duly made and seconded, it was

RESOLVED, that the form of stock certificate presented to this meeting be and hereby is adopted for use by this corporation, and the Secretary of this corporation is directed to annex a copy thereof to the minutes of this meeting.

ACCOUNTING PERIOD

The chairperson informed the board that the next order of business was the selection of the accounting period of the corporation. After discussion and upon motion duly made and seconded, it was

RESOLVED, that the accounting period of this corporation shall end on _____ *(ending date of the accounting period of the corporation)* _____ ❾ of each year.

PRINCIPAL EXECUTIVE OFFICE

After discussion as to the exact location of the corporation's principal executive office, upon motion duly made and seconded, it was

RESOLVED, that the principal executive office of this corporation shall be located at _____ *(address, including city, county, and state of principal executive office)* _____ .❿

BANK ACCOUNT

The chairperson recommended that the corporation open a bank account with _____ *(name of bank(s) and branch office(s))* _____ .⓫ Upon motion duly made and seconded, it was

RESOLVED, that the funds of this corporation shall be deposited with the bank and branch office indicated just above.

RESOLVED FURTHER, that the treasurer of this corporation is hereby authorized and directed to establish an account with said bank and to deposit the funds of this corporation therein.

RESOLVED FURTHER, that any officer, employee, or agent of this corporation is hereby authorized to endorse checks, drafts, or other evidences of indebtedness made payable to this corporation, but only for the purpose of deposit.

RESOLVED FURTHER, that all checks, drafts and other instruments obligating this corporation to pay money shall be signed on behalf of this corporation by any _____*(number)*_____ ⓬ of the following:

(name of person authorized to sign checks)   ⓭
(name of person authorized to sign checks)
(name of person authorized to sign checks)

RESOLVED FURTHER, that said bank is hereby authorized to honor and pay any and all checks and drafts of this corporation signed as provided herein.

RESOLVED FURTHER, that the authority hereby conferred shall remain in force until revoked by the board of directors of this corporation and until written notice of such revocation shall have been received by said bank.

RESOLVED FURTHER, that the secretary of this corporation be and is hereby authorized to certify as to the continuing authority of these resolutions, the persons authorized to sign on behalf of this corporation and the adoption of said bank's standard form of resolution, provided that said form does not vary materially from the terms of the foregoing resolutions.

PAYMENT, DEDUCTION AND AMORTIZATION OF ORGANIZATIONAL EXPENSES ⓮

The board next considered the question of paying the expenses incurred in the formation of this corporation. A motion was made, seconded, and unanimously approved, and it was

RESOLVED, that the president and the treasurer of this corporation are authorized and empowered to pay all reasonable and proper expenses incurred in connection with the organization of the corporation, including, among others, filing, licensing, and attorney's and accountant's fees, and to reimburse any persons making any such disbursements for the corporation, and it was

FURTHER RESOLVED, that the treasurer is authorized to elect to deduct and amortize the foregoing expenditures pursuant to, and as permitted by, Section 248 of the Internal Revenue Code of 1986, as amended.

FEDERAL S CORPORATION TAX TREATMENT ⓯

The board of directors next considered the advantages of electing to be taxed under the provisions of Subchapter S of the Internal Revenue Code of 1986, as amended. After discussion, upon motion duly made and seconded, it was unanimously

RESOLVED, that this corporation hereby elects to be treated as a Small Business Corporation for federal income tax purposes under Subchapter S of the Internal Revenue Code of 1986, as amended.

RESOLVED FURTHER, that the officers of this corporation take all actions necessary and proper to effectuate the foregoing resolution, including, among other things, obtaining the requisite consents from the shareholders of this corporation and executing and filing the appropriate forms with the Internal Revenue Service within the time limits specified by law.

QUALIFICATION OF STOCK AS SECTION 1244 STOCK ⓰

The board next considered the advisability of qualifying the stock of this corporation as Section 1244 Stock as defined in Section 1244 of the Internal Revenue Code of 1986, as amended, and of organizing and managing the corporation so that it is a Small Business Corporation as defined in that section. Upon motion duly made and seconded, it was unanimously

RESOLVED, that the proper officers of the corporation are, subject to the requirements and restrictions of federal, California, and any other applicable securities laws, authorized to sell and issue shares of stock in return for the receipt of an aggregate amount of money and other property, as a contribution to capital and as paid-in surplus, which does not exceed $1,000,000.

RESOLVED FURTHER, that the sale and issuance of shares shall be conducted in compliance with Section 1244 so that the corporation and its shareholders may obtain the benefits of that section.

RESOLVED FURTHER, that the proper officers of the corporation are directed to maintain such records as are necessary pursuant to Section 1244 so that any shareholder who experiences a loss on the transfer of shares of stock of the corporation may determine whether he or she qualifies for ordinary loss deduction treatment on his or her individual income tax return.

AUTHORIZATION OF ISSUANCE OF SHARES ❶❼

The board of directors next took up the matter of the sale and issuance of stock to provide capital for the corporation. Upon motion duly made and seconded, it was unanimously

RESOLVED, that the corporation sell and issue the following number of its authorized common shares to the following persons, in the amounts and for the consideration set forth under their names below. The board also hereby determines that the fair value to the corporation of any consideration for such shares issued other than for money is as set forth below:

Name	Number of Shares	Consideration	Fair Value
_____	_____	_____	$ _____
_____	_____	_____	$ _____
_____	_____	_____	$ _____
_____	_____	_____	$ _____
_____	_____	_____	$ _____
_____	_____	_____	$ _____

RESOLVED FURTHER, that these shares shall be sold and issued by this corporation strictly in accordance with the terms of the exemption from qualification of these shares as provided for in Section 25102(f) of the California Corporations Code.

RESOLVED FURTHER, that the appropriate officers of this corporation are hereby authorized and directed to take such actions and execute such documents as they may deem necessary or appropriate to effectuate the sale and issuance of such shares for such consideration.

Since there was no further business to come before the meeting, upon motion duly made and seconded, the meeting was adjourned.

_____
(signature of secretary)
(typed name of secretary)
                              ,Secretary ❶❽

Instructions

Waiver of Notice and Consent to Holding of First Meeting of Board of Directors

This form is included as the first page of the tear-out minutes in Appendix B and the Minutes form on the CD-ROM. This page is necessary in order to dispense with formal director notice requirements that apply to special board meetings (see Article III, Section 7, of your bylaws). Here are the special instructions associated with this page of your minutes:

❶ Name of Corporation

Type the name of your corporation in the heading to this page and in the first blank of the first paragraph.

❷ Address, Date, and Time of Meeting

Insert the address, date, and time of your first directors' meeting. Normally, you will show the address of the corporation here as the place of your board meeting. As you'll see below, we think it's wise for your first meeting to be more than just a paper meeting. In other words, if you have more than one director, you should actually sit down with the other directors at the place, date, and time indicated here to review and agree to the provisions in your completed minutes.

❸ Signatures of All Directors and Date of Waiver

Complete the date line on the waiver of notice page and have each director sign his or her name. If you have more than one director, the date shown can be the date the first director signs the form.

Title Page

The next page of your minutes (page 2) contains the title of the document and begins

by reciting the facts necessary for you to hold your meeting, repeating the name of your corporation and the address, date, and time of the meeting given above. Fill in these blanks as explained just above.

❹ Present and Absent Directors

List the names of all your directors in these blanks. You will check the appropriate box to the right of each name when you hold your first board meeting to show whether each director is present or absent. Although we suggest that all of your directors be present at your first meeting, only a quorum of the board (as specified in Article III, Section 8, of your bylaws) actually need attend the meeting.

❺ Temporary Chairperson and Secretary

These blanks relate to a minor, but logically necessary, formality. You have not yet elected officers, but someone has to preside over the meeting and keep track of what happens. Type (or print) the name of one of your directors as your temporary chairperson in the first blank and another director as your temporary secretary in the second. If your corporation has only one director, you can enter this person's name in both these blanks.

Articles of Incorporation Resolution

This is the first resolution of your minutes and appears just after the introductory material on your title page. This resolution serves as a formal record of the date of filing of your articles of incorporation and indicates the first day of the legal existence of your corporation.

❻ Date of Filing of Articles

Type the date on which your articles were filed by the secretary of state—this is the "endorsed-filed" date stamped on the first page of the certified copies of your articles of incorporation (see Step 2, above, for further information on filing your articles).

Bylaws Resolution

This resolution shows the formal adoption of your bylaws by the directors. The bylaws require you to keep your corporate records book (and a copy of your bylaws) at the principal executive office of the corporation. You will establish the location of this office in a separate minute resolution discussed below.

Election of Officers Resolution

This resolution allows you to elect the officers of your corporation and to authorize any officer salaries you feel appropriate.

When filling in these blanks, remember the following points (for a further discussion, see "How Many People May Organize the Corporation?" in Chapter 2):

- Under California law you must fill the offices of president, secretary, and treasurer (referred to in the California Corporations Code as the chief financial officer).

- You are not required to elect a vice president, although many incorporators will wish to do so.

- One person may be elected to all, or any number of, these officer positions. For example, in a one-person corporation, this individual will be elected as president, secretary, and treasurer (and vice president, if this person wants to add this optional title to her name). Although less common, the same rule applies if you have more than one person in your corporation.

EXAMPLE:
Joan, Gary, and Matthew form their own corporation. Because it's really Joan's business (her spouse Gary and her brother Matthew are simply investing as shareholders), Joan fills the officer positions of president, secretary, and treasurer.

- An officer need not be a director or shareholder in your corporation (although, for small corporations, the officer usually will be both).

❼ Election of Officers and Optional Officers' Salaries

List the name of your president, secretary, and treasurer (chief financial officer) and any salary you wish to authorize for each officer. If you wish to fill the optional officer position of vice president, list the name of the person who will fill this office.

Filling in the salary blank is optional. Many corporations will not wish to provide for officer salaries (and will not fill in these blanks) because the individuals who will actively work for the corporation, whether they are also directors, officers, or shareholders, will not be paid a salary for their duties as an officer but will be paid in some other capacity.

EXAMPLE:
Betty Bidecker is a 75% shareholder and the president and treasurer of her incorporated software publishing company. Bix Bidecker, her spouse, is a 25% shareholder and the vice president and secretary of the corporation. Rather than being paid for serving in any officer capacity, both are paid annual salaries as executive employees of the corporation: Betty as the publisher, and Bix as the associate publisher.

If you do provide for officer salaries, remember that these salaries must be reasonable in view of the actual duties performed by the officer and to compensation paid to others with similar skills in similar businesses. (See

"Officers" in Chapter 2 for a further discussion of this issue.) But don't worry too much about overpayment. If you are active in your business and can afford to pay yourself a large salary because of the profitability of your corporation, your salary will most likely be reasonable in view of your success and, generally, in view of the trend towards paying higher corporate salaries these days.

Corporate Seal Resolution

This resolution is included in your minutes in case you wish to order and use a corporate seal. If you don't order and use one, just leave the space to the right of this resolution blank.

❽ Impression of Corporate Seal

Stamp or impress the corporate seal in the space provided to the right of this resolution. If you don't buy a corporate seal, just leave this space blank.

Stock Certificate Resolution

This resolution is included in your minutes to adopt the form of stock certificate you will use (either the certificates included in Appendix B of this book or those which you have purchased on your own as part of a Nolo corporate kit— see Step 3, above—or purchased separately).

Accounting Period Resolution

This resolution allows you to specify the accounting period of your corporation. You should normally select this period with the help of your corporate tax advisor. (See Chapter 4 for a discussion of the rules that apply to selecting a corporate accounting period and tax year.)

❾ Ending Date of Corporate Accounting Period

Indicate the date (month and day) of the end of your corporation's accounting period in this blank. For example, if you choose a calendar year accounting period for your corporation, the ending date is "December 31."

The California Franchise Tax Board and the IRS will look to your initial tax returns (not your bylaws) to determine the ending date of your corporate accounting period and tax year. For example, if your first corporate tax returns are submitted for a period ending on July 30th, this date will be taken as the end date of your corporate tax year. In other words, you are not bound by this initial minute resolution, although your answer here should reflect your reasonable expectations for your ultimate accounting period and tax year.

After you file your initial returns, you may need the consent of the IRS and the California Franchise Tax Board to change your tax year. For further information on filing your initial returns and fixing your corporate tax year, see Chapter 4 and "Corporate Income Tax Return" in Chapter 6.

Principal Executive Office Resolution

This resolution allows you to formally specify the principal executive office of your corporation. This is a term used in the Corporations Code to indicate the legal address of the corporation. Most corporations will use their principal place of business (the active address where all or most of its business is carried out) as its legal principal executive office. Although not required, most incorporators will have a principal executive office within California (see Article I, Section 1, of the bylaws).

⑩ Full Address of Principal Executive Office

Type the street address, including the city, county, and state (California), of the principal executive office of your corporation (for example, "1212 Market Street, River City, Humboldt County, California"). Do not use a post office box.

Bank Account Resolution

This resolution authorizes the opening of the corporation's bank account(s) with one or more banks, showing the names of individuals authorized to sign checks and the number of signatures required on corporate checks. Typically, you will also have to fill out, and impress the corporate seal on, a separate bank account authorization form provided by your bank. Banks customarily require your corporation to have a federal employer identification number. You can obtain this number by filing Form SS-4 with the IRS (see "Federal Employer Identification Number" in Chapter 6). All corporations will also need to obtain a state employer number and make deposits of state and federal withholding and employment taxes with an authorized bank, as explained more fully in Chapter 6.

⑪ Name of Bank(s) and Branch Office(s)

Type the name(s) of the bank(s) and branch office(s) where the corporation will maintain its accounts (for example, "Second Multistate Savings; West Covina branch").

⑫ Number of Signatures on Corporate Checks

State how many individual signatures will be required on each corporate check. For example, if you wish to have your president and secretary sign all corporate checks, type "two" in this blank.

⑬ Names of Individuals Who May Sign Checks

List the names of all individuals who are authorized to sign checks on behalf of your corporation. For example, although you may only require one authorized signature on corporate checks, you may wish to allow both your corporate treasurer and your president to sign corporate checks. Generally, you will list the name of one or more officers or key employees here (such as your salaried in-house bookkeeper).

⑭ Payment and Deduction of Organizational Expenses Resolution (Optional)

This resolution is optional. If you do not wish to use this resolution, do not include this page in your completed minutes.

Whether to Include This Resolution in Your Minutes
Many incorporators will wish to use this resolution to allow the corporation to reimburse the incorporators for, and have the corporation pay and deduct over a period of time, the expenses incurred in organizing the corporation under Section 248 of the Internal Revenue Code. This resolution is simply a statement that you intend to make the tax return election. Without a specific election to deduct these expenses over a specified period of time, such a deduction is normally not possible. To make this election, you attach a statement to your first federal corporate income tax return indicating that you are choosing to deduct and amortize organization expenses and you provide a description of the expenses together with other required details. Check with your tax advisor for help in deciding whether to use this resolution (and for help in preparing the statement to send to the IRS).

A corporation can deduct up to $5,000 of organizational (plus up to $5,000 of start-up) expenses in its first corporate tax year. You can ownership to their shares jointly as community property or in joint tenancy—see Step 8, "Taking Title to Property," below), you will need to complete a separate shareholder representation letter for each of the joint owners.

Below is a sample of the tear-out shareholder representation letter and instructions for filling in the blanks.

Instructions

❶ Insert the name of your corporation and street address of the principal executive office of the corporation in these blanks.

❷ Print or type the name of the shareholder in the first blank in this paragraph. In the second blank, indicate the percentage of interest the shareholder will receive in the shares (in most cases, you will simply show a "full" interest here—see the next paragraph if the shares will be co-owned). In the third blank, insert the number of shares that will be issued individually or jointly to the shareholder.

If the shareholder will be taking title to his or her shares individually (without any co-owners), insert "full" here to show that the shareholder will receive a full interest in the shares. If you are issuing a block of shares jointly to two shareholders (whether in joint tenancy or tenancy in common or as part of a business partnership), then you will insert "undivided half" interest here to indicate that the shareholder for whom you are preparing the letter will receive a half-interest in the block of shares together with another co-owner. (For a discussion of ways to take title to shares and the basic characteristics of each type of ownership, see "Taking Title to Stock" in Step 8, below.)

EXAMPLE:

Gregg Walker and his friend and business associate Frank Federman form their own corporation. Gregg will own 500 shares

individually. Frank will take title to his 500 shares jointly with his wife, Tracy Federman (for legal and tax reasons, the Federmans will take title to their shares in joint tenancy—see "Taking Title to Stock" in Step 8, below). In this instance, the corporation would prepare three shareholder representation letters: one for Gregg, one for Frank, and one for Tracy. Here's how this paragraph would be prepared for each shareholder:

Shareholder Letter 1 (Gregg Walker)

"I, _____*Gregg Walker*_____, in connection with my purchase of a/an ___*full*___ interest in ___*500*___ common shares of the corporation named above, hereby make the following representations:"

Shareholder Letter 2 (Frank Federman)

"I, _____*Frank Federman*_____, in connection with my purchase of a/an ___*undivided half*___ interest in ___*500*___ common shares of the corporation named above, hereby make the following representations:"

Shareholder Letter 3 (Tracy Federman)

"I, _____*Tracy Federman*_____, in connection with my purchase of a/an ___*undivided half*___ interest in ___*500*___ common shares of the corporation named above, hereby make the following representations:"

❸ Complete Section A of the letter. The purpose of this section is to indicate that the shareholder fits within one of the shareholder suitability categories of the limited offering exemption. Check the box to the left of one of the six suitability clauses in this section to show which requirement the shareholder meets.

SHAREHOLDER REPRESENTATION LETTER

To: _(name of corporation)_ ❶

(address)

(city, state, zip)

I, _(name of shareholder)_, ❷ in connection with my purchase of a/an _____ ❷

interest in _(number of shares)_ ❷ common shares of the corporation named above, hereby make the following representations:

A. I am a suitable purchaser of these shares under the California limited offering exemption because:

[Check the box to the left of one of the following clauses which describes how you qualify as a suitable purchaser of shares under the California limited offering exemption. The number and name of the limited offering suitability category associated with each clause is indicated above each clause in the sample below.] ❸

Category 1. Inside Shareholder:

1. [ ] I am a director, officer, or promoter of the corporation, or because I occupy a position with the corporation with duties and authority substantially similar to those of an executive officer of the corporation.

Category 2. Existing Relationship:

2. [ ] I have a preexisting personal and/or business relationship with the corporation, or one or more of its directors, officers, or controlling persons, consisting of personal or business contacts of a nature and duration which enables me to be aware of the character, business acumen, and general business and financial circumstances of the person (including the corporation) with whom such relationship exists.

Category 3. Sophisticated Shareholder:

3. [ ] I have the capacity to protect my own interests in connection with my purchase of the above shares by reason of my own business and/or financial experience.

Category 4. Major Shareholders:

(Check box 4(a) or box 4(b) below: check both if both apply)

4(a). [ ] Pursuant to Section 260.102.13(e) of Title 10 of the California Code of Regulations, I am purchasing $150,000 or more of the corporation's shares, and either 1) my investment (including mandatory assessments) does not exceed 10% of my net worth or joint net worth with my spouse, or 2) by reason of my own business and/or financial experience, or the business and/or financial experience of my professional advisor (who is unaffiliated with and not compensated by the corporation or any of its affiliates or selling agents), I have, or my professional advisor has, the capacity to protect my own interests in connection with the purchase of these shares

4(b). [ ] Pursuant to Section 260.102.13(g) of Title 10 of the California Code of Regulations, I am an "accredited investor" under Rule 501(a) of Regulation D adopted by the Securities and Exchange Commission under the Securities Act of 1933. This means either 1) my individual net worth, or joint net worth with my spouse, at the time of the purchase of these shares, exceeds $ 1,000,000; 2) my individual income is in excess of $200,000 in each of the two most recent years or my joint income with my spouse is in excess of $300,000 in each of those years, and I have a reasonable expectation of reaching the same income level in the current year; or 3) I qualify under one of the other accredited investor categories of Rule 501(a) of SEC Regulation D.

Category 5. Reliance on Professional Advisor:

5(a). [ ] I have the capacity to protect my own interests in connection with my purchase of the above shares by reason of the business and/or financial experience of _____*(name of professional advisor)*_____,❸ whom I have engaged and hereby designate as my professional advisor in connection with my purchase of the above shares.

5(b). REPRESENTATION OF PROFESSIONAL ADVISOR

_____*(Name of professional advisor)*_____ ❸ hereby represents:

(1) I have been engaged as the professional advisor of _____*(name of shareholder)*_____ ❸ and have provided him or her with investment advice in connection with the purchase of _____*(number of shares)*_____ ❸ common shares in _____*(name of corporation)*_____ ❸.

(2) As a regular part of my business as a/an _____*(profession)*_____ ❸, I am customarily relied upon by others for investment recommendations or decisions and I am customarily compensated for such services, either specifically or by way of compensation for related professional services.

(3) I am unaffiliated with and am not compensated by the corporation or any affiliate or selling agent of the corporation, directly or indirectly. I do not have, nor will I have (a) a relationship of employment with the corporation, either as an employee, employer, independent contractor, or principal; (b) the beneficial ownership of securities of the corporation, its affiliates, or selling agents, in excess of 1% of its securities; or (c) a relationship with the corporation such that I control, am controlled by, or am under common control with the corporation, and, more specifically, a relationship by which I possess, directly or indirectly, the power to direct, or cause the direction, of the management, policies, or actions of the corporation.

Dated: _(date of signing)_ ❸ _(signature of professional advisor)_
(typed name of advisor)

Category 6. Relative of Another Suitable Shareholder:

I am the spouse, relative, or relative of the spouse of another purchaser of shares and I have the same principal residence as this purchaser.❸

❹ B. I represent that I am purchasing these shares for investment for my own account and not with a view to, or for, sale in connection with any distribution of the shares. I understand that these shares have not been qualified or registered under any state or federal securities law and that they may not be transferred or otherwise disposed of without such qualification or registration pursuant to such laws or an opinion of legal counsel satisfactory to the corporation that such qualification or registration is not required.❺

❹ C. I have not received any advertisement or general solicitation with respect to the sale of the shares of the above-named corporation.

❹ D. I represent that, before signing this document, I have been provided access to, or been given, all material facts relevant to the purchase of my shares, including all financial and written information about the corporation and the terms and conditions of the stock offering and that I have been given the opportunity to

```
ask questions and receive answers concerning any additional terms
and conditions of the stock offering or other information which I,
or my professional advisor if I have designated one, felt necessary
to protect my interests in connection with the stock purchase
transaction.
```
Dated: _(date of signing)_ ❻ _(signature of shareholder)_ ❻

Oct 1, 2010

(typed name of shareholder)

EXAMPLE:

If you are preparing a letter for a director or officer of your corporation, check Box 1 to show that the shareholder fits within the exemption as an Inside Shareholder (Category 1).

If you are preparing a letter for a spouse of one of these directors or officers (and the spouse shares the same principal residence as the director or officer), check the box next to Category 6 to show that this shareholder is a Relative of Another Suitable Shareholder (Category 6).

You only need to check one box for each shareholder. However, if a shareholder fits within more than one suitability category, you can check each box that applies, if you wish. A shareholder can meet the requirements of Category 4 by checking either or both Boxes 4(a) and/or 4(b) in the shareholder representation letter.

Check Box 5(a) for a shareholder who is relying on the financial or business experience of a professional advisor to protect his or her interests in the stock purchase transaction. In this case, you and your professional advisor need to complete the separate page in the shareholder representation letter that contains Sections 5(a) and 5(b). To do this, check Box 5(a) and indicate the name of the professional

advisor on the blank line in this paragraph. Then complete Section 5(b) by typing the name of the shareholder who is being represented, the number of shares the shareholder will purchase, and the name of the corporation in the appropriate blanks in Paragraph 1 of 5(b). The advisor should state his or her profession in Paragraph 2 of 5(b) (see "Who Can Be a Professional Advisor?" below) and sign and date the advisor representation at the bottom of Section 5(b) (type the advisor's name directly under the signature line).

❹ Paragraphs B, C, and D of each shareholder letter contain important representations and disclosures that each shareholder must make. Make sure each shareholder reads these paragraphs and understands their effect before he or she signs the letter. (See "The Limited Offering Exemption" and "Federal Securities Act" in Chapter 3 for further information on these representations.)

❺ The stock certificates in Appendix B of this book contain a legend that alerts your shareholders to the restrictions contained in this paragraph. If you order other stock certificates, you can type this legend on the face of your printed certificates. (See the tear-out certificates at the back of this book for the language to use for this legend.)

❻ Each shareholder should sign and date his or her representation letter. Remember, if you have checked Category 5 for any shareholder, make sure the shareholder has his or her professional advisor date and sign the Representation of Professional Advisor section of the letter. Make a copy of each completed letter to place in your corporate records book, and give each shareholder the completed original.

> **WARNING**
>
> **Check the shareholder representation letter.** This letter is an important legal document, in which the shareholder makes a number of important statements. We suggest that you advise your shareholders to check with their lawyer before signing it.

Step 7. Prepare and File Notice of Stock Transaction Form

When issuing your initial shares under the California limited offering exemption, you must prepare and file a Notice of Transaction Pursuant to Corporations Code Section 25102(f). This form must be filed online through the California Department of Corporation's website, unless you qualify for a hardship exception (for example, you cannot gain access to a computer or you are otherwise unable to answer the online questions). If you qualify for a hardship exception, you can file the paper notice form located in Appendix B or available for downloading from the California Department of Corporation's website at www.corp.ca.gov. To file the notice form and pay the associated filing fees online, go to the California Department of Corporation's website at www.corp.ca.gov, click on the link titled "File Your Corporations Code 25102(f) Notice Online," and follow the instructions.

The notice form must be filed within 15 calendar days "after the first sale of the securities in the transaction in this state." Make sure to file on time. If you don't, the department can make you pay the fees that would normally be due if you issued your shares under a permit (ouch!). Your first sale of shares happens when the corporation first receives payment from any shareholder for any of your initial shares.

Legally, the first sale occurs "when the issuer [corporation] has obtained a contractual commitment in this state to purchase one or more of the securities [shares] the issuer intends to sell in connection with the transaction." We assume that you have not entered into any such preissuance commitment (such as a shareholder's subscription agreement). If you follow the steps in this chapter in sequence, you will receive all of the payments for your shares (consideration) in return for the issuance of all of your shares as part of Step 8, below. To be absolutely sure, however, you should prepare and file the Notice of Stock Transaction form now, before you sell your shares. This way you will be certain your notice form is filed with the department of corporations in advance of the 15-day deadline.

> **WARNING**
>
> **Don't miss this filing deadline.** If you intentionally disregard the timely filing of the Notice of Stock Transaction form, the Commissioner of Corporations can make you pay the full filing fee that would have been owed if you had qualified your stock issuance. This can be a very hefty fee so make sure to file your notice on time. If you have any questions, see a lawyer immediately.

Who Can Be a Professional Advisor?

Attorneys, certified public accountants (CPAs), persons licensed or registered as broker-dealers, agents, investment advisors, and banks and savings and loan associations have been specifically designated by the regulations to the limited offering exemption as qualified to act as professional advisors. This list is not exhaustive, however. You may also rely on and designate a person "who, as a regular part of such person's business, is customarily relied upon by others for investment recommendations or decisions, and who is customarily compensated for such services, either specifically or by way of compensation for related professional services."

Professional advisors must not be affiliated with, or compensated by, the corporation or by any of the corporation's affiliates or selling agents. Paragraph 3 of Section 5(b) of the professional advisor's representation repeats the specific language of the regulations related to these requirements and asks the professional advisor to represent that he or she meets these requirements. (For a further discussion of this category under the limited offering exemption, see "Special Shareholder Suitability Rules" in Chapter 3.)

A few additional points before you do your notice form:

- Prepare and file this form after you have pinned down all of the details of your initial stock issuance (who will purchase your shares, the type and amount of payment to be received, and so on). These details should be contained in the stock issuance resolution of your minutes, prepared as part of Step 5 of this chapter. Your stock issuance information is also contained in your shareholder representation letters, prepared as part of Step 6, above.)

- You will need to have your federal Employer Identification Number (EIN) before you do your notice form online. (See "Federal Employer Identification Number" in Chapter 6 for instructions on how to get your federal EIN.)

- The information provided in this notice form should relate to your entire initial stock issuance transaction. No subsequent notices need to be filed with the state for sales of shares in connection with the same transaction. Remember, you will need to obtain a permit or seek another exemption (file another notice with the help of a lawyer) for any subsequent issuances of shares.

- If you decide to file a federal notice form notifying the SEC of your initial stock offering under one of the rules of Regulation D or Section 4(6) of the federal Securities Act, you can dispense with the notice form shown here and send the Department of Corporations a copy of your federal notice form instead, together with a cover letter and the proper filing fee. (See Section 260.102.14 of Title 10 of the California Code of Regulations for further information.) As we indicate in "Federal Securities Act" in Chapter 3, we don't expect most small, closely held corporations to make this federal filing, and we therefore assume that you will have to file the California notice form discussed in this section.

- This California notice form is not required if none of your shares are purchased in California. We assume, however, that all or most of your shares will be purchased in this state by California residents. (See "Securities Laws and Exemptions" in Chapter 3, for a brief discussion of some of the technicalities involved with out-of-state sales of shares.)

Done   10/06/10

Prepare Your Notice of Stock Transaction Form

You must file your Notice of Transaction Pursuant to Corporations Code Section 25102(f) online, unless you qualify for a hardship exception (for example, you cannot gain access to a computer or are otherwise unable to answer the online questions). To file online, go to the California Department of Corporations' website at www.corp.ca.gov. There is a link from the department's homepage to the Notice of Transaction Pursuant to Corporations Code Section 25102(f). Follow the online instructions for completing and filing the notice form. To get started, you will need your federal Employer Identification Number (EIN). (See "Federal Employer Identification Number in Chapter 6 for instructions on how to obtain your federal EIN.) You will also need a credit card to pay your filing fee online.

You can refer to the sample Notice of Transaction form and instructions below for help with filling out the form. These instructions assume that you qualify for the hardship exception and will be completing and mailing the paper form of the notice. We have included a blank copy of the Notice of Transaction Pursuant to Corporations Code Section 25102(f) in Appendix B and on the CD-ROM in case you qualify for the hardship exception and decide to do a paper notice. If you do file a paper copy of the notice, make sure you use the most recent version of the notice form. You can check online at the Department of Corporations website (www.corp.ca.gov) or call one of the offices of the department listed in Appendix B and ask them to send you the most recent version of the form.

Instructions

❶ **Top of Form:** Ignore the blanks at the upper-left and -right portions of the form. The blanks at the upper left will be filled out by the Department of Corporations. The blank at the upper right is only for corporations that have previously qualified securities with the department and have been issued a department file number.

❷ **Heading:** Circle or mark the amount of the filing fee (see "Your Notice Form Filing Fee," below).

❸ **Item A:** Check the box titled "Section 25102(f)"—this means that you are using the form to provide notice of your stock issuance under the California limited offering exemption.

❹ **Item 1:** Type the name of your corporation exactly as it appears in your articles of incorporation.

❺ **Item 2:** Type the address of the principal executive office of your corporation (this is the address specified in the principal executive office resolution of your minutes prepared in Step 5, above). Make sure to provide a full street address (no P.O. boxes), including the city, state, and Zip code. If you use a mailing address different from your principal executive office, show this address on the second line of this item.

❻ **Item 3:** Type the telephone number of the corporation, including the area code.

❼ **Item 4:** Type "California" in this blank to indicate California as the state of your incorporation.

❽ **Item 5:** Type "Common Stock" in this blank to indicate that you are issuing only one class of common shares. The articles of incorporation included with this book provide for one class of common shares.

SAMPLE FORM

(Department of Corporations Use Only)

Fee paid $ _(leave these_

lines blank) ❶

Receipt No. _____

DEPARTMENT OF CORPORATIONS FILE NO., if any:

(leave this line blank) ❶

Insert File number(s) of Previous Filings Before the Department, if any.

❷

Fee: $25.00 $35.00 $50.00 $150.00 $300.00
(Circle the appropriate amount of fee. See Corporations Code Section 25608(c))

COMMISSIONER OF CORPORATIONS
STATE OF CALIFORNIA

NOTICE OF TRANSACTION PURSUANT TO CORPORATIONS CODE SECTION 25102(f)
A. Check one: Transaction under (X ❸ Section 25102(f) (   ) Rule 260.103.

ELECTRONIC FILING REQUIREMENT AND HARDSHIP EXCEPTION:
This notice must be filed electronically through the Internet process made available by the
Department of Corporations on www.corp.ca.gov, unless the issuer claims the hardship exception as
described in Number 8 below.

1. Name of Issuer:

   (name of corporation) ❹ _____

2. Address of Issuer:

   (address of principal executive office) ❺ _____

              Street   City   State   Zip

   Mailing Address:
   (mailing address, if different) ❺ _____

              Street   City   State   Zip

3. Area Code and Telephone Number: _(telephone number of corporation)_ ❻ _____

4. Issuer's state (or other jurisdiction) of incorporation or organization:

   California ❼ _____

5. Title of class or classes of securities sold in transaction:

   Common Stock ❽ _____

6. The value of the securities sold or proposed to be sold in the transaction, determined in accordance with Corporations Code Sec. 25608(g) in connection with the fee required upon filing this notice, is (fee based on amount shown in line (iii) under "Total Offering"):

		California	_Total Offering_
❾	(a)(i) in money	$_____	$_____
	(ii) in consideration other than money	$_____	$_____
❿	(iii) total of (i) and (ii)	$_____	$_____

    (b) (   ) Change in rights, preferences, privileges or restrictions of or on outstanding securities
    ($25.00 fee.) (See Rule 260.103.)

260.102.14(c) (8-05)

7. Type of filing under Securities Act of 1933, if applicable: _____

    None ⓫ _____

8. **Hardship Exception for electronic filing.** An issuer may file this paper notice in person or by mail only if either of the following exceptions apply. The issuer shall check applicable box and include the reason(s) and description(s) for the hardship exception in the space provided.

⓬ ☐ Computer equipment including hardware and software is unavailable to the issuer without unreasonable burden or expense. If this is the case, describe below both of the following; the reason(s) that the computer equipment including hardware and software is unavailable without unreasonable burden or expense, and the description(s) of the unreasonable burden or expense.

⓬ ☐ The issuer cannot obtain and provide information (including credit card or other identifying information) requested on the Department's electronic notice or through the Internet filing process. If this is the case, describe below both of the following: the reason(s) that the issuer cannot obtain and provide the requested information on the electronic notice or through the Internet filing process without unreasonable burden or expense, and the description(s) of the unreasonable burden or expense to the issuer to make the electronic filing.

After checking the applicable hardship exception above, the issuer shall describe below the reason(s) and description(s) for that hardship exception. (If additional space is needed, attach a separate sheet to this notice.)

_____
_____
_____
_____
_____
_____

⓭ 9. ( ) Check if issuer already has a consent to service of process on file with the Commissioner. (Instruction: Each issuer (other than a California Corporation) filing a notice under Section 25102(f) must file a consent to service of process (Form 260.265), unless it already has a consent to service on file with the Commissioner. If no consent to service of process is on file with the Commissioner, attach the consent to this notice.)

10. *(signature of officer or director)* ⓮ _____
    Authorized Signature on behalf of issuer

    (typed name of officer or director) ⓮ _____
    Print name and title of signatory

    (date of signing) _____
    Date

Name, Address and Phone number of contact person:

    (typed name, address, and telephone number of signer, above) ⓮ _____
_____
_____

260.102.14(c) (8-05)   2

❾ **Item 6(a):** In these blanks, show the value of the shares that you will sell to your shareholders. For most small, closely held corporations, the value of the corporation's initial shares is the same as the value of the cash or noncash payments that will be made for the shares (see "The Value of Your Shares," below).

You have already prepared a list of the fair value of the payments to be made by your shareholders in the Stock Issuance Resolution in your minutes. Simply add up the cash payment and noncash payment amounts from the Fair Value column of your stock issuance resolution and place these totals in the blanks here. (We assume that the fair value figures in your stock issuance resolution do, in fact, reflect the actual value of any nonmonetary consideration to be received for your shares.)

Here's how to fill in each of the blanks in this section of the form:

- Indicate the total amount of all cash payments to be made by your California shareholders in the California column of Blank 6(a)(i).

- Indicate the total value of all noncash payments to be made by your California shareholders in the California column of Blank 6(a)(ii)—again, the actual value of any noncash payments made by your shareholders is shown in the stock issuance resolution in your minutes.

- Total the above amounts and place the result in the California column of Blank 6(a)(iii).

- If all your initial shareholders will be California shareholders, simply carry over the three California amounts to the corresponding row of the Total Offering column in Item 6(a). If you will sell shares outside of California, add the out-of-state cash and noncash figures to the California figures and place these totals in the corresponding rows in the "Total Offering" column. Then provide a new overall total in the Blank 6(a)(iii) of the Total Offering column.

The calculations here are really quite easy and are best demonstrated with an example or two.

EXAMPLE 1:

You plan to issue a total of 30,000 initial shares for cash and property totalling $30,000: $10,000 in cash, $20,000 as the fair value of all the property to be transferred for shares. All your prospective shareholders are California residents. You would fill out this item in the notice form as follows:

	California	Total Offering
(a)(i) in money	$ _10,000_	$ _10,000_
(ii) in consideration other than money	$ _20,000_	$ _20,000_
(iii) total of (i) and (ii)	$ _30,000_	$ _30,000_

EXAMPLE 2:

Assume the same facts as the previous example except that 5,000 shares will also be issued to an out-of-state shareholder in return for $5,000 cash. In this case, the Total Offering column figures will be changed to reflect this out-of-state amount as follows:

	California	Total Offering
(a)(i) in money	$ _10,000_	$ _15,000_
(ii) in consideration other than money	$ _20,000_	$ _20,000_
(iii) total of (i) and (ii)	$ _30,000_	$ _35,000_

⑩ **Item 6(b):** Ignore this box ("Change in rights, preferences, privileges or restrictions of or on outstanding securities"). It applies to types of transactions we don't discuss here.

⑪ **Item 7:** In answer to the "Type of filing under Securities Act of 1933, if applicable," type "None." This question relates to the federal securities laws. If you are actually registering your stock offering or filing a notice with the SEC (with the help of a lawyer), the attorney who is helping you with your federal filing will indicate "Registered" or show the number of the rule under which the federal filing was made on the separate notice form he is preparing for you. (See Chapter 3 for a discussion of the federal securities laws.)

⑫ **Item 8:** If you are completing a paper notice because you qualify under the a hardship exception, you must check the applicable box and state your reasons for qualifying in the space provided.

⑬ **Item 9:** Leave this item blank. As stated in the instructions, California corporations don't need to file a consent to service with the Department of Corporations.

⑭ **Item 10:** Type the name of a corporate officer or director who will sign your notice form (on the line marked "Print name and title of signatory"); and this person's name, address, and phone number as the contact person for your corporation in the blanks indicated in the sample notice form. The contact person is the person the department will notify in the event there are any questions concerning your notice form.

Make sure to complete the date and signature lines in this part of the form on all copies of your notice form; these are the lines marked "Date" and "Authorized Signature on behalf of issuer."

The Value Of Your Shares

The total value figure of all of the securities (shares) you are issuing under the limited offering exemption is used to compute the filing fee for your notice form (as explained in Step 7, "Your Notice Form Filing Fee," below). As you might guess, there are legal guidelines for determining the fair value of your shares. The value of your initial shares is: (1) the price to be paid for the shares (money) or the actual value of any consideration other than money to be received for the shares; or (2) the value of the shares when issued; whichever is greater. In our instructions on filling in these blanks on your notice form, we assume that the value of your shares is (1) the actual price to be paid for the shares (if the shares are purchased for cash), or (2) the actual value of any consideration other than money (such as property) to be received for the shares. Most, if not all, privately held corporations can follow this rule to determine the fair value of their shares. However, if the value of your shares when issued is greater than the actual cash price or value of the noncash received for the shares, then this higher figure should be used when filling in these blanks on the notice form.

But don't worry—it is very unlikely that this alternative rule will apply to you. Your corporation's initial shares should have no value in and of themselves—there's no market for such shares. In other words, in the absence of outside market pressures driving up share values or outside investors vying for your initial shares, these shares should only be worth the actual amount your shareholders pay for them.

Your Notice Form Filing Fee

Below is the latest fee schedule for filing the notice form. The filing fee is based upon the total value of the securities to be sold, as shown on Line 6(a)(iii) of your printed form in the "Total Offering" column.

Value of Securities Proposed to Be Sold (from "Total Offering" column, Line 6(a)(iii))	*Filing Fee*
$25,000 or less	$25
$25,001 to $100,000	$35
$100,001 to $500,000	$50
$500,001 to $1,000,000	$150
Over $1,000,000	$300

As you might guess, the fee for smaller corporations normally will be $25 or $35. Make sure you have the correct fee amount indicated at the top of the notice.

Filing Your Notice Form

After you submit the notice form and filing fee electronically to the Department of Corporations, you will have completed your filing. Be sure to print out, sign, and date a copy of your notice when you are done. Keep this signed copy in your corporate records book. The Department of Corporations can ask you to produce this paper copy later to prove you filed your notice form on time.

If you requested a hardship exception and are filing a paper copy, send two signed copies of the final form and a stamped, self-addressed envelope to the Department of Corporations at its main Sacramento address (the Department of Corporations addresses are listed in Appendix B). (You can mail the notice to any branch office address, but it will be forwarded to the Sacramento address.) Include a check payable to the "California Department of Corporations" for the amount of your filing fee. In a brief cover letter, ask the department to send you a file-stamped copy of the notice in your enclosed return envelope. You can also file your notice in person at any of the branch offices of the department (assuming you qualify to file a paper notice under the hardship exception). See Appendix B for these addresses.

Step 8. Issue Shares of Stock

The final step in your incorporation process is to issue stock to your shareholders. Issuing shares of stock is an essential step—as a general rule, you should not begin doing business as a corporation until you have issued your stock. (See "Piercing the Corporate Veil" in Chapter 2.)

Ten blank, ready-to-use stock certificates are included in Appendix B at the back of this book. They are specifically designed for use by corporations issuing their initial shares under the California limited offering exemption. If you want to order specially printed certificates for your corporation, you can do so by ordering through a legal stationery store. (For a further discussion on choosing the right certificates, see Step 3, above.)

A Few Reminders When You Issue Shares

- All of your initial shares should be sold for the same price per share. For example, if someone pays the corporation $1,000 cash for ten shares, then another person selling the corporation a machine worth $10,000 should receive 100 shares.

- Your corporation cannot issue more shares than you have authorized in your articles of incorporation. (As explained in Step 2, above, it's common for corporations to authorize more shares in their articles than they will actually issue here.)

- You must issue your initial shares under the California limited offering exemption when following the procedure contained in this book. (See "The Limited Offering Exemption" in Chapter 3 to refresh yourself on these rules.)

Comply With California's Bulk Sales Law

Before getting to the details of your stock issuance, we must make a slight detour to mention a preliminary formality that may apply to some readers—complying with California's bulk sales law. (See Division 6 of the California Commercial Code, starting with Section 6101.)

Generally, this law applies to you only if you meet all of these conditions:

- You are transferring more than half the value of the inventory and equipment of an unincorporated business located in California to your new corporation (if you are incorporating an existing sole proprietorship or partnership).

- The value of the business assets being transferred is at least $10,000 but no more than $5 million.

- The business being incorporated is a restaurant or is engaged in the principal business of selling inventory from stock (such as a retail or wholesale business, including a business that manufactures what it sells).

FAST TRACK

If each the above conditions doesn't apply to your incorporation, you can ignore this section and skip ahead to "Taking Title to Stock," below.

Even if you do meet all three conditions, you may still be exempt from most of the provisions of California's bulk sales law. The exemption most often available to incorporators of small businesses applies if your corporation:

- assumes the debts of the unincorporated business

- is not insolvent after the assumption of these debts, and

- publishes and files a notice to creditors within 30 days of the transfer of assets (normally, the assets are transferred when shares are issued to the initial shareholders).

To comply with this exemption to the bulk sales law, call a local legal newspaper. The paper will send you a notice of bulk transfer form to prepare and will publish and file this form with the county recorder's and tax collector's offices for a fee.

Other exemptions also exist. (See Division 6 of the California Commercial Code for specifics.) If your corporation is not eligible for an exemption from the bulk sales provisions, the publication and filing procedures must be accomplished at least 12 business days *prior* to the transfer of business assets.

RECORDING REQUESTED BY:

AND WHEN RECORDED MAIL TO:

Name

Address

City, State, Zip _____

Space Above This Line for Recorder's Use

NOTICE TO CREDITORS OF BULK SALE

[SECS. 6103(c)(10), (11), 6105 U.C.C.]

Escrow No. _____

Notice is hereby given to creditors of the within-named seller that a sale that may constitute a bulk sale has been or will be made.

The individual, partnership, or corporate names and the business addresses of the seller are:

As listed by the seller, all other business names and addresses used by the seller within three years before the date such list was sent or delivered to the buyer are: (if "none," so state)

The address to which inquiries about the sale may be made, if different from the seller's address: (if "same," so state)

The individual, partnership, or corporate names and the business addresses of the buyer are:

The assets sold or to be sold are described in general as:

and are located at:

The date or prospective date of the bulk sale was/is _____ ,

at _____ .

The buyer has assumed or will assume in full the debts that were incurred in the seller's business before the date of the bulk sale.

Dated: _____ , 20 _____

_____
(Signature of Buyer)

_____
(Type or Print Name)

This form is provided at no charge as an accommodation to our customers. Any questions concerning its use should be referred to an attorney.

California Newspaper Service Bureau, Inc.

What Are the Bulk Sales Provisions?

The purpose of the bulk sales provisions in California (and other states) is to prevent business owners from secretly transferring the "bulk" of the assets of their business to another person or entity in an attempt to avoid creditors and to prevent schemes whereby the prior business owners sell out (usually to a relative at bargain prices) and come back into the business through a back door later on. Of course, we assume you are simply changing the form of your unincorporated business, not trying to convince others that you are disassociated from their prior business (and its debts). In other words, if the bulk sales law applies to you, you should be complying with its notice and filing procedures only as formalities. If, on the other hand, your unincorporated business will have debts outstanding at the time of its incorporation and your corporation does not plan, or may not be able, to assume and promptly pay these debts as they become due, then compliance with the bulk sales procedures is more than a mere formality and you should see a lawyer.

There are various notice forms that fit specific provisions of the bulk sales law. To rely on the exemption described above, prepare and have the newspaper publish and file a Notice to Creditors under Section 6013(c)(10) of the Uniform Commercial Code. This notice will usually include a heading indicating that it is a Bulk Sale and Assumption form. In any case, it must include a clause to the effect that "the buyer has assumed or will assume in full the debts that were incurred in the seller's business before the date of the bulk sale."

Above is a sample Notice to Creditors under Section 6103(c)(10) of the bulk sales law.

If you don't comply with the requirements of the bulk sales law, a claimant against the prior business can collect the amount owed from the corporation. Of course, if the unincorporated business does not owe any money or have potential liabilities, or if you are sure that your corporation will pay any outstanding debts and claims as they become due, you may not be concerned with this penalty. Even so, we recommend that incorporators to whom the bulk sales law applies attend to these simple publication and filing formalities. Besides helping you avoid claims in the future, compliance with the bulk sales law is additional proof that you have perfected the separate legal existence of your corporation.

Taking Title to Stock

In the next section, you will actually fill out your stock certificates. Before you do, however, you need to know how your shareholders will take title to their stock—that is, whose name or names, and what additional descriptive language, if any, should be put on the stock certificates. If all shareholders will take title to stock in their own names, individually, you can skip most of this section. However, if joint ownership is involved, read this section carefully.

Taking title to stock, essentially, means putting the owner's name on the ownership line of the stock certificate. Often a married person will take title to stock in his or her name alone. This is perfectly legal, even if community property is used to buy the shares. The other (nonlisted) spouse has a half interest in the stock even if the spouse's name doesn't appear, and can enforce this interest against the named spouse if necessary (at death or divorce). The names that appear on the certificates are of concern primarily to the shareholders, not the corporation.

Prepare a Bill of Sale and/or Receipts for Your Shareholders

After filling out your stock certificates, you may wish to prepare receipts and, if incorporating a prior business, a bill of sale for your shareholders, before actually distributing your stock certificates. You are not legally required to prepare these forms, but we think it's a sensible precaution to avoid later confusion over who paid what for shares in your corporation.

A tear-out bill of sale and separate receipts are contained in Appendix B to this book and on the CD-ROM. Make copies of the appropriate forms and prepare them according to the sample forms and instructions below.

Prepare a Bill of Sale for Assets of a Business

If you are transferring the assets of an unincorporated business to your corporation in return for the issuance of shares to the prior owners, you may wish to prepare a bill of sale. If not, skip to the next section below, "Prepare Receipts for Your Shareholders."

Below is a sample of the bill of sale form with instructions.

As indicated in the form, you should attach an inventory of the assets of the prior business that will be transferred to the corporation. If you have any questions, your tax advisor can help you prepare this inventory and choose among the options offered in this form.

Instructions

❶ Type (or print) the names of the prior business owners.

❷ Insert the name of your corporation.

❸ Enter the total number of shares to be issued to all prior owners of the business in return for the transfer of the business to the corporation.

Extra Steps Are Required to Transfer Real Property or Leases

If you are transferring real property or a lease to your corporation, you will have to prepare and execute new corporate ownership papers, such as deeds, leases, assignments of leases, and so on. An excellent California guide to transferring property interests and preparing new deeds (with tear-out forms) is *Deeds for California Real Estate*, by Mary Randolph (Nolo).

For rental property, you should talk to the landlord about having a new lease prepared showing the corporation as the new tenant. Or you can have the prior tenants assign the lease to the corporation; however, read your lease carefully before trying to do this, as many leases are not assignable without the landlord's permission.

If the property being transferred is mortgaged, you will most likely need the permission of the lender to transfer the property. If your real property note agreement contains a "due on sale or transfer" clause, you may even be required to refinance your mortgage if rates have gone up substantially since the existing deed of trust was executed. This, of course, may be so undesirable that you decide not to transfer the real property to the corporation, preferring to keep it in the name of the original owner and lease it to the corporation. And, don't forget that the transfer of real property to your corporation may trigger a Proposition 13 reassessment of the property; check with your tax advisor before completing a real property transfer to your corporation.

Prepare and execute these new ownership papers, lease documents, and so on before you give the prior property owners their shares. (See "Distribute Your Stock Certificates," below.)

BILL OF SALE FOR ASSETS OF A BUSINESS

This is an agreement between:

_____ *(name of prior business owner)* ❶

_____ *(name of prior business owner)* , ❶

herein called "transferor(s)," and _____ *(name of corporation)* , ❷ a California corporation, herein called "the corporation."

In return for the issuance of _____ *(number of shares)* ❸ shares of stock of the corporation, transferor(s) hereby sell(s), assign(s), and transfer(s) to the corporation all right, title, and interest in the following property:

All the tangible assets listed on the inventory attached to this bill of sale and all stock in trade, goodwill, leasehold interests, trade names, and other intangible assets [except _____ *(any nontransferred assets shown here)* ❹] of _____ *(name of prior business)* ❺, located at _____ *(address of prior business)* ❻.

In return for the transfer of the above property to it, the corporation hereby agrees to assume, pay, and discharge all debts, duties and obligations that appear on the date of this agreement on the books and owed on account of said business [except _____ *(any unassumed liabilities shown here)* ❼]. The corporation agrees to indemnify and hold the transferor(s) of said business and their property free from any liability for any such debt, duty, or obligation and from any suits, actions, or legal proceedings brought to enforce or collect any such debt, duty, or obligation.

❽ The transferor(s) hereby appoint(s) the corporation as representative to demand, receive, and collect for itself any and all debts and obligations now owing to said business. The transferor(s) further authorize(s) the corporation to do all things allowed by law to recover and collect any such debts and obligations and to use the transferor's(s') name(s) in such manner as it considers necessary for the collection and recovery of such debts and obligations, provided, however, without cost, expense, or damage to the transferor(s).

Dated: _____ *(date)* ❾   *(signature of prior business owner)* _____ ❾
                                           (typed name) , Transferor
                                           (signature of prior business owner) _____ ❾
                                           (typed name) , Transferor
                                           (signature of prior business owner) _____ ❾
                                           (typed name) , Transferor

Dated: _____ *(date)* ❾   *(name of corporation)* _____ ❾
Name of Corporation

By: *(signature of president)* _____ ❾
        (typed name) , President
        (signature of treasurer) _____ ❾
        (typed name) , Treasurer

Receipt for Services Rendered to the Corporation

If you are transferring shares in return for past services performed by a shareholder for the corporation, prepare the receipt form as explained below. Have the shareholder date and sign a bill for these services as "Paid in Full" showing the date of payment (the date you distribute the shares in return for these services—see "Distribute Your Stock Certificates," below). Remember, you cannot issue shares in return for services that will be performed in the future by a shareholder (see "Selling Stock," in Chapter 2).

This is not a common type of stock issuance transaction for newly formed corporations, since (1) most work done for the corporation will occur after your stock issuance, and (2) most contractors or other professionals who have performed services will want cash (not shares of stock) as payment for their services. However, if one of the principals of your closely held corporation has performed services for the corporation prior to your stock issuance, this type of stock issuance transaction may make

sense. Of, course, to avoid unfairness to your other stockholders, you will want to make sure that the shareholder charges no more than the prevailing rate for the services performed. For a further discussion of this type of payment for shares, see the "Stock Issuance Resolution" section in Step 5 of this chapter.

Instructions

❶, ❷, and ❸ Show the name of the corporation, the name of the shareholder, and the number of shares this person will receive in the blanks.

❹ Provide a short description in this space of the past services performed by the shareholder (for example, the date(s), description, and value of (amount billed for) past services performed by the shareholder).

❺ and ❻ When you distribute the shares in return for the past services (see "Distribute Your Stock Certificates," below), provide the date of issuance of the shares and have the shareholder sign the receipt on the lines indicated above.

RECEIPT FOR SERVICES RENDERED

In consideration of the performance of the following services actually rendered to, or labor done for, _____ *(name of corporation)* ❶ , _____ *(name of shareholder)* ❷ , the provider of such services or labor done, hereby acknowledges the receipt of _____ *(number of shares)* ❸ shares of stock in _____ *(name of corporation)* ❶ as payment in full for these services:

*(description of past services)*❹

Dated: _____ *(date of issuance)* ❺   _____ *(signature of shareholder)* ❻

*(name of shareholder)*❸

Distribute Your Stock Certificates

Now that you've filled in your stock certificates and prepared receipts for your shareholders (and a bill of sale if you are incorporating a prior business), it's time to distribute your stock certificates to your shareholders. Distribute your shares after receiving payment from each shareholder. To complete this step, do the following:

- Have each shareholder (or both shareholders, for jointly issued shares) sign his or her stock certificate stub. Indicate the date of stock issuance on each stub.

- Date each stock certificate and have your president and secretary sign each one, and impress your corporate seal in the circular space at the bottom of each certificate.

- Complete the date and signature lines on your receipts (and bill of sale for the assets of a business if you have prepared this form) as explained above. Give each shareholder a copy of his or her receipt(s) and/or a copy of the bill of sale.

- Make sure to place all your completed stock stubs and completed copies of all receipts, bills of sale, and any attachments (inventory of assets of the prior business, cancelled notes, paid-in-full bills for services, and the like) in your corporate records book.

- If you have not already done so, prepare and file your Notice of Stock transaction with the California Department of Corporations (see Step 7 of this chapter). Remember, you are required to file this notice form within 15 calendar days of your sale of stock.

TIP

Throw out extra certificates. If you have stock certificates left over after filling out and distributing the certificates for your initial limited offering stock issuance, we suggest you tear them up and throw them away. Remember, future stock issuances or transfers may require a permit from the California Commissioner of Corporations, and you will need to consult a lawyer to ensure compliance with state and federal securities laws.

Signing Corporate Documents

From now on, whenever you sign a document on behalf of the corporation, be certain to do so in the following manner:

(name of corporation), a California corporation

By : *(signature of corporate officer)*

(typed name), (corporate title, for example, president)

If you fail to sign documents this way (on behalf of the corporation in your capacity as a corporate officer or director), you may be leaving yourself open to personal liability for corporate obligations. This is but one example designed to illustrate a basic premise of corporate life: From now on, it is extremely important for you to maintain the distinction between the corporation and those of you who are principals of the corporation. As we've said, the corporation is a separate legal person, and you want to make sure that other people, businesses, the IRS, and the courts respect this distinction (see "Piercing the Corporate Veil" in Chapter 2 for a further discussion).

CONGRATULATIONS!

You have completed your last incorporation step! Please read through the post-incorporation procedures in Chapter 6 to see how they may apply to your new corporation.

After You Incorporate

Postincorporation Paperwork and Tasks 161

    File Annual Statement of Information 161

    File and Publish Fictitious Business Name Statement (If Appropriate) 161

    File Final Papers on Prior Business 162

    Notify Creditors and Others of Dissolution of Prior Business 163

    Adopt a Shareholders' Buy-Sell Agreement 163

Tax Forms—Federal 167

    S Corporation Tax Election 167

    Federal Employer Identification Number 168

    Employee's Withholding Certificate 168

    Income and Social Security Tax Withholding 168

    Quarterly Withholding Returns and Deposits 168

    Annual Wage and Tax Statement 169

    Federal Unemployment Tax 169

    Corporate Income Tax Return 169

    S Corporation Income Tax Return 170

    Corporate Employee and Shareholder Returns 170

    Estimated Corporate Income Tax Payments 170

Tax Forms—State 170

    Corporate Estimated Tax Return 170

    Annual Corporate Franchise Tax Return 171

    Employer Registration Forms 171

    State Withholding Allowance Certificate 171

    Personal Income Tax Withholding 171

    California Unemployment and Disability Insurance 171

    Withholding Returns 172

    Annual Wage and Tax Statement 172

    Annual Reconciliation of Income Tax Withholding 172

    Sales Tax Permits and Returns 172

Licenses and Permits 173

Workers' Compensation Insurance 173

Private Insurance Coverage 173

t this point, you have formed your corporation. But as you know, operating any business, regardless of its size, involves ongoing attention to paperwork. In this chapter, we briefly cover some important steps you should take after organizing your corporation. We discuss how to comply with the various ongoing state and federal tax requirements that may apply to your corporation. We also recommend adopting a shareholder buy-sell agreement that helps control what happens to your small corporation when an owner dies or decides to leave. And we discuss other formalities related to hiring employees and conducting corporate business.

Postincorporation Paperwork and Tasks

There are a few formalities you should take care of shortly after you organize your corporation. Some of these apply to all incorporators; others apply only to those who have incorporated an existing business.

10-4-10 mailed dated 10-1-10

File Annual Statement of Information

Shortly after you file your articles of incorporation, you will receive an Initial Statement of Information (Domestic Stock Corporation) from the California Secretary of State's office. This form (Form SI-200 C) must be filled out and sent back to the secretary with a small filing fee within 90 days after your articles were filed. The purpose of this form is to provide the public with current information about the corporation, including the location of its principal executive office and the identities of its directors and officers.

Every year, you will receive a new Statement of Information (Form SI-200 C), which you must fill out and return by the due date

indicated. If there has been no change in the information given in the last statement, the corporation may file a simplified form, Form SI-200 N/C.

WEBSITE

You can file your Statement of Information online. Go to the secretary of state's website at www.ss.ca.gov. In the California Business Portal, click on the "E-File" link and you can fill in and file Form SI-200C or SI-200N/C online.

In addition to filing a statement every year, the corporation may file a new statement any time the information contained in the last annual statement becomes inaccurate (for example, if new directors or officers are selected). You must file a new statement whenever the name or address of the corporation's agent for service of process changes. (Use Form SI-200 C for this.)

If the corporation fails to file the initial or annual statements on time, it is subject to a fine and a possible suspension of corporate powers. So make sure to follow this simple formality.

File and Publish Fictitious Business Name Statement (If Appropriate)

If your corporation will do business under a name other than the exact corporate name given in your articles of incorporation, you must file and publish a fictitious business name statement in the county of the corporation's principal place of business. For instance, if the name stated in your articles is "Acme Business Computers, Inc.," and you plan to do business under the acronym "ABC, Inc.," you should file and publish a fictitious business name statement. Remember, if you are the first to file this statement for a particular name in a particular county and if you actually engage in business in this county under this name, you are presumed to have the exclusive right to use this name in connection with your business in this county. Although another business can overcome this presumption if it was using the same or a similar name first, it doesn't hurt to stake your claim by getting your name on file.

You must file this statement within 40 days after you start doing business under your fictitious name. Also, you can be barred from using the courts to sue another business or person involving a transaction or contract in which you used your fictitious name unless you first file and publish this statement.

To file and publish your fictitious business name statement, do the following:

1. Obtain a fictitious business name statement and instructions from a legal newspaper or from your local county clerk's office. You can get to the website of each county clerk's office from a link on the Name Availability page of the corporation division's website—see Appendix B. If you haven't already done so (see Chapter 5, Step 1), you should check the county clerk's files to make sure that another business is not already using your fictitious name in the county.

2. Prepare the statement following the instructions for corporations. If your fictitious business name includes a corporate designator such as "Incorporated," "Inc.," "Corporation," or "Corp.," you may have to provide proof that you are a corporation (by showing the county clerk a certified copy of your articles).

3. File the original statement with the county clerk of the county in which the principal executive office of the corporation is located, along with the current filing fee. Obtain a file-endorsed copy of the statement from the county clerk.

4. Mail a copy of the statement to a qualified legal newspaper of general circulation in the county where the corporation's principal place of business is located. Ask the paper to publish your fictitious name statement and file an affidavit of publication with the county clerk (you will have to pay the newspaper's fee for this service). The newspaper will publish the statement once a week for four successive weeks, and should be willing to file an affidavit of publication with the county clerk for you. If you wish to make this filing yourself, follow the instructions accompanying the statement.

5. Place a copy of the endorsed-filed fictitious business name statement and endorsed-filed affidavit of publication in your corporate records book.

6. Make a note in your corporate records book to file another statement five years after your original filing (as explained in the instructions). The county clerk will not notify you of this renewal date.

7. Make similar filings (and publications of the statement), if you wish, in other counties in which you plan to use this name.

File Final Papers on Prior Business

If you have incorporated a preexisting business (transferred the assets of a business to the corporation in return for shares), the prior business owners should file all papers needed to terminate their prior business, including final sales tax and employment tax returns, if appropriate. Of course, you should close your previous business bank accounts and open the corporate bank accounts indicated in the bank account resolution of your minutes. In addition, if the old business holds any licenses or permits, you may need to cancel them and take out new licenses or permits in the name of the corporation.

Notify Creditors and Others of Dissolution of Prior Business

If you have incorporated a prior business, you should notify the creditors of the prior business and other interested parties (for example, suppliers, vendors, and others with whom you have open-book accounts or lines of credit), in writing, that the prior business is now a corporation.

If the prior business was a partnership, use the following notification procedure. Nonpartnership businesses can simply send out a notification letter as discussed in Paragraph 4, below.

1. Obtain at least two copies of a Notice of Dissolution of a Partnership form from a legal newspaper.

2. Fill out the notice following the instructions on the form.

3. Send the completed notice to a legal newspaper circulated in the place or places where the partnership regularly did business, with the request that it publish the notice and file an affidavit of publication with the county clerk within 30 days afterwards. Include publication and filing fees with your request. Place copies of the notice form and the endorsed-filed affidavit of publication in your corporate records book.

4. Notify creditors (and other interested parties) by mail of the dissolution of the partnership or other type of prior business. This notice should be in letter form, addressed and sent to each creditor, and should contain the same information included in the published notice. However, you will want to modify the information in the letter to show that it is directed to a particular individual or business, rather than the general public. Indicate that your prior business has been dissolved and that you are now doing business as a corporation under your new corporate name. Indicate your new corporate address if you have changed the location of your principal place of business. Place a copy of each letter in your corporate records book.

Adopt a Shareholders' Buy-Sell Agreement

By now you're surely tired of incorporation paperwork, and are ready to get down to business. Not so fast—there is one postincorporation formality we want you to seriously consider: adopting a shareholder buy-sell agreement to control who can own shares in your corporation in the future and how much they must pay for them.

You may be wondering, why deal with these issues while our corporation is still in the start-up phase? The answer is as simple as it is scary (potentially, at least): If all shareholders don't sign a buy-sell agreement when they begin corporate life, you could end up in a nasty dispute when a shareholder departs, dies, or divorces and his or her shares are transferred to an outsider the rest of you can't stand.

Some Shareholders Don't Need to Adopt a Buy-Sell Agreement

If you and your longtime spouse own 100% of corporate shares and you agree there is virtually no possibility that you will divorce, there normally is little reason to go to the trouble of creating a buy-sell agreement. After all, if one of you dies while you still own the business, chances are excellent that the other person will inherit the deceased spouse's shares—or that they will be left to a child or children according to a mutually agreed upon estate plan.

A buy-sell agreement may also be unnecessary if shares are all owned by parents and their compatible children in a situation where all agree that the children will eventually be given or inherit the parents' interests.

Here's the problem: When a shareholder in a closely held corporation dies, sells his or her shares, gives them away, or (in some cases) gets a divorce, this brings an outsider into the shareholder ranks. Think about it: Do you really want to have to deal with another shareholder's spoiled child, or hostile ex-spouse? Remember, a shareholder in a small corporation not only gets to vote at annual meetings for the election of the board, he or she also has a say in all major decisions brought before the shareholders for a vote. These decisions may include major structural changes to the corporation, such as amending the articles of incorporation or the corporate bylaws. But that isn't the worst part. A shareholder in a small corporation also may be able to elect him- or herself to a board position. This is true because, in most smaller corporations, a plurality—not a majority—shareholder vote is all that is needed to elect a person to the board. An outsider who gets elected to the board is given a management vote equal to all other board members (each board member has one vote), and thereby gets to participate in all major corporate decisions (and even if outvoted, will have to be heard).

A good shareholder buy-sell agreement deals with these and other issues in advance, when everyone is in a good mood. The agreement usually allows the corporation and remaining shareholders to buy shares offered to an outsider for sale. It also spells out whether the corporation and/or remaining shareholders get a chance, or are required, to buy the shares of a shareholder who stops working for the corporation, dies, divorces, or, under provisions in some agreements, becomes disabled. And it handles the important issue of setting a price, or a procedure to price, shares when the corporation and shareholders decide to buy shares under the buy-sell agreement. This is crucial, since one of the most potentially

contentious issues involved in any buyback is how much the shares are worth. Without an advance agreement, arriving at a fair value can be murky—after all, with no ready market for the shares of a privately held corporation, their value is in the eye of the beholder (the holder of shares). And can't you just imagine how much an angry ex-spouse who receives shares as part of a divorce may claim they are worth?

Fortunately, armed with good information and forms, you can prepare a sound buy-sell agreement for your corporation. But to do so, you'll need more material than we have space to include here. One source, designed for use by self-help incorporators who want a basic buy-sell agreement to handle future buyback problems, is Nolo's publication *Business Buyout Agreements: A Step-by-Step Guide for Co-Owners,* by Anthony Mancuso and Bethany K. Laurence (Nolo). This book takes you step by step through the process of adopting buy-sell provisions for your small corporation, limited liability company, or partnership, with particular attention paid to the concerns and issues of the small, closely held business. Ready-to-use agreements are included as tear-outs and on the CD-ROM to help you accomplish this task efficiently.

Of course, you may find other sources for a buy-sell agreement, including other business or legal titles in bookstores or business or law libraries. But no matter how you prepare your agreement, the range of technical legal and tax considerations that may apply to your agreement and to any buy-sell transaction that later occurs under it makes it sensible to check with your legal or tax advisor before adopting your agreement. This will help ensure that the practical procedure you have agreed upon will not have any unwanted tax or legal effects later.

Issues Covered in Shareholder Buy-Sell Agreements

Here are some of the basic issues most corporate buy-sell agreements cover, and typical ways they are handled:

- **Shareholder tries to sell to an outside buyer.** Agreements often provide that either the corporation or the other shareholders have a right to buy the shares before an outside shareholder gets a chance.

- **Shareholder wants to give or transfer shares to relatives.** Some agreements restrict all gifts or other transfers of shares. Others allow gifts to family members, as long as certain conditions are met (less than one-half of a shareholder's stock may be gifted to relatives).

- **Shareholder dies.** Some agreements give the corporation or remaining shareholders a right to purchase the shares from a deceased shareholder's estate within a specified number of days from the date of the shareholder's death. Other agreements require the corporation, if financially able, to buy back the shares from the estate or heirs of a deceased shareholder upon request by the representative of the estate or an heir.

- **Shareholder leaves the corporation.** Many agreements adopted by closely held corporations require a shareholder who quits the corporation to sell the shares back to the corporation. Other agreements simply give the corporation a right to require such a buyback, or let the ex-shareholder-employee demand a buyback if he or she wishes to sell the shares.

- **Current shareholder asks to be cashed out.** Some agreements let a shareholder request a buy-out of his or her shares, even if he or she remains an employee of the corporation. The corporation has the choice whether to do so or not (and the approval of the other shareholders also may be required).

- **Shareholder divorces.** Agreements often provide that if a shareholder divorces, and shares are transferred to the shareholder's ex-spouse by court order as part of a marital settlement agreement, the corporation can demand a buyback of the shares from the ex-spouse. Typically, spouses of shareholders also sign the shareholder buy-sell agreements.

- **Shareholder becomes disabled.** Some agreements say nothing specific about the disability of a shareholder; the provisions of the agreement that deal with an employee who stops working for the corporation (whether due to quitting, firing, disability, or any other cause) handle the buyback. Other agreements require or permit the corporation to buy out the shares of a disabled shareholder, if a written statement of disability is submitted by one or two doctors.

- **Shareholder has debt problems.** If a shareholder files for personal bankruptcy, many agreements require the corporation, if financially able, to buy the shares back from the bankruptcy trustee. Some agreements prohibit a shareholder from pledging shares as collateral for a personal loan, and require a buyback from the creditor if shares have been pledged contrary to the agreement and the creditor gets possession of the shares due to the shareholder's default on the loan.

- **Buyback price or formula.** All agreements specify a default price or procedure that will be used to value shares for purposes of any buyout covered in the agreement. Typically, this provision only applies if a buyback price or procedure is not specified for a particular type of buyout covered elsewhere in the agreement (for example, it is common for agreements to

Issues Covered in Shareholder Buy-Sell Agreements (cont'd)

allow the buyback of shares offered for sale by a shareholder to an outsider at the price the outsider is willing to pay). Different formulas are used, depending on the type of business and the profit history of the corporation. Agreements adopted at the beginning of corporate life typically value shares at book value (the depreciated value of assets on the balance sheet of your corporation, minus liabilities). Later, after several years of continuing profits, corporations typically switch to a share valuation method based upon a multiple of the corporation's earnings (for example, the shares of a successful corporation may be valued at five times average annual earnings in the corporation's buy-sell agreement). Other valuation methods used in agreements include a share valuation made at the time of buyback by an independent appraiser or a price agreed to by the shareholders and specified in the agreement.

- **Different buyback prices.** Some agreements specify different buyback prices and terms for different buyback scenarios. For example, if a shareholder leaves the corporation within one year of its formation, the shareholder may get a discounted buyback price, such as 80% of the standard buyback price specified elsewhere in the agreement.

- **Buyback payment method.** Agreements also set out the terms for payment of the buyback price. All cash upfront may be specified if the shareholders know the corporation will be able to afford it. More often, agreements provide for the payment of the buyout price in stages, with part cash paid at the time of buyback and the balance, plus interest, payable by the corporation in monthly installments.

- **Life insurance funding of buyback.** Often the corporation and/or shareholders are required to take out and pay for life insurance policies on each shareholder. If a shareholder dies, the cash proceeds from these policies are used to purchase the deceased shareholder's shares.

TIP

Don't wait too long to adopt a buy-sell agreement. Many incorporators are tempted to avoid discussing and deciding on buy-sell issues, particularly at this early stage of corporate operations. One bit of advice is in order: Don't give in to the temptation. Once your corporation begins to make money, the questions of who owns its shares and how much they are worth will quickly become loaded, and not just to your fellow shareholders. Spouses, children, and other eventual transferees or successors to the shares may also get agitated. In other words, trying to settle the basic questions of who can own shares and how much they are worth at the time of a buyout may be fraught with controversy, requiring the hiring of expensive lawyers (and accountants) to sort them out. Much better to agree, ahead of time, on a reasonable procedure to handle these possibilities.

Tax Forms—Federal

Another basic corporate formality is reporting and paying taxes. Here, we discuss the basic federal tax issues and forms that a corporation might need to handle. Because each corporation is different, we can't anticipate every tax your business might have to pay. Instead, this section is intended as a general guide to the routine tax questions corporations face.

You can get most of the tax forms discussed below from the IRS.

S Corporation Tax Election

If you have decided to elect federal S corporation tax status, and have included an authorizing resolution in your minutes, you must make a timely election by filing IRS Form 2553 and the consents of your shareholders. (See "S Corporation Tax Status" in Chapter 4.) If you haven't made your election yet (and haven't consulted a tax advisor as to the timing of the election), call your advisor now and make sure the S corporation election form is sent in on time—you don't want to miss the deadline for this election.

TIP

Make tax year elections, too. Remember, S corporations must generally select a calendar tax year unless they are eligible to elect a fiscal tax year under IRS rules and regulations. (See "Corporate Accounting Periods and Tax Years" in Chapter 4.) Check with your tax advisor when you make your S corporation tax election to figure out whether you can, and should, elect a fiscal tax year.

Tax and Business Resources

An excellent source of legal information on starting a small business, generally, is *Legal Guide for Starting & Running a Small Business,* by Fred S. Steingold (Nolo). Another excellent sourcebook of practical information, including financial ledgers and worksheets, is *Small Time Operator,* by Bernard Kamoroff (Bell Springs Publishing).

Federal tax forms and information are available over the Internet at www.irs.gov. California tax forms and information are available from www.ftb.ca.gov.

We suggest all incorporators obtain IRS Publication 509, *Tax Calendars,* prior to the beginning of each year. This pamphlet contains tax calendars showing the dates for corporate and employer filings during the year.

Information on withholding, depositing, reporting, and paying federal employment taxes can be found in IRS Publication 15, *Circular E,* *Employer's Tax Guide,* and the Publication 15-A and 15-B Supplements. Further federal tax information can be found in IRS Publication 542, *Corporations,* and Publication 334, *Tax Guide for Small Business.*

Helpful information on accounting methods and bookkeeping procedures is contained in IRS Publication 538, *Accounting Periods and Methods,* and Publication 583, *Starting a Business and Keeping Records.*

For information on withholding, contributing, paying, and reporting California employment taxes, obtain the *California Employer's Tax Guide* (Publication DE 44) and *Employer's Guide* (Publication DE 4525—for unemployment and disability tax information). This guide can be downloaded from www.edd.cahwnet.gov, Forms and Publications pages.

Federal Employer Identification Number

As soon as possible after your articles are filed, your corporation must apply for a federal Employer Identification Number (EIN) by filling out IRS Form SS-4 and sending it to the nearest IRS center. The IRS should call back within a day or two with your assigned number. Form SS-4 is available online at the IRS website at www.irs.gov. You can fill in and file an SS-4 form online in a few minutes—just type "SS-4" in the top search box on the main IRS Web page ("Search IRS Site for" box), then select the "Online EIN" link. If you are incorporating a preexisting sole proprietorship or partnership, you will need to apply for a new EIN. You need this number for the employment tax returns and deposits discussed below. You will also need this number before you do your Notice of Transactions Pursuant to Corporation Code Section 25102(f) online (see Step 7 in Chapter 5).

Employee's Withholding Certificate

Each employee of the corporation must fill out and give the corporation an Employee's Withholding Exemption Certificate (IRS Form W-4) on or before starting work. This form is used in determining the amount of income taxes to be withheld from the employee's wages.

Generally, any individual who receives compensation for services rendered the corporation and who is subject to the control of the corporation, both as to what shall be done and how it should be done, is considered an employee. All shareholders of the corporation who receive salaries or wages for services as directors, officers, or nontitled personnel are considered employees of the corporation and must furnish a W-4.

 TIP

Directors are not considered employees if they are paid only for attending board meetings. However, if they are paid for other services or are salaried employees of the corporation, they will be considered employees whose wages are subject to the employment taxes discussed below—check with the IRS and your local state employment tax district office for more information.

Income and Social Security Tax Withholding

The corporation must withhold federal income tax and Social Security tax (FICA) from wages paid to each employee. These, as well as other employment taxes, are withheld and reported on a calendar year basis, regardless of the tax year of the corporation, and returns and deposits must be submitted on a quarterly or more frequent basis.

The amount of federal income tax withheld is based upon the employee's wage level and marital status and the number of allowances claimed on the employee's W-4.

Social Security taxes are withheld at a specific rate on an employee's wage base (the rate and wage base figures change constantly). The corporation is required to make matching Social Security tax contributions for each employee.

Quarterly Withholding Returns and Deposits

The corporation is required to prepare and file a Withholding Return (IRS Form 941) for each quarter of the calendar year, showing all income and Social Security taxes withheld from employees' wages as well as matching corporation Social Security tax contributions.

The corporation is required to deposit federal income and Social Security taxes on a monthly (or more frequent) basis in an authorized commercial or federal reserve bank. You must submit payment for undeposited taxes owed at the end of a calendar quarter with the quarterly return. Consult IRS Publication 15 for specifics.

Annual Wage and Tax Statement

The corporation is required to furnish two copies of the Wage and Tax Statement (IRS Form W-2) to each employee if income tax has been withheld from this person's wages or would have been withheld if the employee had claimed no more than one withholding exemption on his or her W-4. This form must show total wages paid and amounts deducted for income and Social Security taxes. A special six-part W-2 should be used in California to show state income tax and disability insurance contributions in addition to the required federal withholding information. W-2 forms must be furnished to employees no later than January 31 following the close of the calendar year.

The corporation must submit the original of each employee's previous year's W-2 form and an annual Transmittal of Income and Tax Statement (Form W-3) to the Social Security Administration on or before the last day of February following the close of the calendar year.

Federal Unemployment Tax

Most corporations are subject to the federal unemployment tax provisions. Under the tax statutes, your corporation is subject to paying Federal Unemployment Tax (FUTA) if, during the current or preceding calendar year, the corporation:

- paid wages of $1,500 or more during any calendar quarter, or
- had one or more employees for some portion of at least one day during each of 20 different calendar weeks. These 20 weeks do not have to be consecutive.

FUTA taxes are paid by the corporation and are not deducted from employees' wages. The FUTA tax is determined by the employee wage base and is paid by the corporation (as usual, rates and wage base figures are subject to change). The corporation receives a credit for a percentage of this tax for California unemployment taxes paid or for receiving a favorable experience rating by the state.

Generally, the corporation must deposit the tax in an authorized commercial or federal reserve bank within one month following the close of the quarter. For help in computing your quarterly FUTA tax liability, see the instructions in IRS Publication 15. An annual FUTA return (IRS Form 940) must be filed by the corporation with the nearest IRS center by January 31 following the close of the calendar year for which the tax is due. Any tax still due is payable with the return.

Corporate Income Tax Return

A regular business corporation must file an annual Corporation Income Tax Return (IRS Form 1120) on or before the 15th day of the third month following the close of its tax year. A two-page Short-Form Corporation Income Tax Return (IRS Form 1120-A) is available for use by smaller corporations with gross receipts, total income, and total assets of less than $500,000. The corporation's tax year must correspond with the corporation's accounting period (the period for which corporate books are kept as specified in your minutes). The tax year is established by the first income tax return filed by the corporation.

Your first corporate tax year may be a short year—that is, a year of less than 12 months. For example, if the corporate accounting period selected in the minutes is the calendar year, January 1 to December 31, and the corporate existence began on March 13 (the date the articles were filed), the corporation would establish its calendar tax year and report income for its first tax year by filing its first annual return on or before March 15 of the following year.

Note that this first return would be for the short year, March 13 to December 31. If the minutes select a fiscal tax year, say from July 1 to June 30, and the corporate existence begins on May 1, the first return would be filed on or before August 15 for the first short year of May 1 to June 30.

S Corporation Income Tax Return

Even though federal S corporations are, for the most part, not subject to the payment of corporate income taxes, such corporations must file an annual U.S. Small Business Corporation Income Tax Return (IRS Form 1120-S) on or before the 15th day of the third month following the close of the tax year for which the S corporation election is effective.

Corporate Employee and Shareholder Returns

Corporate employees and shareholders report employment and dividend income on their annual individual income tax returns (IRS Form 1040). S corporation shareholders report their pro rata share of undistributed corporate taxable income on Form 1040, Schedule E. (As noted in "S Corporation Tax Status" in Chapter 4, S corporation shareholders may be required to estimate and pay taxes on this undistributed taxable income during the year—check with your tax advisor.)

Estimated Corporate Income Tax Payments

Corporations that expect to owe federal corporate income taxes at the end of their tax year (and most will) are required to make estimated tax payments. Estimated tax payments must be deposited in an authorized commercial or federal reserve bank. The due date and amount of each installment are computed by a formula based upon the corporation's income tax liability.

To determine corporate estimated tax liability and the date and amount of deposits, obtain IRS Form 1120-W. This form is to be used for computational purposes only and should not be filed with the IRS.

Tax Forms—State

These are the basic state tax forms you will have to use in forming and running your corporation. You can get copies of these forms from the Franchise Tax Board.

Corporate Estimated Tax Return

A California profit corporation is required to pay an annual California franchise tax based on its annual net taxable income. It usually also must pay the minimum annual franchise tax each year. Corporations formed on or after January 1, 2000 are exempt from paying the minimum tax for their first tax year. For all tax years, the corporation is required to estimate its franchise tax liability at the beginning of the tax year and make advance franchise tax payments each quarter. At least the minimum $800 annual amount must be submitted with the corporation's first-quarter estimated tax payment each year (if the minimum applies for the year).

Annual Corporate Franchise Tax Return

Your corporation must submit an annual California Corporate Franchise Tax Return (Form 100) on or before the 15th day of the third month following the close of its tax year. With the return, you must submit payment for any portion of the tax due that wasn't estimated and paid during the year, as explained above.

Employer Registration Forms

All California corporations that have employees must register with the California Employment Development Department within 15 days of becoming subject to the California personal income tax withholding provisions and the California Unemployment Insurance Code (most are subject to these provisions immediately). If you have employees, register right now if you haven't done so. Registration forms can be obtained by calling the nearest California employment tax district office. If you are incorporating a preexisting business, you'll need to reregister with the Employment Development Department (even though you may be given the same account number). See the *Employer's Guide* mentioned in "Tax and Business Resources," above, and contact your local employment tax district office for more information—you can visit their website at www.edd.ca.gov.

> ! **WARNING**
>
> **Be sure to comply with unemployment insurance code provisions.** Be careful about classifying people who perform services for your corporation as independent contractors. The EDD is particularly aggressive when it comes to collecting state unemployment taxes from businesses. The office routinely investigates employee complaints and conducts field audits to monitor compliance with California's Unemployment Insurance Code

provisions. This includes making sure that employers are paying unemployment taxes for all of their workers who are really employees, regardless of how the employer has classified them.

State Withholding Allowance Certificate

Although the corporation can use the information contained in the federal W-4 form to compute the amount of state personal income taxes to be withheld from employees' wages, it is required to make a special California Withholding Allowance Certificate (DE-4) available to all its employees. Use of this form by the employee is optional. If not used, the corporation withholds state personal income tax from an employee's wages in accordance with the allowances on his or her federal W–4.

Personal Income Tax Withholding

The amount the corporation withholds from employee wages for state personal income tax is based on tax tables that take into account the marital status, claimed allowances, and wages of the employee. These tables automatically allow for applicable exemptions and the standard deduction.

California Unemployment and Disability Insurance

California unemployment insurance contributions are paid by the corporation at its employer contribution rate shown on the Quarterly Withholding Return (DE-3), discussed below. Employer contributions are payable on the current employee wage base amount.

The employer contribution rates vary and, except for new businesses, are based upon the employer's experience rating for each year.

Experience ratings vary, depending upon the extent of unemployment benefits paid to former employees of the corporation.

While officers are employees for purposes of unemployment insurance contributions, unemployment benefits may be denied to them if they are laid off or terminated by the corporation and the corporation pays them any fringes while they are not working (such as profit-sharing or pension benefits). Also, if the officers and directors are the only shareholders of the corporation, they won't be eligible for benefits unless the corporation has to pay federal unemployment taxes. Check with your local employment tax district office about this when you first contact them.

Disability insurance contributions are paid by the employee—the employer has to withhold a certain amount from the employee's paycheck to make these payments.

Withholding Returns

Most corporations are required to file Monthly Withholding Returns (Form DE-3M) with the state, indicating California personal income tax withholding and disability and unemployment tax contributions for each employee.

The corporation must file a Quarterly Withholding Return (Form DE-3) reporting personal income tax withholding and disability and unemployment insurance contributions for the previous quarter and pay any balance not already paid with monthly returns. For more specific information, consult the *California Employer's Tax Guide* available from your local employment tax district office, mentioned in "Tax and Business Resources," above.

Annual Wage and Tax Statement

The corporation should prepare a six-part combined federal/state Annual Wage and Tax Statement, Form W-2, as discussed in "California Unemployment and Disability Insurance," above. One copy must be filed with the state.

Annual Reconciliation of Income Tax Withholding

The corporation must file a completed Reconciliation of Income Tax Withheld Form (Form DE-43 or DE-43A) together with one copy of each employee's W-2 form, copies of California unemployment insurance filings, and a total listing of all personal income tax withheld, with the California Employment Development Department on or before February 28 following the close of each calendar year.

Sales Tax Permits and Returns

Subject to a few exceptions, every corporation that has gross receipts from the sale of personal property in California (that is, merchandise sold to customers) must apply for a seller's permit by filing an application (Form BT-400) with the nearest office of the California Board of Equalization. This form also registers you as an employer with the Employment Development Department. No fee is required.

Some applicants may be required to post a bond or other security for payment of future sales taxes, although this amount may be waived if you indicate that you plan to do very little resale business. A separate permit is required for each place of business where transactions generating sales tax are customarily entered into with customers. You must add sales tax to the price of certain goods and collect them from the purchaser.

Wholesalers, as well as retailers, must obtain a permit. A wholesaler, however, is not required to collect sales tax from a retailer who holds a valid seller's permit and who buys items for resale to customers, provided a resale certificate is completed in connection with the transaction.

Sellers must file periodic sales and use tax returns to report and pay sales tax collected from customers. A seller must keep complete records of all business transactions, including sales, receipts, purchases, and other expenditures, and have them available for inspection by the board at all times.

The State Board of Equalization also collects an annual environmental fee from corporations with 50 or more employees doing business in California. Corporations with 50 to 100 employees pay $100 per year. Call the excise tax division of the Board of Equalization in Sacramento for more information or visit its website at www.boe.ca.gov.

Licenses and Permits

Many businesses, whether operating as corporations or not, are required to obtain state licenses or permits before commencing business. To get a license or permit, you generally have to meet one or more requirements relating to registration, experience, education, examination scores, and adequate bonding.

Your corporation should obtain all proper licenses before commencing corporate operations. Even if you are incorporating an already licensed business, you must comply with any corporate license requirement in your field. Some businesses must obtain licenses in the name of the corporation, while others must obtain them in the name of supervisory corporate personnel. For specific information relating to corporate licensing requirements, check with a local department of Consumer Affairs office. They will either refer you to one of their boards or to an appropriate outside agency.

Workers' Compensation Insurance

With some exceptions, all employees of a corporation, whether officers or otherwise, must be covered by workers' compensation insurance. Rates vary depending on the salary level and risk associated with an employee's job. Generally, if all of the officers are the only shareholders of the corporation, they do not have to be covered by workers' compensation. Also, if directors are only paid travel expenses for attending meetings, they may be exempt from coverage (although flat per-meeting payments will generally make them subject to coverage). This is a blurry area, so check with your local state compensation insurance commission office for names of carriers, rates, and extent of required coverage in all cases.

For online workers' compensation information, go to the California Department of Insurance website at www.insurance.ca.gov.

Private Insurance Coverage

Corporations, like other businesses, should carry the usual kinds of insurance to prevent undue loss in the event of an accident, fire, theft, and so on. Although the corporate form may insulate shareholders from personal loss, it won't prevent corporate assets from being jeopardized by such hazards. You can obtain basic commercial coverage, which often includes coverage for autos, inventory, and personal injuries on premises. Additional coverage for product liability and directors' and officers' liability, and other specialized types of insurance, may also be appropriate (of course, these policies may be more costly for a closely held corporation to obtain). Many smaller companies elect to have a large deductible to keep premium payments down. Obviously, there are a number of options to consider when putting together your corporate insurance package. Talk to a few experienced commercial insurance brokers and compare rates, areas, and extent of coverage before deciding. Look for someone who suggests ways to get essential coverage for an amount you can live with—not someone who wants to sell you a policy that will protect you from all possible risks. This type of policy really doesn't exist—and even if it did, you probably wouldn't want to pay the price.

Lawyers and Accountants

Lawyers 176

Accountants and Tax Advisors 177

Lawyers

It often makes sense to consult an experienced attorney to review your incorporation papers and suggest any specific modifications you might want to consider before you file your incorporation papers. Reviewing your incorporation papers with an attorney is a sensible way to ensure that all of your papers are up to date and meet your specialized needs.

But remember: Asking a lawyer to review the forms and organizational aspects of your incorporation is quite different from having him or her do, or redo, all the work for you. The lawyer should have experience in small business incorporations, should be prepared to answer your specific, informed questions, and should review, not rewrite (unless absolutely necessary), the forms you have prepared.

Throughout this book, we have flagged areas of potential complexity that may require a lawyer's help. If any of these issues come up for you, go over them with an experienced lawyer before filing your articles of incorporation. For example, the following areas will require a lawyer's (or other professional's) services:

- One of your proposed shareholders needs (or wishes) to designate and rely on the advice of a lawyer, accountant, or other professional advisor in order to be eligible as a suitable shareholder under Category 5 of the California limited offering exemption—see Chapter 5, Step 6, and "The Limited Offering Exemption" in Chapter 3.

- You wish to have a lawyer prepare or review a shareholders' buy-sell agreement for the repurchase of shares in your corporation—see "Adopt a Shareholders' Buy-Sell Agreement" in Chapter 6.

- You wish to form a California statutory close corporation, in which case you will need a lawyer's help in preparing a special close corporation shareholders' agreement and adding the required close corporation provisions to your articles of incorporation and stock certificates—see Chapter 5, Step 2, and "The Close Corporation" in Chapter 2.

If you decide to consult a lawyer, you may well ask, "What type of lawyer should I consult?" The best lawyer to choose is someone whom you personally know and trust and who has lots of experience advising small businesses. The next best is usually a small business expert whom a friend (with his or her own business experience) recommends. If you make some calls, you can almost always find someone via this reliable word-of-mouth approach. You can try to find an attorney through a lawyer referral service, but make sure the service is certified by the State Bar of California. For more information on certified lawyer referral services, call the state bar or check their website at www.calbar.ca.gov. You can also check Nolo's online Lawyer Directory at www.nolo.com for information on lawyers in your area.

When you call a prospective lawyer (not just his or her law office), you can probably get a good idea of how the person operates by paying close attention to the way your call is handled. Is the lawyer available? Is your call returned promptly? Is the lawyer willing to spend at least a few minutes talking to you to determine if he or she is really the best person for the job? Do you get a good personal feeling from your conversation? Oh, and one more thing: Be sure to get the hourly rate the lawyer will charge set in advance.

Rules of the state bar require a lawyer to provide you with a written fee agreement in advance if the fee for services will exceed a certain amount (or in contingency fee cases).

If you are using this book, you will probably not be impressed by—or need—someone who charges $350 per hour to support an office at the top of the tallest building in town.

RESOURCES

Look up the law yourself. Some incorporators may wish to research legal information not covered in this book. County law libraries are open to the public and are not difficult to use once you understand how the information is categorized and stored. They are an invaluable source of corporate and general business forms, corporate tax procedures, and information. Research librarians will usually go out of their way to help you find the right statute, form, or background reading on any corporate or tax issue. If you are interested in doing self-help legal research, an excellent source on how to break the code of the law libraries is *Legal Research: How to Find & Understand the Law,* by Stephen Elias and Susan Levinkind (Nolo).

WEBSITE

Check the California Corporations Code online. If you want to browse the Corporations Code, go to the following Internet website: www. leginfo.ca.gov, click "California Law," then select "Corporations Code" and click on "Search." The General Corporation law, which applies to California business corporations, is contained in Title 1, Division 1.

Accountants and Tax Advisors

As you already know, organizing and operating a corporation involves a significant amount of financial and tax work and decisions. Again, we have flagged tricky areas involving financial planning and corporate tax issues throughout this book, including:

- Does it make more sense to form an LLC for your California unlicensed business (and possibly elect corporate tax treatment for your LLC) instead of incorporating?—see "The Limited Liability Company" in Chapter 1.

- Should you elect federal S corporation tax status?—see "S Corporation Tax Status" in Chapter 4.

- Are you eligible for Section 351 tax-free exchange treatment?—see "Tax Treatment When an Existing Business Is Incorporated" in Chapter 4.

- Do you need help in selecting your corporate tax year?—see Chapter 5, Step 5.

- Do you wish to set up IRS-qualified fringe benefit packages for yourself and other employees?—see "Tax Treatment of Employee Compensation and Benefits" in Chapter 4.

- Will you rely on an accountant or other professional in setting up your corporate books (double-entry journals and general ledger) and in making ongoing corporate and employment tax filings?—see the discussion below and "Tax Forms–Federal" and "Tax Forms–State" in Chapter 6.

- Do you need to obtain a valuation of the assets before transferring a prior business to your corporation in return for shares?—see Chapter 5, Step 8.

Although we tend to use the terms tax advisor, financial consultant, and accountant interchangeably, you may want to refer these initial incorporation considerations to a certified public accountant with corporate experience. For general assistance and advice, a qualified financial planner may also be very helpful.

Once your initial incorporation questions have been answered, your corporation is set up, and your books established, you may want to have routine tax filings and bookkeeping tasks performed by corporate personnel or independent contractors who have been trained in bookkeeping and tax matters (in many instances trained or recommended by the accountant you have previously consulted). Most corporations will have at least their annual corporate returns handled by their accountant or other tax return preparer.

For future financial advice, you may wish to contact an officer in the corporate department of the bank where you keep your corporate account(s). Banks are an excellent source of financial advice, particularly if they will be corporate creditors—after all, they will have a stake in the success of your corporation. Further, the Small Business Administration can be an ideal source of financial and tax information and resources (as well as financing, in some cases).

Whatever your arrangement for financial or tax advice and assistance, you may wish to order the IRS publications listed in "Tax and Business Resources" in Chapter 6 to familiarize yourself with some of the tax and bookkeeping aspects of operating a corporation.

When you select an accountant, bookkeeper, or financial advisor, the same considerations apply as when selecting a lawyer. Choose someone you know or whom a friend with business experience recommends. Be as specific as you can regarding the services you wish performed, and find someone with experience in corporate taxation and corporate and employee tax returns and requirements. And find out ahead of time how much you will have to pay.

How to Use the CD-ROM

Installing the Form Files Onto Your Computer..180

    Windows 2000, XP, and Vista Users 180

    Macintosh Users..180

Using the Word Processing Files to Create Documents..181

Using California Secretary of State Forms..183

Files Included on the Forms CD..185

The tear-out forms in Appendix B are included on a CD-ROM in the back of the book. This CD-ROM, which can be used with Windows computers, installs files that you use with software programs that are already installed on your computer. It is not a stand-alone software program. Please read this appendix and the README.TXT file included on the CD-ROM for instructions on using the Forms CD.

Note to Mac users: This CD-ROM and its files should also work on Macintosh computers. Please note, however, that Nolo cannot provide technical support for non-Windows users.

How to View the README File

If you do not know how to view the file README.TXT, insert the Forms CD-ROM into your computer's CD-ROM drive and follow these instructions:

- **Windows 2000, XP, and Vista:** (1) On your PC's desktop, double click the My Computer icon; (2) double click the icon for the CD-ROM drive into which the Forms CD-ROM was inserted; (3) double click the file README.TXT.
- **Macintosh:** (1) On your Mac desktop, double click the icon for the CD-ROM that you inserted; (2) double click on the file README.TXT.

Two different kinds of forms are on the CD-ROM:

- Word processing (RTF) forms that you can open, complete, print, and save with your word processing program (see Using the Word Processing Files to Create Documents, below), and
- Forms from California Secretary of State (PDF) that can be viewed only with *Adobe*

Acrobat Reader (see "Using California Secretary of State Forms," below). Some of these forms have fill-in text fields and can be completed using your computer. You will not, however, be able to save the completed forms with the filled-in data. PDF forms without fill-in text fields must be printed out and filled in by hand or with a typewriter.

See Appendix B for a list of forms, their file names, and file formats.

Installing the Form Files Onto Your Computer

Before you can do anything with the files on the CD-ROM, you need to install them onto your hard disk. In accordance with U.S. copyright laws, remember that copies of the CD-ROM and its files are for your personal use only.

Insert the Forms CD and do the following:

Windows 2000, XP, and Vista Users

Follow the instructions that appear on the screen. (If nothing happens when you insert the Forms CD-ROM, then (1) double click the My Computer icon; (2) double click the icon for the CD-ROM drive into which the Forms CD-ROM was inserted; and (3) double click the file WELCOME.EXE.)

By default, all the files are installed to the \California Corporation Forms folder in the \ Program Files folder of your computer. A folder called California Corporations Forms is added to the Programs folder of the Start menu.

Macintosh Users

Step 1: If the CA Corporation Forms CD window is not open, open it by double clicking the CA Corporation Forms CD icon.

Install : C:\ ProgramFiles\ California Corporation Files

Step 2: Select the California Corporation Forms folder icon.

Step 3: Drag and drop the folder icon onto the icon of your hard disk.

Using the Word Processing Files to Create Documents

This section concerns the files for forms that can be opened and edited with your word processing program.

All word processing forms come in rich text format. These files have the extension ".RTF." For example, the form for the articles of incorporation discussed in Chapter 5 is on the file ARTICLES.rtf. All forms, their file names, and file formats are listed in Appendix B.

RTF files can be read by most recent word processing programs including all versions of MS Word for Windows and Macintosh, WordPad for Windows, and recent versions of WordPerfect for Windows and Macintosh.

To use a form from the CD to create your documents you must: (1) open a file in your word processor or text editor; (2) edit the form by filling in the required information; (3) print it out; and (4) rename and save your revised file.

Following are general instructions, however, each word processor uses different commands to open, format, save, and print documents. Please read your word processor's manual for specific instructions on performing these tasks.

Do not call Nolo's technical support if you have questions on how to use your word processor or your computer.

Step 1: Opening a File

There are three ways to open the word processing files included on the CD-ROM after you have installed them onto your computer.

- Windows users can open a file by selecting its shortcut as follows: (1) Click the Windows Start button; (2) open the Programs folder; (3) open the California Corporation Forms subfolder; (4) open the RTF subfolder; and (5) click on the shortcut to the form you want to work with.

- Both Windows and Macintosh users can open a file directly by double clicking on it. Use My Computer or Windows Explorer (Windows 2000, XP, or Vista) or the Finder (Macintosh) to go to the folder you installed or copied the CD-ROM's files to. Then, double click on the specific file you want to open.

- You can also open a file from within your word processor. To do this, you must first start your word processor. Then, go to the File menu and choose the Open command. This opens a dialog box where you will tell the program (1) the type of file you want to open (*.RTF); and (2) the location and name of the file (you will need to navigate through the directory tree to get to the folder on your hard disk where the CD's files have been installed).

Where Are the Files Installed?

Windows Users

- RTF files are installed by default to a folder named \California Corporation Forms\ RTF in the \Program Files folder of your computer.

Macintosh Users

- RTF files are located in the RTF folder within the California Corporation Forms folder.

Step 2: Editing Your Document

Fill in the appropriate information according to the instructions and sample agreements in the book. Underlines are used to indicate where you need to enter your information, frequently followed by instructions in brackets. Be sure to delete the underlines and instructions from your edited document. You will also want to make sure that any signature lines in your completed documents appear on a page with at least some text from the document itself.

Editing Forms That Have Optional or Alternative Text

Some of the forms have check boxes before text. The check boxes indicate:

- optional text, where you choose whether to include or exclude the given text, or
- alternative text, where you select one alternative to include and exclude the other alternatives.

If you are using the tear-out forms in Appendix B, you simply mark the appropriate box to make your choice.

If you are using the Forms CD, however, we recommend that instead of marking the check boxes, you do the following:

Optional text

If you don't want to include optional text, just delete it from your document.

If you do want to include optional text, just leave it in your document.

In either case, delete the check box itself as well as the italicized instructions that the text is optional.

Alternative text

First delete all the alternatives that you do not want to include.

Then delete the remaining check boxes, as well as the italicized instructions that you need to select one of the alternatives provided.

Step 3: Printing Out the Document

Use your word processor's or text editor's Print command to print out your document.

Step 4: Saving Your Document

After filling in the form, use the Save As command to save and rename the file. Because all the files are read-only, you will not be able to use the Save command. This is for your protection. *If you save the file without renaming it, the underlines that indicate where you need to enter your information will be lost, and you will not be able to create a new document with this file without recopying the original file from the CD-ROM.*

Using California Secretary of State Forms

Electronic copies of useful forms from the California Secretary of State are included on the CD-ROM in Adobe Acrobat PDF format. You must have the *Adobe Acrobat Reader* installed on your computer to use these forms. *Adobe Reader* is available for all types of Windows and Macintosh systems. If you don't already have this software, you can download it for free at www.adobe.com.

All forms, their file names, and file formats are listed in Appendix B. These form files were created by California Secretary of State, not by Nolo.

Some of these forms have fill-in text fields. To create your document using these files, you must: (1) open a file; (2) fill in the text fields using either your mouse or the tab key on your keyboard to navigate from field to field; and (3) print it out. **Note:** While you can print out your completed form, you will not be able to save your completed form to disk.

Forms without fill-in text fields cannot be filled out using your computer. To create your document using these files, you must: (1) open the file; (2) print it out; and (3) complete it by hand or typewriter.

Step 1: Opening a Form

PDF files, like the word processing files, can be opened one of three ways.

- Windows users can open a file by selecting its shortcut as follows: (1) Click the Windows Start button; (2) open the Programs folder; (3) open the California Corporation Forms subfolder; (4) open the PDF folder; and (5) click on the shortcut to the form you want to work with.

- Both Windows and Macintosh users can open a file directly by double clicking on it. Use My Computer or Windows Explorer (Windows 2000, XP, or Vista) or the Finder (Macintosh) to go to the folder you created and copied the CD-ROM's files to. Then, double click on the specific file you want to open.

- You can also open a PDF file from within *Adobe Reader*. To do this, you must first start *Reader*. Then, go to the File menu and choose the Open command. This opens a dialog box where you will tell the program the location and name of the file (you will need to navigate through the directory tree to get to the folder on your hard disk where the CD's files have been installed).

Where Are the PDF Files Installed?

Windows Users

- PDF files are installed by default to a folder named \California Corporation Forms\ PDF in the \Program Files folder of your computer.

Macintosh Users

- PDF files are located in the PDF folder within the California Corporation Forms folder.

Step 2: Filling in a Form

Use your mouse or the Tab key on your keyboard to navigate from field to field within these forms. Be sure to have all the information you will need to complete a form on hand because you will not be able to save a copy of the filled-in form to disk. You can, however, print out a completed version.

Note: This step is only applicable to forms that have been created with fill-in text fields. Forms without fill-in fields must be completed by hand or typewriter after you have printed them out.

Step 3: Printing a Form

Choose Print from the *Acrobat Reader* File menu. This will open the Print dialog box. In the Print Range section of the Print dialog box, select the appropriate print range, then click OK.

Files Included on the Forms CD

The following files are in rich text format (RTF):

File Name	Document Title
ARTICLES.RTF*	Articles of Incorporation
COVERLET.RTF	Cover Letter for Filing Articles
BYLAWS.RTF	Bylaws
MINUTES.RTF	Waiver of Notice and Consent to Holding of First Meeting of Board of Directors
MINUTES.RTF	Minutes of First Meeting of the Board of Directors
SHARELET.RTF	Shareholder Representation Letter
BILLSALE.RTF	Bill of Sale for Assets of a Business
RECEIPTS.RTF	Receipt for Cash Payment
RECEIPTS.RTF	Form for Cancellation of Indebtedness
RECEIPTS.RTF	Bill of Sale for Items of Property
RECEIPTS.RTF	Receipt for Services Rendered

*IF YOU REFORMAT THE ARTICLES: If you reformat the ARTICLES.RTF file, make sure to leave a 3-inch-square space in the upper right-hand corner of the first page of this form for the California Secretary of State's file stamp. We have inserted hard carriage returns at the top of the first page of the articles in the CD-ROM form to leave space for this stamp.

The following files are in portable document format (PDF):

File Name	Document Title
NAAVINQUIRYFORM.PDF	Name Availability Inquiry Letter
NAAVRESERVFORM.PDF	Name Reservation Order Form
25102f.PDF**	Notice of Transaction Pursuant to Corporations Code Section 25102(f)

**USING THE STOCK NOTICE FORM: You must prepare and file this notice online unless you qualify for a hardship exemption. For more information, see Chapter 5, Step 7. If you qualify for the exemption and are filing a paper copy, we suggest you go to www.corp.ca.gov, to see if the version of this form included in this book is the latest. If not, use the form provided on the website.

Contact Information and Incorporation Forms

Incorporation Forms	Chapter/Step
Name Availability Inquiry Letter	5/1
Name Reservation-Order Form	5/1
Articles of Incorporation	5/2
Cover Letter for Filing Articles	5/2
Bylaws	5/4

Notice and Meeting Forms

Waiver of Notice and Consent to Holding of First Meeting of Board of Directors	5/5
Minutes of First Meeting of the Board of Directors	5/5
Shareholder Representation Letter	5/6
Notice of Transaction Pursuant to Corporations Code Section 25102(f)*	5/7
Bill of Sale for Assets of a Business	5/8
Receipt for Cash Payment	5/8
Form for Cancellation of Indebtedness	5/8
Bill of Sale for Items of Property	5/8
Receipt for Services Rendered	5/8
Share Register and Transfer Ledger (not on disk)	5/8
Stock Certificates (not on disk)	5/8

*USING THE STOCK NOTICE FORM: You must prepare and file this notice online unless you qualify for a hardship exemption. For more information, see Chapter 5, Step 7. If you qualify for the exemption and are filing a paper copy, we suggest you go to www.corp.ca.gov, to see if the version of this form included in this book is the latest. If not, use the form provided on the website.

CALIFORNIA SECRETARY OF STATE CONTACT INFORMATION

www.ss.ca.gov/business/corp/corporate.htm
Office hours for all locations are Monday through Friday
8:00 a.m. to 5:00 p.m.

Sacramento Office

1500 11th Street
Sacramento, CA 95814
(916) 657-5448*

- Name Availability Unit
  (*recorded information on how to obtain)

- Document Filing Support Unit

- Legal Review Unit

- Information Retrieval and Certification Unit

- Status
  (*recorded information on how to obtain)

- Statement of Information Unit
  (filings only)
  P.O. Box 944230
  Sacramento, CA 94244-2300

- Substituted Service of Process
  (must be hand delivered to the Sacramento office)

San Francisco Regional Office

455 Golden Gate Avenue, Suite 14500
San Francisco, CA 94102-7007
415-557-8000

Fresno Regional Office

1315 Van Ness Ave., Suite 203
Fresno, CA 93721-1729
559-445-6900

Los Angeles Regional Office

300 South Spring Street, Room 12513
Los Angeles, CA 90013-1233
213-897-3062

San Diego Regional Office

1350 Front Street, Suite 2060
San Diego, CA 92101-3609
619-525-4113

CALIFORNIA DEPARTMENT OF CORPORATIONS CONTACT INFORMATION

www.corp.ca.gov

Contact Information

The Department of Corporations, the office that receives your Notice of Stock Issuance, as explained in Chapter 5, Step 7, has four offices. The hours of operation are Monday through Friday, 8:00 a.m. to 5:00 p.m., excluding state holidays:

320 West 4th Street, Suite 750
Los Angeles, CA 90013-2344
213-576-7500

1515 K Street, Suite 200
Sacramento, CA 95814-4052
916-445-7205 or 866-275-2677 (886-ASK-CORP)

1350 Front Street, Room 2034
San Diego, CA 92101-3697
619-525-4233

71 Stevenson Street, Suite 2100
San Francisco, CA 94105-2980
415-972-8559

Name Availability Inquiry Letter
Corporations, Limited Partnerships, Limited Liability Companies

To inquire as to the availability of a corporation, limited partnership or limited liability company name, complete the order form below, listing up to three names to be checked. Submit your request by mail, along with a self-addressed envelope, to:

Secretary of State
Name Availability Unit
1500 11th Street, 3rd Floor
Sacramento, CA 95814

Email and/or online inquiries regarding name availability cannot be accepted at this time.

REQUESTOR'S INFORMATION	
YOUR NAME:	
FIRM NAME, IF ANY:	
ADDRESS:	
CITY/STATE/ZIP:	
TELEPHONE #:	FAX #:

SELECT ENTITY TYPE (choose only one)

☐ Corporation   ☐ Limited Partnership   ☐ Limited Liability Company

NAME(S) TO BE CHECKED

1st Choice	
FOR OFFICE USE ONLY	( ) is available. ( ) is not available. We have:
2nd Choice	
FOR OFFICE USE ONLY	( ) is available. ( ) is not available. We have:
3rd Choice	
FOR OFFICE USE ONLY	( ) is available. ( ) is not available. We have:

Note: Checking the availability of a corporation, limited partnership or limited liability company name does not reserve the name and has no binding effect on the Secretary of State, nor does it confer any rights to a name. A name reservation request can be made over-the-counter at any Secretary of State office location or can be addressed in writing to the Sacramento office. Fees and instructions for reserving a name are included on the Name Reservation Request Form.

THE SPACE BELOW IS RESERVED FOR OFFICE USE ONLY

Date:	I #	By:

Secretary of State
Business Programs Division

1500 11th Street, 3rd Floor
Sacramento, CA 95814

Business Entities
(916) 657-5448

Name Reservation Request
Corporations, Limited Partnerships, and Limited Liability Companies

To request the reservation of a corporation, limited partnership or limited liability company name, complete the Name Reservation Request Form on the following page and attach a check in the amount of $10.00 (made payable to the Secretary of State) and submit the request:

- **By mail**, along with a self-addressed envelope, to Secretary of State, Name Availability Unit, 1500 11th Street, 3rd Floor, Sacramento, CA 95814. Please refer to Business Entities Mail Processing Times for current mail processing times.

- **In person** (over-the-counter) at the Secretary of State's office in Sacramento. *Corporation* names can also be reserved, in person, at any of the Secretary of State's regional offices. Please refer to Contact Information for regional office locations and addresses. A special handling fee of $10.00 is applicable for each name reserved in person. The special handling fee must be remitted by separate check (made payable to the Secretary of State) as it will be retained whether the proposed name is accepted or denied for reservation. The special handling fee is not applicable to requests submitted by mail.

Only one reservation will be made per request form. You may list up to three names, in order of preference, and the first available name will be reserved for a period of 60 days. The remaining names will not be researched.

A name reservation is made for a period of 60 days, and can be renewed, but not for consecutive periods, to the same applicant or for the benefit of the same party.

Email and/or online requests for name reservations cannot be accepted at this time. Please complete the Name Reservation Request Form on the following page.

Name Reservation Request Form
Corporations, Limited Partnerships, and Limited Liability Companies

THE PROPOSED NAME IS TO BE RESERVED FOR USE BY:

YOUR NAME:	
FIRM NAME (IF ANY):	
ADDRESS:	
CITY/STATE/ZIP:	
TELEPHONE #:	FAX #:

TYPE OF ENTITY (choose only one)

☐ Corporation   ☐ Limited Partnership   ☐ Limited Liability Company

NAME TO BE RESERVED

Enter the name to be reserved. Only one reservation will be made per name reservation request form. You may list up to three names, in order of preference, and the first available name will be reserved for a period of 60 days. The remaining names will not be researched.

1st Choice:

FOR OFFICE USE ONLY: ( ) is available.   ( ) is available only with consent from * :   ( ) is not available. We have * :
*

2nd Choice:

FOR OFFICE USE ONLY: ( ) is available.   ( ) is available only with consent from ** :   ( ) is not available. We have ** :
**

3rd Choice:

FOR OFFICE USE ONLY: ( ) is available.   ( ) is available only with consent from *** :   ( ) is not available. We have *** :
***

SUSPENDED/FORFEITED CORPORATION

☐ If the proposed name is being reserved for the purpose of reviving a suspended/forfeited corporation, check the box and include the corporate number.   CORPORATION NUMBER

MAIL BACK RESPONSE

☐ If the name reservation request form is submitted in person and if you would like the reservation to be mailed back, check the box and include a self-addressed envelope.

FEES
Make check(s) payable to the Secretary of State.

Reservation Fee: The fee for reserving a corporation, limited partnership or limited liability company name is $10.00 (per reserved name).

Special Handling Fee: A $10.00 special handling fee is applicable for processing requests delivered in person to the Secretary of State's office. The $10.00 special handling fee must be remitted by separate check for each submittal and will be retained whether the proposed name is accepted or denied for reservation. The special handling fee does not apply to name reservation requests submitted by mail.

THE SPACE BELOW IS RESERVED FOR OFFICE USE ONLY

Date:	Amt Rec'd:	R #:	By:

NAME RESERVATION REQUEST FORM (REV 07/2005)

ARTICLES OF INCORPORATION

ONE: The name of this corporation is _____
_____ .

TWO: The purpose of the corporation is to engage in any lawful act or activity for which a corporation may be organized under the General Corporation Law of California other than the banking business, the trust company business or the practice of a profession permitted to be incorporated by the California Corporations Code.

THREE: The name and address in the State of California of this corporation's initial agent for service of process is _____
_____
_____ .

FOUR: This corporation is authorized to issue only one class of shares of stock, which shall be designated common stock. The total number of shares which this corporation is authorized to issue is _____
_____ shares.

FIVE: The names and addresses of the persons who are appointed to act as the initial directors of this corporation are:

Name   Address

_____   _____

_____   _____

_____   _____

_____   _____

_____   _____

SIX: The liability of the directors of the corporation for monetary damages shall be eliminated to the fullest extent permissible under California law.

SEVEN: The corporation is authorized to indemnify the directors and officers of the corporation to the fullest extent permissible under California law.

IN WITNESS WHEREOF, the undersigned, being all the persons named above as the initial directors, have executed these Articles of Incorporation.

Dated: _____   _____

                              _____

                              _____

                              _____

                              _____

The undersigned, being all the persons named above as the initial directors, declare that they are the persons who executed the foregoing Articles of Incorporation, which instrument is their act and deed.

Dated: _____   _____

                              _____

                              _____

                              _____

                              _____

COVER LETTER FOR FILING ARTICLES

_____

_____

_____

Secretary of State
Business Programs Division
1500 11th Street
Sacramento, CA 95814
Attention: Document Filing Support Unit

Re: _____

Dear Secretary of State:

    I enclose an original and two copies of the proposed Articles of Incorporation of _____ .

    Also enclosed is a check/money order in payment of the following fees:

        Filing Articles of Incorporation $ 100.00

    Please file the original Articles and return the certified copies to me at the above address.

Very truly yours,

_____

             , Incorporator

BYLAWS

of

_____

ARTICLE I
OFFICES

SECTION 1. PRINCIPAL EXECUTIVE OFFICE

The location of the principal executive office of the corporation shall be fixed by the board of directors. It may be located at any place within or outside the state of California. The secretary of this corporation shall keep the original or a copy of these bylaws, as amended to date, at the principal executive office of the corporation if this office is located in California. If this office is located outside California, the bylaws shall be kept at the principal business office of the corporation within California. The officers of this corporation shall cause the corporation to file an annual statement with the Secretary of State of California as required by Section 1502 of the California Corporations Code specifying the street address of the corporation's principal executive office.

SECTION 2. OTHER OFFICES

The corporation may also have offices at such other places as the board of directors may from time to time designate, or as the business of the corporation may require.

ARTICLE II
SHAREHOLDERS' MEETINGS

SECTION 1. PLACE OF MEETINGS

All meetings of the shareholders shall be held at the principal executive office of the corporation or at such other place as may be determined by the board of directors.

SECTION 2. ANNUAL MEETINGS

The annual meeting of the shareholders shall be held each year on

_____ ,

at which time the shareholders shall elect a board of directors and transact any other proper business. If this date falls on a legal holiday, then the meeting shall be held on the following business day at the same hour.

SECTION 3. SPECIAL MEETINGS

Special meetings of the shareholders may be called by the board of directors, the chairperson of the board of directors, the president, or by one or more shareholders holding at least 10 percent of the voting power of the corporation.

SECTION 4. NOTICES OF MEETINGS

Notices of meetings, annual or special, shall be given in writing to shareholders entitled to vote at the meeting by the secretary or an assistant secretary or, if there be no such officer, or in the case of his or her neglect or refusal, by any director or shareholder.

Such notices shall be given either personally or by first-class mail or other means of written communication, addressed to the shareholder at the address of such shareholder appearing on the stock transfer books of the corporation or given by the shareholder to the corporation for the purpose of notice. Notice shall be given not less than ten (10) nor more than sixty (60) days before the date of the meeting.

Such notice shall state the place, date, and hour of the meeting and (1) in the case of a special meeting, the general nature of the business to be transacted, and that no other business may be transacted, or (2) in the case of an annual meeting, those matters which the board at the time of the mailing of the notice, intends to present for action by the shareholders, but, subject to the provisions of Section 6 of this Article, any proper matter may be presented at the annual meeting for such action. The notice of any meeting at which directors are to be elected shall include the names of the nominees which, at the time of the notice, the board of directors intends to present for election. Notice of any adjourned meeting need not be given unless a meeting is adjourned for forty-five (45) days or more from the date set for the original meeting.

SECTION 5. WAIVER OF NOTICE

The transactions of any meeting of shareholders, however called and noticed, and wherever held, are as valid as though had at a meeting duly held after regular call and notice, if a quorum is present, whether in person or by proxy, and if, either before or after the meeting, each of the persons entitled to vote, not present in person or by proxy, signs a written waiver of notice or a consent to the holding of the meeting or an approval of the minutes thereof. All such waivers or consents shall be filed with the corporate records or made part of the minutes of the meeting. Neither the business to be transacted at the meeting, nor the purpose of any annual or special meeting of shareholders, need be specified in any written waiver of notice, except as provided in Section 6 of this Article.

SECTION 6. SPECIAL NOTICE AND WAIVER OF NOTICE REQUIREMENTS

Except as provided below, any shareholder approval at a meeting, with respect to the following proposals, shall be valid only if the general nature of the proposal so approved was stated in the notice of meeting, or in any written waiver of notice:

a. Approval of a contract or other transaction between the corporation and one or more of its directors or between the corporation and any corporation, firm, or association in which one or more of the directors has a material financial interest, pursuant to Section 310 of the California Corporations Code;

b. Amendment of the articles of incorporation after any shares have been issued pursuant to Section 902 of the California Corporations Code;

c. Approval of the principal terms of a reorganization pursuant to Section 1201 of the California Corporations Code;

d. Election to voluntarily wind up and dissolve the corporation pursuant to Section 1900 of the California Corporations Code;

e. Approval of a plan of distribution of shares as part of the winding up of the corporation pursuant to Section 2007 of the California Corporations Code.

Approval of the above proposals at a meeting shall be valid with or without such notice, if it is by the unanimous approval of those entitled to vote at the meeting.

SECTION 7. ACTION WITHOUT MEETING

Any action that may be taken at any annual or special meeting of shareholders may be taken without a meeting and without prior notice if a consent, in writing, setting forth the action so taken, shall be signed by the holders of outstanding shares having not less than the minimum number of votes that would be necessary to authorize or take such action at a meeting at which all shares entitled to vote thereon were present and voted.

Unless the consents of all shareholders entitled to vote have been solicited in writing, notice of any shareholders' approval, with respect to any one of the following proposals, without a meeting, by less than unanimous written consent shall be given at least ten (10) days before the consummation of the action authorized by such approval:

a. Approval of a contract or other transaction between the corporation and one or more of its directors or another corporation, firm, or association in which one or more of its directors has a material financial interest, pursuant to Section 310 of the California Corporations Code;

b. To indemnify an agent of the corporation pursuant to Section 317 of the California Corporations Code;

c. To approve the principal terms of a reorganization, pursuant to Section 1201 of the California Corporations Code; or

d. Approval of a plan of distribution as part of the winding up of the corporation pursuant to Section 2007 of the California Corporations Code.

Prompt notice shall be given of the taking of any other corporate action approved by shareholders without a meeting by less than a unanimous written consent to those shareholders entitled to vote who have not consented in writing.

Notwithstanding any of the foregoing provisions of this section, and except as provided in Article III, Section 4, of these bylaws, directors may not be elected by written consent except by the unanimous written consent of all shares entitled to vote for the election of directors.

A written consent may be revoked by a writing received by the corporation prior to the time that written consents of the number of shares required to authorize the proposed action have been filed with the secretary of the corporation, but may not be revoked thereafter. Such revocation is effective upon its receipt by the Secretary of the corporation.

SECTION 8. QUORUM AND SHAREHOLDER ACTION

A majority of the shares entitled to vote, represented in person or by proxy, shall constitute a quorum at a meeting of shareholders. If a quorum is present, the affirmative vote of the majority of shareholders represented at the meeting and entitled to vote on any matter shall be the act of the shareholders, unless the vote of a greater number is required by law and except as provided in the following paragraphs of this section.

The shareholders present at a duly called or held meeting at which a quorum is present may continue to transact business until adjournment notwithstanding the withdrawal of enough shareholders to leave less than a quorum, if any action is approved by at least a majority of the shares required to constitute a quorum.

In the absence of a quorum, any meeting of shareholders may be adjourned from time to time by the vote of a majority of the shares represented either in person or by proxy, but no other business may be transacted except as provided in the foregoing provisions of this section.

SECTION 9. VOTING

Only shareholders of record on the record date fixed for voting purposes by the board of directors pursuant to Article VIII, Section 3, of these bylaws or, if there be no such date fixed, on the record dates given below, shall be entitled to vote at a meeting.

If no record date is fixed:

a. The record date for determining shareholders entitled to notice of, or to vote, at a meeting of shareholders, shall be at the close of business on the business day next preceding the day on which notice is given or, if notice is waived, at the close of business on the business day next preceding the day on which the meeting is held.

b. The record date for determining the shareholders entitled to give consent to corporate actions in writing without a meeting, when no prior action by the board is necessary, shall be the day on which the first written consent is given.

c. The record date for determining shareholders for any other purpose shall be at the close of business on the day on which the board adopts the resolution relating thereto, or the 60th day prior to the date of such other action, whichever is later.

Every shareholder entitled to vote shall be entitled to one vote for each share held, except as otherwise provided by law, by the articles of incorporation or by other provisions of these bylaws. Except with respect to elections of directors, any shareholder entitled to vote may vote part of his or her shares in favor of a proposal and refrain from voting the remaining shares or vote them against the proposal. If a shareholder fails to specify the number of shares he or she is affirmatively voting, it will be conclusively presumed that the shareholder's approving vote is with respect to all shares the shareholder is entitled to vote.

At each election of directors, shareholders shall not be entitled to cumulate votes unless the candidates' names have been placed in nomination before the commencement of the voting and a shareholder has given notice at the meeting, and before the voting has begun, of his or her intention to cumulate votes. If any shareholder has given such notice, then all shareholders entitled to vote may cumulate their votes by giving one candidate a number of votes equal to the number of directors to be elected multiplied by the number of his or her shares or by distributing such votes on the same principle among any number of candidates as he or she thinks fit. The candidates receiving the highest number of votes, up to the number of directors to be elected, shall be elected. Votes cast against a candidate or which are withheld shall have no effect. Upon the demand of any shareholder made before the voting begins, the election of directors shall be by ballot rather than by voice vote.

SECTION 10. PROXIES

Every person entitled to vote shares may authorize another person or persons to act by proxy with respect to such shares by filing a proxy with the secretary of the corporation. For purposes of these bylaws, a "proxy" means a written authorization signed or an electronic transmission authorized by a shareholder or the shareholder's attorney in fact giving another person or persons power to vote with respect to the shares of the shareholder. "Signed" for the purpose of these bylaws means the placing of the shareholder's name or other authorization on the proxy (whether by manual signature, typewriting, telegraphic or electronic transmission, or otherwise) by the shareholder or the shareholder's attorney in fact. A proxy may be transmitted by an oral telephonic transmission if it is submitted with information from which it may be determined that the proxy was authorized by the shareholder, or his or her attorney in fact.

A proxy shall not be valid after the expiration of eleven (11) months from the date thereof unless otherwise provided in the proxy. Every proxy shall continue in full force and effect until revoked by the person executing it prior to the vote pursuant thereto, except as otherwise provided in Section 705 of the California Corporations Code.

ARTICLE III
DIRECTORS

SECTION 1. POWER

Subject to any limitations in the articles of incorporation and to the provisions of the California Corporations Code, the business and affairs of the corporation shall be managed and all corporate powers shall be exercised by, or under the direction of, the board of directors.

SECTION 2. NUMBER

The authorized number of directors shall be _____ .

After issuance of shares, this bylaw may only be amended by approval of a majority of the outstanding shares entitled to vote; provided, moreover, that a bylaw reducing the fixed number of directors to a number less than five (5) cannot be adopted unless in accordance with the additional requirements of Article IX of these bylaws.

SECTION 3. ELECTION AND TENURE OF OFFICE

The directors shall be elected at the annual meeting of the shareholders and hold office until the next annual meeting and until their successors have been elected and qualified.

SECTION 4. VACANCIES

A vacancy on the board of directors shall exist in the case of death, resignation, or removal of any director or in case the authorized number of directors is increased, or in case the shareholders fail to elect the full authorized number of directors at any annual or special meeting of the shareholders at which any director is elected. The board of directors may declare vacant the office of a director who has been declared of unsound mind by an order of court or who has been convicted of a felony.

Except for a vacancy created by the removal of a director, vacancies on the board of directors may be filled by approval of the board or, if the number of directors then in office is less than a quorum, by (1) the unanimous written consent of the directors then in office, (2) the affirmative vote of a majority of the directors then in office at a meeting held pursuant to notice or waivers of notice complying with this article of these bylaws, or (3) a sole remaining director. Vacancies occurring on the board by reason of the removal of directors may be filled only by approval of the shareholders. Each director so elected shall hold office until the next annual meeting of the shareholders and until his or her successor has been elected and qualified.

The shareholders may elect a director at any time to fill a vacancy not filled by the directors. Any such election by written consent other than to fill a vacancy created by the removal of a director requires the consent of a majority of the outstanding shares entitled to vote.

Any director may resign effective upon giving written notice to the chairperson of the board of directors, the president, the secretary, or the board of directors, unless the notice specifies a later time for the effectiveness of the resignation. If the resignation is effective at a later time, a successor may be elected to take office when the resignation becomes effective. Any reduction of the authorized number of directors does not remove any director prior to the expiration of such director's term in office.

SECTION 5. REMOVAL

Any or all of the directors may be removed without cause if the removal is approved by a majority of the outstanding shares entitled to vote, subject to the provisions of Section 303 of the California Corporations Code. Except as provided in Sections 302, 303, and 304 of the California Corporations Code, a director may not be removed prior to the expiration of the director's term of office.

The superior court of the proper county may, on the suit of shareholders holding at least 10 percent of the number of outstanding shares of any class, remove from office any director in case of fraudulent or dishonest acts or gross abuse of authority or discretion with reference to the corporation and may bar from re-election any director so removed for a period prescribed by the court. The corporation shall be made a party to such action.

SECTION 6. PLACE OF MEETINGS

Meetings of the board of directors shall be held at any place, within or without the state of California, which has been designated in the notice of the meeting or, if not stated in the notice or if there is no notice, at the principal executive office of the corporation or as may be designated from time to time by resolution of the board of directors. Meetings of the board may be held through use of conference telephone, electronic video screen communication, or other communications equipment, as long as all of the following apply:

(a) Each member participating in the meeting can communicate with all members concurrently.

(b) Each member is provided the means of participating in all matters before the board, including the capacity to propose, or to interpose, an objection to a specific action to be taken by the corporation.

(c) The corporation adopts and implements some means of verifying both of the following:

(1) A person communicating by telephone, electronic video screen, or other communications equipment is a director entitled to participate in the board meeting.

(2) All actions of, or votes by, the board are taken or cast only by the directors and not by persons who are not directors.

SECTION 7. ANNUAL, REGULAR, AND SPECIAL DIRECTORS' MEETINGS

An annual meeting of the board of directors shall be held without notice immediately after and at the same place as the annual meeting of the shareholders.

Other regular meetings of the board of directors shall be held at such times and places as may be fixed from time to time by the board of directors. Call and notice of these regular meetings shall not be required.

Special meetings of the board of directors may be called by the chairperson of the board, president, vice president, secretary, or any two directors. Special meetings of the board of directors shall be held upon four (4) days' notice by mail, or forty-eight (48) hours' notice delivered personally or by telephone or telegraph or by other electronic means including facsimile or electronic mail message. Mailed notice shall be sent by first-class mail to the director's address that appears on the records of the corporation, or the address given by the director for the purpose of mailing such notice. Notice by voice or facsimile telephone shall be to the telephone number given by a director for such notice. Notice to an electronic mail message system shall be sent to the electronic mail address designated by the director for such mail. A notice or waiver of notice need not specify the purpose of any special meeting of the board of directors.

If any meeting is adjourned for more than 24 hours, notice of the adjournment to another time or place shall be given before the time of the resumed meeting to all directors who were not present at the time of adjournment of the original meeting.

SECTION 8. QUORUM AND BOARD ACTION

A quorum for all meetings of the board of directors shall consist of _____ of the authorized number of directors until changed by amendment to this article of these bylaws.

Every act or decision done or made by a majority of the directors present at a meeting duly held at which a quorum is present is the act of the board, subject to the provisions of Section 310 (relating to the approval of contracts and transactions in which a director has a material financial interest); the provisions of Section 311 (designation of committees); and Section 317(e) (indemnification of directors) of the California Corporations Code. A meeting at which a quorum is initially present may continue to transact business notwithstanding the withdrawal of directors, if any action taken is approved by at least a majority of the required quorum for such meeting.

A majority of the directors present at a meeting may adjourn any meeting to another time and place, whether or not a quorum is present at the meeting.

SECTION 9. WAIVER OF NOTICE

The transactions of any meeting of the board, however called and noticed or wherever held, are as valid as though undertaken at a meeting duly held after regular call and notice if a quorum is present and if, either before or after the meeting, each of the directors not present signs a written waiver of notice, a consent to holding the meeting, or an approval of the minutes thereof. All such waivers, consents, and approvals shall be filed with the corporate records or made a part of the minutes of the meeting. Waivers of notice or consents need not specify the purpose of the meeting.

SECTION 10. ACTION WITHOUT MEETING

Any action required or permitted to be taken by the board may be taken without a meeting, if all members of the board shall individually or collectively consent in writing to such action. Such written consent or consents shall be filed with the minutes of the proceedings of the board. Such action by written consent shall have the same force and effect as a unanimous vote of the directors.

For purposes of this section of the bylaws only, "all members of the board" shall include an "interested director" as described in Subdivision (a) of Section 310 of the California Corporations Code or a "common director" as described in Subdivision (b) of said Section 310 who abstains in writing from providing consent, where 1) the disclosures required by said Section 310 have been made to the noninterested or noncommon directors, as applicable, prior to their execution of the written consent or consents, 2) the specified disclosures are conspicuously included in the written consent or consents executed by the noninterested or noncommon directors, and 3) the noninterested or noncommon directors, as applicable, approve the action by a vote that is sufficient without counting the votes of the interested or common directors. If written consent is provided by the directors in accordance with the immediately preceding sentence and the disclosures made regarding the action that is the subject of the consent do not comply with the requirements of said Section 310, the action that is the subject of the consent shall be deemed approved, but in any suit brought to challenge the action, the party asserting the validity of the action shall have the burden of proof in establishing that the action was just and reasonable to the corporation at the time it was approved.

SECTION 11. COMPENSATION

No salary shall be paid directors, as such, for their services but, by resolution, the board of directors may allow a reasonable fixed sum and expenses to be paid for attendance at regular or special meetings. Nothing contained herein shall prevent a director from serving the corporation in any other capacity and receiving compensation therefor. Members of special or standing committees may be allowed like compensation for attendance at meetings.

ARTICLE IV

OFFICERS

SECTION 1. OFFICERS

The officers of the corporation shall be a president, a vice president, a secretary, and a treasurer who shall be the chief financial officer of the corporation. The corporation also may have such other officers with such titles and duties as shall be determined by the board of directors. Any number of offices may be held by the same person.

SECTION 2. ELECTION

All officers of the corporation shall be chosen by, and serve at the pleasure of, the board of directors.

SECTION 3. REMOVAL AND RESIGNATION

An officer may be removed at any time, either with or without cause, by the board. An officer may resign at any time upon written notice to the corporation given to the board, the president, or the secretary of the corporation. Any such resignation shall take effect at the date of receipt of such notice or at any other time specified therein. The removal or resignation of an officer shall be without prejudice to the rights, if any, of the officer or the corporation under any contract of employment to which the officer is a party.

SECTION 4. PRESIDENT

The president shall be the chief executive officer and general manager of the corporation and shall, subject to the direction and control of the board of directors, have general supervision, direction, and control of the business and affairs of the corporation. He or she shall preside at all meetings of the shareholders and directors and be an ex-officio member of all the standing committees, including the executive committee, if any, and shall have the general powers and duties of management usually vested in the office of president of a corporation and shall have such other powers and duties as may from time to time be prescribed by the board of directors or these bylaws.

SECTION 5. VICE PRESIDENT

In the absence or disability of the president, the vice presidents, in order of their rank as fixed by the board of directors (or if not ranked, the vice president designated by the board) shall perform all the duties of the president and, when so acting, shall have all the powers of, and be subject to all the restrictions upon, the president. Each vice president shall have such other powers and perform such other duties as may from time to time be prescribed by the board of directors or these bylaws.

SECTION 6. SECRETARY

The secretary shall keep, or cause to be kept, at the principal executive office of the corporation, a book of minutes of all meetings of directors and shareholders. The minutes shall state the time and place of holding of all meetings; whether regular or special, and if special, how called or authorized; the notice thereof given or the waivers of notice received; the names of those present at directors' meetings; the number of shares present or represented at shareholders' meetings; and an account of the proceedings thereof.

The secretary shall keep, or cause to be kept, at the principal executive office of the corporation, or at the office of the corporation's transfer agent, a share register, showing the names of the shareholders and their addresses, the number and classes of shares held by each, the number and date of certificates issued for shares, and the number and date of cancellation of every certificate surrendered for cancellation.

The secretary shall keep, or cause to be kept, at the principal executive office of the corporation, the original or a copy of the bylaws of the corporation, as amended or otherwise altered to date, certified by him or her.

The secretary shall give, or cause to be given, notice of all meetings of shareholders and directors required to be given by law or by the provisions of these bylaws.

The secretary shall have charge of the seal of the corporation and have such other powers and perform such other duties as may from time to time be prescribed by the board or these bylaws.

In the absence or disability of the secretary, the assistant secretaries if any, in order of their rank as fixed by the board of directors (or if not ranked, the assistant secretary designated by the board of directors), shall have all the powers of, and be subject to all the restrictions upon, the secretary. The assistant secretaries, if any, shall have such other powers and perform such other duties as may from time to time be prescribed by the board of directors or these bylaws.

SECTION 7. TREASURER

The treasurer shall be the chief financial officer of the corporation and shall keep and maintain, or cause to be kept and maintained, adequate and correct books and records of accounts of the properties and business transactions of the corporation.

The treasurer shall deposit monies and other valuables in the name and to the credit of the corporation with such depositories as may be designated by the board of directors. He or she shall disburse the funds of the corporation in payment of the just demands against the corporation as authorized by the board of directors; shall render to the president and directors, whenever they request it, an account of all his or her transactions as treasurer and of the financial condition of the corporation; and shall have such other powers and perform such other duties as may from time to time be prescribed by the board of directors or the bylaws.

In the absence or disability of the treasurer, the assistant treasurers, if any, in order of their rank as fixed by the board of directors (or if not ranked, the assistant treasurer designated by the board of directors), shall perform all the duties of the treasurer and, when so acting, shall have all the powers of and be subject to all the

WAIVER OF NOTICE AND CONSENT TO HOLDING OF
FIRST MEETING OF BOARD OF DIRECTORS

of

_____

We, the undersigned, being all the directors of
_____ ,
a California corporation, hereby waive notice of the first meeting of the
board of directors of the corporation and consent to the holding of said
meeting at _____

_____ ,
on _____ , at _____ ,
and consent to the transaction of any and all business by the directors
at the meeting including, without limitation, the adoption of bylaws, the
election of officers, the selection of the corporation's accounting period,
the designation of the principal executive office of the corporation,
the selection of the place where the corporation's bank account will be
maintained, and the authorization of the sale and issuance of the initial
shares of stock of the corporation.

Dated: _____ , Director

_____ , Director

_____ , Director

PAYMENT, DEDUCTION, AND AMORTIZATION OF ORGANIZATIONAL EXPENSES

The board next considered the question of paying the expenses incurred in the formation of this corporation. A motion was made, seconded, and unanimously approved, and it was

RESOLVED, that the president and the treasurer of this corporation are authorized and empowered to pay all reasonable and proper expenses incurred in connection with the organization of the corporation, including, among others, filing, licensing, and attorney's and accountant's fees, and to reimburse any persons making any such disbursements for the corporation, and it was

FURTHER RESOLVED, that the treasurer is authorized to elect to deduct and amortize the foregoing expenditures, pursuant to, and as permitted by, Section 248 of the Internal Revenue Code of 1986, as amended.

The board of directors next considered the advantages of electing to be taxed under the provisions of Subchapter S of the Internal Revenue Code of 1986, as amended. After discussion, upon motion duly made and seconded, it was unanimously

RESOLVED, that this corporation hereby elects to be treated as a small business corporation for federal income tax purposes under Subchapter S of the Internal Revenue Code of 1986, as amended.

RESOLVED FURTHER, that the officers of this corporation take all actions necessary and proper to effectuate the foregoing resolution, including, among other things, obtaining the requisite consents from the shareholders of this corporation and executing and filing the appropriate forms with the Internal Revenue Service within the time limits specified by law.

QUALIFICATION OF STOCK AS SECTION 1244 STOCK

The board next considered the advisability of qualifying the stock of this corporation as Section 1244 Stock as defined in Section 1244 of the Internal Revenue Code of 1986, as amended, and of organizing and managing the corporation so that it is a small business corporation as defined in that section. Upon motion duly made and seconded, it was unanimously

RESOLVED, that the proper officers of the corporation are, subject to the requirements and restrictions of federal, California, and any other applicable securities laws, authorized to sell and issue shares of stock in return for the receipt of an aggregate amount of money and other property, as a contribution to capital and as paid-in surplus, which does not exceed $1,000,000.

RESOLVED FURTHER, that the sale and issuance of shares shall be conducted in compliance with Section 1244 so that the corporation and its shareholders may obtain the benefits of that section.

RESOLVED FURTHER, that the proper officers of the corporation are directed to maintain such records as are necessary pursuant to Section 1244 so that any shareholder who experiences a loss on the transfer of shares of stock of the corporation may determine whether he or she qualifies for ordinary loss deduction treatment on his or her individual income tax return.

AUTHORIZATION OF ISSUANCE OF SHARES

The board of directors next took up the matter of the sale and issuance of stock to provide capital for the corporation. Upon motion duly made and seconded, it was unanimously

RESOLVED, that the corporation sell and issue the following number of its authorized common shares to the following persons, in the amounts and for the consideration set forth under their names below. The board also hereby determines that the fair value to the corporation of any consideration for such shares issued other than for money is as set forth below:

Name	Number of Shares	Consideration	Fair Value
_____	_____	_____	$_____
_____	_____	_____	$_____
_____	_____	_____	$_____
_____	_____	_____	$_____
_____	_____	_____	$_____
_____	_____	_____	$_____
_____	_____	_____	$_____
_____	_____	_____	$_____
_____	_____	_____	$_____
_____	_____	_____	$_____

RESOLVED FURTHER, that these shares shall be sold and issued by this corporation strictly in accordance with the terms of the exemption from qualification of these shares as provided for in Section 25102(f) of the California Corporations Code.

RESOLVED FURTHER, that the appropriate officers of this corporation are hereby authorized and directed to take such actions and execute such documents as they may deem necessary or appropriate to effectuate the sale and issuance of such shares for such consideration.

Since there was no further business to come before the meeting, upon motion duly made and seconded, the meeting was adjourned.

_____
, Secretary

SHAREHOLDER REPRESENTATION LETTER

To: _____

_____

_____

I, _____ , in connection with my purchase of a/an _____ interest in _____ common shares of the corporation named above, hereby make the following representations:

A. I am a suitable purchaser of these shares under the California limited offering exemption because:

1. [ ] I am a director, officer, or promoter of the corporation, or because I occupy a position with the corporation with duties and authority substantially similar to those of an executive officer of the corporation.

2. [ ] I have a preexisting personal and/or business relationship with the corporation, or one or more of its directors, officers, or controlling persons, consisting of personal or business contacts of a nature and duration which enables me to be aware of the character, business acumen, and general business and financial circumstances of the person (including the corporation) with whom such relationship exists.

3. [ ] I have the capacity to protect my own interests in connection with my purchase of the above shares by reason of my own business and/or financial experience.

4(a). [ ] Pursuant to Section 260.102.13(e) of Title 10 of the California Code of Regulations, I am purchasing $150,000 or more of the corporation's shares, and either 1) my investment (including mandatory assessments) does not exceed 10% of my net worth or joint net worth with my spouse, or 2) by reason of my own business and/or financial experience, or the business and/or financial experience of my professional advisor (who is unaffiliated with and not compensated by the corporation or any of its affiliates or selling agents), I have, or my professional advisor has, the capacity to protect my own interests in connection with the purchase of these shares

4(b). [ ] Pursuant to Section 260.102.13(g) of Title 10 of the California Code of Regulations, I am an "accredited investor" under Rule 501(a) of Regulation D adopted by the Securities and Exchange Commission under the Securities Act of 1933. This means either 1) my individual net worth, or joint net worth with my spouse, at the time of the purchase of these shares, exceeds $ 1,000,000; 2) my individual income is in excess of $200,000 in each of the two most recent years or my joint income with my spouse is in excess of $300,000 in each of those years, and I have a reasonable expectation of reaching the same income level in the current year; or 3) I qualify under one of the other accredited investor categories of Rule 501(a) of SEC Regulation D.

5(a). [ ]   I have the capacity to protect my own interests in connection with my purchase of the above shares by reason of the business and/or financial experience of _____ , whom I have engaged and hereby designate as my professional advisor in connection with my purchase of the above shares.

5(b).   REPRESENTATION OF PROFESSIONAL ADVISOR

_____ hereby represents:

(1) I have been engaged as the professional advisor of _____ and have provided him or her with investment advice in connection with the purchase of _____ common shares in _____ .

(2) As a regular part of my business as a/an _____ _____ I am customarily relied upon by others for investment recommendations or decisions and I am customarily compensated for such services, either specifically or by way of compensation for related professional services.

(3) I am unaffiliated with and am not compensated by the corporation or any affiliate or selling agent of the corporation, directly or indirectly. I do not have, nor will I have (a) a relationship of employment with the corporation, either as an employee, employer, independent contractor, or principal; (b) the beneficial ownership of securities of the corporation, its affiliates, or selling agents, in excess of 1% of its securities; or (c) a relationship with the corporation such that I control, am controlled by, or am under common control with the corporation, and, more specifically, a relationship by which I possess, directly or indirectly, the power to direct, or cause the direction, of the management, policies, or actions of the corporation.

Dated: _____   _____

                                          , Professional Advisor

6. [ ] I am the spouse, relative, or relative of the spouse of another purchaser of shares and I have the same principal residence as this purchaser.

B. I represent that I am purchasing these shares for investment for my own account and not with a view to, or for, sale in connection with any distribution of the shares. I understand that these shares have not been qualified or registered under any state or federal securities law and that they may not be transferred or otherwise disposed of without such qualification or registration pursuant to such laws or an opinion of legal counsel satisfactory to the corporation that such qualification or registration is not required.

C. I have not received any advertisement or general solicitation with respect to the sale of the shares of the above-named corporation.

D. I represent that, before signing this document, I have been provided access to, or been given, all material facts relevant to the purchase of my shares, including all financial and written information about the corporation and the terms and conditions of the stock offering and that I have been given the opportunity to ask questions and receive answers concerning any additional terms and conditions of the stock offering or other information which I, or my professional advisor if I have designated one, felt necessary to protect my interests in connection with the stock purchase transaction.

Dated: _____   _____

Fee paid $_____

_____
Receipt No. _____

DEPARTMENT OF CORPORATIONS FILE NO., if any:

_____

_____
Insert File number(s) of Previous Filings Before the
Department, if any.

Fee: $25.00 $35.00 $50.00 $150.00 $300.00
(Circle the appropriate amount of fee. See Corporations Code Section 25608(c))

COMMISSIONER OF CORPORATIONS
STATE OF CALIFORNIA

NOTICE OF TRANSACTION PURSUANT TO CORPORATIONS CODE SECTION 25102(f)
A. Check one: Transaction under (   ) Section 25102(f) (   ) Rule 260.103.

ELECTRONIC FILING REQUIREMENT AND HARDSHIP EXCEPTION:
**This notice must be filed electronically through the Internet process made available by the
Department of Corporations on www.corp.ca.gov, unless the issuer claims the hardship exception as
described in Number 8 below.**

1. Name of Issuer:

_____

2. Address of Issuer:

	Street	City	State	Zip
Mailing Address:

	Street	City	State	Zip

3. Area Code and Telephone Number: _____

4. Issuer's state (or other jurisdiction) of incorporation or organization:

_____

5. Title of class or classes of securities sold in transaction:

_____

_____

6. The value of the securities sold or proposed to be sold in the transaction, determined in accordance with
Corporations Code Sec. 25608(g) in connection with the fee required upon filing this notice, is (fee based on
amount shown in line (iii) under "Total Offering"):

	California	*Total Offering*
(a)(i) in money	$_____	$_____
(ii) in consideration other than money	$_____	$_____
(iii) total of (i) and (ii)	$_____	$_____

(b) (   ) Change in rights, preferences, privileges or restrictions of or on outstanding securities
($25.00 fee.) (See Rule 260.103.)

260.102.14(c) (8-05)

7. Type of filing under Securities Act of 1933, if applicable: _____

_____

8. **Hardship Exception for electronic filing.** An issuer may file this paper notice in person or by mail only if either of the following exceptions apply. The issuer shall check applicable box and include the reason(s) and description(s) for the hardship exception in the space provided.

☐ Computer equipment including hardware and software is unavailable to the issuer without unreasonable burden or expense. If this is the case, describe below both of the following; the reason(s) that the computer equipment including hardware and software is unavailable without unreasonable burden or expense, and the description(s) of the unreasonable burden or expense.

☐ The issuer cannot obtain and provide information (including credit card or other identifying information) requested on the Department's electronic notice or through the Internet filing process. If this is the case, describe below both of the following: the reason(s) that the issuer cannot obtain and provide the requested information on the electronic notice or through the Internet filing process without unreasonable burden or expense, and the description(s) of the unreasonable burden or expense to the issuer to make the electronic filing.

After checking the applicable hardship exception above, the issuer shall describe below the reason(s) and description(s) for that hardship exception. (If additional space is needed, attach a separate sheet to this notice.)

_____
_____
_____
_____
_____
_____
_____

9. ( ) Check if issuer already has a consent to service of process on file with the Commissioner. (Instruction: Each issuer (other than a California Corporation) filing a notice under Section 25102(f) must file a consent to service of process (Form 260.265), unless it already has a consent to service on file with the Commissioner. If no consent to service of process is on file with the Commissioner, attach the consent to this notice.)

10. _____
      Authorized Signature on behalf of issuer

_____
      Print name and title of signatory

_____
      Date

Name, Address and Phone number of contact person:

_____
_____
_____

BILL OF SALE FOR ASSETS OF A BUSINESS

This is an agreement between:

_____

_____

_____ ,

herein called "transferor(s)," and _____

_____ ,

a California corporation, herein called "the corporation."

In return for the issuance of _____
shares of stock of the corporation, transferor(s) hereby sell(s),
assign(s), and transfer(s) to the corporation all right, title, and
interest in the following property:

All the tangible assets listed on the inventory attached to this
Bill of Sale and all stock in trade, goodwill, leasehold interests, trade
names, and other intangible assets except _____

_____

_____

_____

_____

of _____ , located at

_____ .

In return for the transfer of the above property to it, the
corporation hereby agrees to assume, pay, and discharge all debts, duties,
and obligations that appear on the date of this agreement on
the books and owed on account of said business except _____

_____

_____

_____

_____

_____ .

The corporation agrees to indemnify and hold the transferor(s) of said
business and their property free from any liability for any such debt,
duty, or obligation and from any suits, actions, or legal proceedings
brought to enforce or collect any such debt, duty, or obligation.

The transferor(s) hereby appoint(s) the corporation as
representative to demand, receive, and collect for itself any and all
debts and obligations now owing to said business. The transferor(s)
further authorize(s) the corporation to do all things allowed by law

to recover and collect any such debts and obligations and to use the transferor's(s') name(s) in such manner as it considers necessary for the collection and recovery of such debts and obligations, provided, however, without cost, expense, or damage to the transferor(s).

Dated: _____   _____
                                                      , Transferor

                          _____
                                                      , Transferor

                          _____
                                                      , Transferor

Dated: _____   _____
                          (name of corporation)

                   By: _____
                                                      , President

                          _____
                                                      , Treasurer

FORM FOR CANCELLATION OF INDEBTEDNESS

The receipt of _____ shares of this corporation to

_____

for the cancellation by _____

of a current loan outstanding to this corporation, dated _____ ,

with a remaining unpaid principal amount and unpaid accrued interest, if

any, totalling $ _____ , is hereby acknowledged.

Dated: _____   _____
                                    Signature

BILL OF SALE FOR ITEMS OF PROPERTY

In consideration of the issuance of _____

shares of stock in and by _____ ,

_____

hereby sells, assigns, conveys, transfers, and delivers to the corporation
all right, title, and interest in and to the following property:

Dated: _____   _____

                                                              , Transferor

RECEIPT FOR SERVICES RENDERED

In consideration of the performance of the following services actually rendered to, or labor done for _____ ,

_____ ,

the provider of such services or labor done, hereby acknowledges the

receipt of _____

shares of stock in _____

as payment in full for these services:

Dated: _____   _____

                           Signature

INCORPORATED UNDER THE LAWS OF CALIFORNIA

Common Shares

NUMBER _____

SHARES _____

THE SHARES REPRESENTED BY THIS CERTIFICATE HAVE NOT BEEN REGISTERED OR QUALIFIED UNDER ANY FEDERAL OR STATE SECURITIES LAW. THEY HAVE BEEN ACQUIRED FOR INVESTMENT PURPOSES AND NOT WITH A VIEW TOWARD RESALE AND MAY NOT BE OFFERED FOR SALE, SOLD, TRANSFERRED, OR PLEDGED WITHOUT REGISTRATION AND QUALIFICATION PURSUANT TO SUCH LAWS OR AN OPINION OF LEGAL COUNSEL SATISFACTORY TO THE CORPORATION THAT SUCH REGISTRATION AND QUALIFICATION IS NOT REQUIRED.

This Certifies that _____ *is the owner of* _____ *fully paid and non-assessable Shares of the above Corporation transferable only on the books of the Corporation by the holder hereof in person or by duly authorized Attorney upon surrender of this Certificate properly endorsed.*

In Witness Whereof, the Corporation has caused this Certificate to be signed by its duly authorized officers and to be sealed with the Seal of the Corporation.

Dated _____

_____ *, President*

_____ *, Secretary*

Certificate Number _____

For _____ Shares

Issued To: _____

Dated _____

From Whom Transferred _____

Dated _____

No. Original Shares	No. Original Certificate	No. of Shares Transferred

Received Certificate Number _____

For _____

This _____ day of _____

_____ SIGNATURE

For value received, the undersigned hereby sells, assigns and transfers to _____

_____

_____ *Shares*

represented by the within Certificate, and does hereby irrevocably constitute and appoint _____

Attorney to transfer the said shares on the books of the within-named Corporation with full power of substitution in the premises.

Dated: _____

In presence of _____

_____

NOTICE: The signature to this assignment must correspond with the name as written upon the face of this certificate in every particular without alteration or enlargement, or any change whatever.

NUMBER _____

SHARES _____

INCORPORATED UNDER THE LAWS OF CALIFORNIA

Common Shares

THE SHARES REPRESENTED BY THIS CERTIFICATE HAVE NOT BEEN REGISTERED OR QUALIFIED UNDER ANY FEDERAL OR STATE SECURITIES LAW. THEY HAVE BEEN ACQUIRED FOR INVESTMENT PURPOSES AND NOT WITH A VIEW TOWARD RESALE AND MAY NOT BE OFFERED FOR SALE, SOLD, TRANSFERRED, OR PLEDGED WITHOUT REGISTRATION AND QUALIFICATION PURSUANT TO SUCH LAWS OR AN OPINION OF LEGAL COUNSEL SATISFACTORY TO THE CORPORATION THAT SUCH REGISTRATION AND QUALIFICATION IS NOT REQUIRED.

This Certifies that _____ *is the owner of* _____ *fully paid and non-assessable Shares of the above Corporation transferable only on the books of the Corporation by the holder hereof in person or by duly authorized Attorney upon surrender of this Certificate properly endorsed.*

In Witness Whereof, the Corporation has caused this Certificate to be signed by its duly authorized officers and to be sealed with the Seal of the Corporation.

Dated _____

_____ *, President*

_____ *, Secretary*

For value received, the undersigned hereby sells, assigns and transfers to _____

PRINT OR TYPE NAME AND ADDRESS OF ASSIGNEE

_____

_____ *Shares*

represented by the within Certificate, and does hereby irrevocably constitute and appoint _____

Attorney to transfer the said shares on the books of the within-named Corporation with full power of substitution in the premises.

Dated: _____

In presence of _____

_____

NOTICE: The signature to this assignment must correspond with the name as written upon the face of this certificate in every particular without alteration or enlargement, or any change whatever.

Certificate Number _____

For _____ Shares

Issued To: _____

Dated _____

From Whom Transferred

Dated _____

No. Original Shares	No. Original Certificate	No. of Shares Transferred

---

Received Certificate Number _____

For _____

This _____ day of _____

_____
SIGNATURE

_____ Shares

NUMBER _____

SHARES _____

INCORPORATED UNDER THE LAWS OF CALIFORNIA

Common Shares

THE SHARES REPRESENTED BY THIS CERTIFICATE HAVE NOT BEEN REGISTERED OR QUALIFIED UNDER ANY FEDERAL OR STATE SECURITIES LAW. THEY HAVE BEEN ACQUIRED FOR INVESTMENT PURPOSES AND NOT WITH A VIEW TOWARD RESALE AND MAY NOT BE OFFERED FOR SALE, SOLD, TRANSFERRED, OR PLEDGED WITHOUT REGISTRATION AND QUALIFICATION PURSUANT TO SUCH LAWS OR AN OPINION OF LEGAL COUNSEL SATISFACTORY TO THE CORPORATION THAT SUCH REGISTRATION AND QUALIFICATION IS NOT REQUIRED.

This Certifies that _____ *is the owner of* _____ *fully paid and non-assessable Shares of the above Corporation transferable only on the books of the Corporation by the holder hereof in person or by duly authorized Attorney upon surrender of this Certificate properly endorsed.*

In Witness Whereof, the Corporation has caused this Certificate to be signed by its duly authorized officers and to be sealed with the Seal of the Corporation.

Dated _____

_____ , *President*

_____ , *Secretary*

For value received, the undersigned hereby sells, assigns and transfers to _____

_____

_____ *Shares*

represented by the within Certificate, and does hereby irrevocably constitute and appoint _____

Attorney to transfer the said shares on the books of the within-named Corporation with full power of substitution in the premises.

Dated: _____

       In presence of _____

_____

NOTICE: The signature to this assignment must correspond with the name as written upon the face of this certificate in every particular without alteration or enlargement, or any change whatever.

For value received, the undersigned hereby sells, assigns and transfers to _____

PRINT OR TYPE NAME AND ADDRESS OF ASSIGNEE

_____

_____ *Shares*

represented by the within Certificate, and does hereby irrevocably constitute and appoint _____

Attorney to transfer the said shares on the books of the within-named Corporation with full power of substitution in the premises.

Dated: _____

In presence of _____

_____

NOTICE: The signature to this assignment must correspond with the name as written upon the face of this certificate in every particular without alteration or enlargement, or any change whatever.

From Whom Transferred

Dated _____

No. Original Shares	No. Original Certificate	No. of Shares Transferred

Received Certificate Number _____

For _____

This _____ day of _____

_____
SIGNATURE

NUMBER _____

SHARES _____

INCORPORATED UNDER THE LAWS OF CALIFORNIA

Common Shares

THE SHARES REPRESENTED BY THIS CERTIFICATE HAVE NOT BEEN REGISTERED OR QUALIFIED UNDER ANY FEDERAL OR STATE SECURITIES LAW. THEY HAVE BEEN ACQUIRED FOR INVESTMENT PURPOSES AND NOT WITH A VIEW TOWARD RESALE AND MAY NOT BE OFFERED FOR SALE, SOLD, TRANSFERRED, OR PLEDGED WITHOUT REGISTRATION AND QUALIFICATION PURSUANT TO SUCH LAWS OR AN OPINION OF LEGAL COUNSEL SATISFACTORY TO THE CORPORATION THAT SUCH REGISTRATION AND QUALIFICATION IS NOT REQUIRED.

This Certifies that _____ *is the owner of* _____ *fully paid and non-assessable Shares of the above Corporation transferable only on the books of the Corporation by the holder hereof in person or by duly authorized Attorney upon surrender of this Certificate properly endorsed.*

In Witness Whereof, the Corporation has caused this Certificate to be signed by its duly authorized officers and to be sealed with the Seal of the Corporation.

Dated _____

_____ *, President*

_____ *, Secretary*

For value received, the undersigned hereby sells, assigns and transfers to _____

_____

_____ *Shares*

represented by the within Certificate, and does hereby irrevocably constitute and appoint _____
Attorney to transfer the said shares on the books of the within-named Corporation with full power of substitution in the premises.

Dated: _____

In presence of _____

_____

NOTICE: The signature to this assignment must correspond with the name as written upon the face of this certificate in every particular without alteration or enlargement, or any change whatever.

Certificate Number ____

For _____ Shares

Issued To: _____

Dated _____

From Whom Transferred

Dated _____

No. Original Shares	No. Original Certificate	No. of Shares Transferred

---

Received Certificate Number ____

For _____ Shares

This _____ day of _____

_____
SIGNATURE

NUMBER _____

SHARES _____

INCORPORATED UNDER THE LAWS OF CALIFORNIA

Common Shares

THE SHARES REPRESENTED BY THIS CERTIFICATE HAVE NOT BEEN REGISTERED OR QUALIFIED UNDER ANY FEDERAL OR STATE SECURITIES LAW. THEY HAVE BEEN ACQUIRED FOR INVESTMENT PURPOSES AND NOT WITH A VIEW TOWARD RESALE AND MAY NOT BE OFFERED FOR SALE, SOLD, TRANSFERRED, OR PLEDGED WITHOUT REGISTRATION AND QUALIFICATION PURSUANT TO SUCH LAWS OR AN OPINION OF LEGAL COUNSEL SATISFACTORY TO THE CORPORATION THAT SUCH REGISTRATION AND QUALIFICATION IS NOT REQUIRED.

This Certifies that _____ *is the owner of* _____ *fully paid and non-assessable Shares of the above Corporation transferable only on the books of the Corporation by the holder hereof in person or by duly authorized Attorney upon surrender of this Certificate properly endorsed.*

In Witness Whereof, the Corporation has caused this Certificate to be signed by its duly authorized officers and to be sealed with the Seal of the Corporation.

Dated _____

_____ *, President*

_____ *, Secretary*

For value received, the undersigned hereby sells, assigns and

transfers to _____

PRINT OR TYPE NAME AND ADDRESS OF ASSIGNEE

_____

_____ *Shares*

represented by the within Certificate, and does hereby irrevocably

constitute and appoint _____

Attorney to transfer the said shares on the books of the within-

named Corporation with full power of substitution in the

premises.

Dated: _____

     In presence of _____

_____

NOTICE: The signature to this assignment must correspond with the name as written upon the face of this certificate in every particular without alteration or enlargement, or any change whatever.

NUMBER _____

SHARES _____

INCORPORATED UNDER THE LAWS OF CALIFORNIA

Common Shares

THE SHARES REPRESENTED BY THIS CERTIFICATE HAVE NOT BEEN REGISTERED OR QUALIFIED UNDER ANY FEDERAL OR STATE SECURITIES LAW. THEY HAVE BEEN ACQUIRED FOR INVESTMENT PURPOSES AND NOT WITH A VIEW TOWARD RESALE AND MAY NOT BE OFFERED FOR SALE, SOLD, TRANSFERRED, OR PLEDGED WITHOUT REGISTRATION AND QUALIFICATION PURSUANT TO SUCH LAWS OR AN OPINION OF LEGAL COUNSEL SATISFACTORY TO THE CORPORATION THAT SUCH REGISTRATION AND QUALIFICATION IS NOT REQUIRED.

This Certifies that _____ *is the owner of* _____ *fully paid and non-assessable Shares of the above Corporation transferable only on the books of the Corporation by the holder hereof in person or by duly authorized Attorney upon surrender of this Certificate properly endorsed.*

In Witness Whereof, the Corporation has caused this Certificate to be signed by its duly authorized officers and to be sealed with the Seal of the Corporation.

Dated _____

_____ *, President*

_____ *, Secretary*

For value received, the undersigned hereby sells, assigns and

transfers to _____

PRINT OR TYPE NAME AND ADDRESS OF ASSIGNEE

_____

_____ *Shares*

represented by the within Certificate, and does hereby irrevocably

constitute and appoint _____

Attorney to transfer the said shares on the books of the within-

named Corporation with full power of substitution in the

premises.

Dated: _____

In presence of _____

_____

**NOTICE: The signature to this assignment must correspond with the
name as written upon the face of this certificate in every particular
without alteration or enlargement, or any change whatever.**

For value received, the undersigned hereby sells, assigns and

transfers to _____

_____

_____ *Shares*

represented by the within Certificate, and does hereby irrevocably ·

constitute and appoint _____

Attorney to transfer the said shares on the books of the within-

named Corporation with full power of substitution in the

premises.

Dated: _____

      In presence of _____

_____

NOTICE: The signature to this assignment must correspond with the name as written upon the face of this certificate in every particular without alteration or enlargement, or any change whatever.

Index

A

Accident insurance, 89
Accountants, 32, 73, 137, 177, 178
  RLLPs for, 9, 33
Accounting methods, 167
Accounting period, 79, 167
  board resolution, 117, 123
  See also Tax year
Accredited investors, 58–59
Actuaries, 32, 73
Acupuncturists, 32
Agents
  changes, 161
  initial agent, 103
  officers as, 40
  partnerships, 10
Age requirements, incorporators, 42
Annual franchise tax. *See* Franchise tax
Annual meetings, 22, 110
  close corporations, 33
Annual Statement of Information filing, 161
Annual wage and tax statement, 169, 172
Apparent authority, 40
Appraisals, existing business assets, 127
Appreciated assets, tax considerations, 18, 77–78
Architects, 12, 32, 73
  RLLPs for, 9, 33
Articles of incorporation, 35, 100–107
  amendment of, 41
  board resolution, 115, 121–122
  cover letter, 104–105, 106
  delayed filing, 105
  filing fees, 22, 104, 105
  filing instructions, 104–105, 107
  immunity/indemnification provisions, 37–38, 39, 103–104
  initial directors in, 101, 103
  online filing, 93
  photocopies, 105
  sample form/instructions, 102–104
  share authorization provisions, 101, 103
  signatures, 104
Articles of organization, LLCs, 139
Assets. *See* Business assets; Corporate assets; Existing business assets
Attorneys. *See* Lawyers
Audiologists, 32
Authorized shares, 103, 127, 144

B

Bank accounts
  board resolution, 117–118, 124–125
  incorporation of prior businesses, 162
Bank loans, 15, 21, 44, 45, 49
Bankruptcy, 47, 165
Basis. *See* Tax basis
Benefits. *See* Employee benefits
Bill of sale, for assets transferred to corporation, 127, 151–153, 156
Board of directors. *See* Board resolutions; Directors; Directors' meetings
Board resolutions
  accounting period, 117, 123

articles of incorporation, 115, 121–122

bank accounts, 117–118, 124–125

corporate seal, 116, 123

employee compensation, 88

officer election and compensation, 122–123

principal executive office, 117, 123–124

S corporation election, 119, 125

Section 1244 stock qualification, 81, 119, 125

stock certificate adoption, 117, 123

Bookkeeping, 177–178

Borrowing money. *See* Loan entries; Promissory notes

Breach of duty, directors, 37, 39

Buildings. *See* Real estate

Bulk sales law, 88, 144–146

Business assets

of deceased sole proprietors, 7

See also Corporate assets; Existing business assets

Business loss deductibility, 17, 28, 77, 78

Business names. *See* Names

Business structures, 6–28

comparison chart, 25–28

conversions, 17, 27

corporation basics, 14–23

LLCs, 12–14

partnerships, 8–12

sole proprietorships, 6–8

See also specific types

Buy-sell agreements, 11, 163–166

Bylaws, 108–112

amendment of, 41, 49

basics, 108–109

board resolution, 115–116, 122

certification by secretary, 129

director provisions, 42, 110, 111–112

indemnification provision, 38–39

sample form/instructions, 109–112

shareholder meeting provisions, 110, 111

C

Calendar tax year, 79, 80, 167

California Corporations Code, online, 30, 177

California law. *See* State law

California taxes. *See* State taxes

Cancellation of debt, as payment for shares, 45, 46, 127, 128, 155

Capital contributions, 26, 43–45. *See also* Investors; Stock issuance

Capital gains

business asset sales/transfers, 82–86

stock sales profits, 81–82

Capitalization, 43–45, 48. *See also* Raising money; Stock issuance

Capital losses, 80–81

asset transfers to corporations, 85, 86

Cash, as payment for shares, 22, 45, 126, 127, 154. *See also* Section 351 exchanges

C corporations, 6. *See also* Corporations

CD-ROM, how to use, 180–185

Certificate of election to dissolve, 48

Certified public accountants, 177

Checks, signatures on, 118, 124

Chief financial officer. *See* Treasurer

Chiropractors, 32

Citizenship requirements, S corporations, 78

Clinical social workers, 32

Close corporations, 30, 32–34, 95, 108

Closely held corporations, 30–31, 44

cautions, 48

Collateral, for shareholder loans, 46

Commingling of funds, 1, 48

Committees, executive, 36

Community property

spousal sole proprietorships, 6–7

stock ownership, 146, 147–148

Compensation

directors, 36, 168

employees, 1–2, 16, 18, 23, 88

officers, 40–41, 116, 122–123

Conflicts of interest. *See* Self-interested transactions

Consideration for shares rule, limited offering exemption, 55

Consultants, 32, 73

Contracts
authority to bind business to, 10, 25, 40
board ratification, 35, 40
contracts benefiting directors, 36–37
pre-incorporation, 35

Controlling persons, 57

Copyrights, 84

Corporate assets
capitalization basics, 43–45
dissolution/sale and, 18, 47, 48, 77–78
dividend payouts and, 46
shareholder approval for sale/lease of, 41

Corporate formalities, 22, 48–49, 158. *See also* Meetings; Paperwork

Corporate franchise tax. *See* Franchise tax

Corporate kits, 107–108

Corporate names. *See* Names

Corporate personnel, 35–42, 122. *See also* Directors; Employees; Incorporators; Officers; Shareholders

Corporate powers, 34

Corporate promoters. *See* Incorporators

Corporate records book, 107–108, 129

Corporate seal, 108, 116, 123, 150

Corporate tax election, partnerships and LLCs, 10, 12–13, 16, 74

Corporations, 14–23
basics, 1–2, 6, 14
close corporations, 30, 32–34, 95
compared to other business structures, 25–28
disadvantages, 20, 22
domestic vs. foreign, 30
funding/capitalization, 2, 19–20, 21, 43–45, 48
limited liability protection, 1, 14–15
nonprofit corporations, 2, 30, 31
officer/director requirements, 42–43

organizational structure, 19–21
out-of-state corporations, 24
paperwork, 20, 22
perpetual existence, 21–22, 31
personal service corporations, 32, 73, 80
pre-incorporation activities, 35, 124
reorganizing as LLC, 17
switching to S corporation, 17
tax basics, 1, 15–18, 70–75, 167–173
termination, 25
types, 30–34
See also Closely held corporations; Incorporation; Professional corporations; S corporations

Court reporters, 32

Court-supervised dissolutions, 47

Cover letter, articles of incorporation, 104, 106

CPAs, 177

Creditors, notifying of incorporation, 144–146, 163

D

Damages
directors' breaches of duty, 37
personal liability for, 15

DBAs. *See* Fictitious business names

Death/withdrawal of owner, 21–22, 25
buy-sell agreements and, 163–164, 165
joint stock ownership and, 147–148
partnerships, 10
sole proprietorships, 7

Debt capital, 43, 44

Debts
bankruptcy, 47, 165
cancellation of, as payment for shares, 45, 46, 127, 128, 155
dissolution and, 47
dividend payouts and, 46
of prior businesses, 85, 87–88, 144–146, 153
tax debts, 15, 48, 87
See also Limited liability; Personal liability

Debt-to-equity ratios, 45

Defined-benefit plans, 89

Defined-contribution plans, 89

Delaware corporations, 24

Dentists, 32

Department of Corporations

  contact information, Appendix B

  Notice of Stock Transaction filing, 136, 138, 143

Dependents, insurance for, 89

Directors, 19, 21, 36–39

  actions benefiting, 36–37, 39

  actions requiring approval of, 40

  actions requiring shareholder approval, 37, 41

  bylaws provisions, 42, 110, 111

  close corporations, 33

  compensation, 36, 168

  duties and conflicts of interest, 36–37

  election, 41, 164

  immunity and indemnification, 37–39, 41, 104

  initial, 101, 103

  as inside shareholders, 46–47

  insurance for, 173

  mismanagement, 37–38, 41–42

  nonprofits, 31

  number of, 42–43, 103, 110

  potential for personal liability, 37, 47

  pre-incorporation contract ratification, 35

  removal, 41

  shareholder suits against, 37–38, 42

  See also Directors' meetings

Directors' meetings, 40, 48–49

  annual, 22, 110

  bylaws provisions, 110, 112

  first meeting, holding, 128–129

  first meeting minutes, instructions, 121–128

  first meeting minutes form, 113–120

  notice/waiver of notice, 114, 121, 129

  recordkeeping, 48

  voting rules, 110

  See also Board resolutions

Disability, of shareholder, 165

Disability insurance, 89, 172

Disclosure rules, stock offers, 56, 65

Dissolution. *See* Termination/dissolution

Dividends, 46–47

  compensation treated as, 88

  interest payments treated as, 45

  payout restrictions, 46–47

  PHC surtax and, 74

  taxation, 16, 44, 70–71, 73

  See also Shareholder distributions

Divorces, 165

Doctors, 12, 32

Domestic corporations, 30

Domestic production activities deduction, 72

Double taxation, 15–16, 44, 70–71

Duty of loyalty, directors, 36

E

EIN (employer identification number), 8, 124, 137, 168

Employee benefits, 18, 23, 28, 88–89

  S corporations, 79

  stock bonuses/options, 1–2, 18, 21, 103

Employees

  compensation, 1–2, 16, 18, 23, 88

  EIN requirement and, 8

  payroll taxes, 15, 167, 168–169, 171–172

  personal income taxes, 16, 70–71, 73, 75, 88–89, 170

  S corporations, 77, 170

  stock sales to, 57, 65

  workers' compensation insurance, 173

  See also Employee benefits

Employee stock ownership plans, 79

Employer Identification Number (EIN), 8, 124, 137, 168

Employers

  legal/tax responsibilities, 168–169, 171–172, 173

  state registration, 171

Employment Development Department (EDD)
  employer registration, 171
  tax reporting, 171–173
Employment taxes. *See* Payroll taxes
Engineers, 32, 73
Environmental fee, 173
Equity capital, 43, 44
Estate planning, 7, 147
Estimated tax payments, 70, 170
Executive committees, 36
Executive officers, 57. *See also* Officers
Executive team, 19. *See also* Officers
Existing business assets, transferring to
  corporation, 43, 82–88, 127–128
  bill of sale for, 127, 151–153
  bulk sales law compliance, 144–146
  for promissory note, 44, 85
  real estate and leases, 86–87, 151
Existing businesses, incorporating
  liabilities/debts, 85, 87–88, 144–146, 153
  names, 94
  postincorporation tasks, 162–163
  tax considerations, 43, 82–87
  timing, 86
  See also Existing business assets
Existing relationship shareholders (limited offering
  exemption), 57–58
Expense reimbursement
  directors, 36
  incorporators, 118, 124

F

Federal corporate income tax, 71–73, 74, 169–
  170
Federal securities law, 52, 53, 63–67, 130
  offering exemptions, 63–66, 130, 137
Federal tax basics, 71–75, 167–170
Fees, 93

articles of incorporation filing, 22, 104, 105
Board of Equalization environmental fee, 173
lawyers, 22, 176–177
LLC formation, 13
name reservation, 96–97
Notice of Stock Transaction filing, 142, 143
public offering filings, 53
SCOR filings, 53
FEIN (employer identification number), 8, 124,
  137, 168
FICA. *See* Social Security tax
Fictitious business names, 7, 94, 100, 161–162
Fiduciary duty
  directors, 36–37
  incorporators, 35
  officers, 40
  shareholders, 41
Filing fees. *See* Fees
Financial advisors. *See* Professional advisors; Tax
  advice
Fiscal year, 79, 80
Foreign citizens, S corporation citizenship
  requirements, 78
Foreign corporations, 30. *See also* Out-of-state
  corporations
Forms
  federal tax forms, 167–170
  Form U-7, 53
  how to use CD-ROM, 180–185
  making changes, 182, 185
  name reservation request, 98
  Statement of Information (Form SI-200 C), 161
  state tax forms, 71, 170–173
  See also IRS forms
Franchise tax, 13, 22, 79, 93
  basics, 70, 71, 170–171
Franchise Tax Board, 170

Form 100, 171
Form 3500, 71
See also State taxes
Franchising, 20–21
Fraud, 15, 42, 87
Fringe benefits. *See* Employee benefits
FUTA tax, 169

G

General partnerships, 9, 10. *See also* Partnership
   entries
Gifts of stock, 148, 165

H

Health care providers, 12, 32, 73
Health insurance, 89
Home-based businesses, 7–8
Home office deduction, 8

I

Immunity, of directors and officers, 37–38, 39, 41
Income splitting, 15–16, 71, 73, 74
Income taxes, business
   California franchise tax, 13, 22, 70, 71, 79, 93,
     170–171
   federal corporate income tax, 71–73, 74, 169–170
Income taxes, personal
   asset transfers to corporations and, 82–86
   business loss deductibility, 17, 28, 77, 78, 79, 86
   California personal income tax, 70–71
   corporate employees, 16, 70–71, 73, 75, 88–89
   dividend income, 16, 44, 70–71, 73, 88, 170
   double taxation, 15–16, 44, 70–71
   on employee benefits, 88–89
   federal income tax, 73–75, 168–169
   income from spousal businesses, 6–7

income splitting, 15–16, 71, 73, 74
   partners, 10
   payroll taxes, 15, 167, 168–169, 171–172
   S corporation income, 170
   self-employment taxes, 6, 77
   shares issued in return for services, 84
   sole proprietors, 1, 6–77
   stock gains/losses, 80–82
Income tax rates. *See* Tax rates
Incorporation
   articles of incorporation preparation/filing,
     100–107
   basics, 20, 22, 93
   bylaws preparation, 108–112
   costs, 22
   fees, 93
   first directors' meeting, 113–129
   name choice, 93–100
   notifying creditors, 144–146, 163
   organizational expenses, 118, 124–125
   out-of-state, 24
   postincorporation tasks, 161–166
   preincorporation activities, 35, 124–125
   professional help, 3
   records organization, 107–108
   shareholder representation letters, 129–136
   software for, 3, 93
   See also Corporations; Existing business entries;
     Stock issuance
Incorporators, 35, 42, 43–44
   expense reimbursement, 118, 124
Indemnification, of directors and officers, 38–39,
   41, 104
Independent contractors, 171
Initial Statement of Information, 161
Inside shareholders (limited offering exemption),
   56–57
Insurance, 8, 173–174
   as employee benefit, 89
   life insurance, 18, 89, 166

state unemployment and disability insurance, 171–172
workers' compensation, 173
Intangible property, as payment for shares, 84, 127
Intentional misconduct, 39
Interest payments, shareholder loans, 44, 45
Internal Revenue Service. *See* IRS
Investment representation rule, limited offering exemption, 54
Investors, 2, 19–20, 21
  limited partnerships, 9
  venture capital, 21
  See also Capitalization
Involuntary dissolutions, 47
IRC (Internal Revenue Code)
  personal holding company surtax, 74
  Section 351 exchanges, 44, 82–86
  Section 1202 capital gains tax exclusion, 81–82
  Section 1244 treatment for stock losses, 80–81
  small business corporation definition, 76
IRS (Internal Revenue Service)
  applying for EIN, 8, 124, 137, 168
  helpful publications, 167, 178
  and loans by shareholders, 45
  personal service corporation definition, 80
  and undercapitalization, 43
  See also IRS forms; Taxes and taxation
IRS forms
  Form 941, 168
  Form 1040, 82, 170
  Form 1065, 10, 13
  Form 1120, 169–170
  Form 1120-S, 170
  Form 1120-W, 170
  Form 1128, 80
  Form 2553, 17, 76, 80, 167
  Form 8832, 10, 12, 74
  Form 8903, 72
  Form SS-4, 124, 168
  Form W-2, 169, 172
  Form W-4, 168, 171
  Schedule C, 6
  Schedules K and K-1, 10, 13
Issued shares, 103

J

Joint ownership of shares, 125–126, 130–131, 146, 147–148, 163–164, 165
Joint tenancy, 147

K

Know-how, 84

L

Lawsuits
  indemnification of directors/officers, 38–39, 41, 104
  by shareholders, 37–38, 41–42
  See also Damages; Liability insurance; Limited liability
Lawyers, 12, 32, 73
  fees, 22, 176–177
  for incorporation help, 3, 22
  as professional advisors for limited offering exemption purposes, 137
  RLLPs for, 9, 33
  selecting and working with, 176–177
  for trademark searches, 99–100
  when to consult, 66–67, 136, 176
Leases, 86–87, 151
Legal obligations, authority to bind business to, 10, 25, 40
Legal research, 30, 53–54, 177
Legal structure. *See* Business structures; specific structures
Liabilities. *See* Debts

Liability
  of incorporators, 35
  issues when incorporating an existing business, 87–88
  malpractice liability, 9, 33
  See also Limited liability; Personal liability
Liability insurance, 8, 173–174
Licensed professionals, 12
  malpractice liability, 9, 33
  See also Professional corporations; Professional partnerships
Licenses and permits, 162, 172–173
Liens, 87
Life insurance, 18, 89, 166
Limited liability, 25
  corporate formalities and, 22, 48–49, 158
  corporate shareholders, 1, 14–15, 41
  denial/loss of, 1, 9, 15, 22, 48–49, 158
  exceptions, 14–15
  limited partners, 9
  LLC members, 12
  nonprofits, 31
  RLLP partners, 9, 33
  See also Personal liability
Limited liability companies. *See* LLCs
Limited offering exemption, 30, 45, 53–63, 144
  basics, 53–56
  examples, 60–63
  Notice of Stock Transaction, 136–143
  researching, 53–54
  shareholder representation letters, 54, 129–136
  shareholder suitability rules, 56–60, 130
  stock certificates and, 108
  35-shareholder rule, 60
Limited partnerships, 9, 13, 33
  RLLPs, 9, 33
Liquidation. *See* Termination/dissolution
Litigation. *See* Lawsuits
Living trusts, 7, 147

LLCs (limited liability companies), 6, 12–14, 16, 17
  compared to other structures, 25–28
  corporate tax status for, 10, 12–13, 16, 74
  vs. S corporations, 76, 78–79
Loan guarantees, 15, 44
  for directors/officers, 37, 41
Loans, 19, 21, 22, 44
  approval/authorization, 49
  to directors or officers, 37, 41
  loss deductibility and, 79
  by shareholders to corporation, 44–45, 79
  stock issuance in return for cancellation of debt, 45, 46, 127, 128, 155
  See also Promissory notes
Losses
  on asset transfers to corporations, 85, 86
  deductibility, 17, 28, 86
  deductibility, S corporation shareholders, 77, 78, 79
  stock losses, 80–81

M

Major shareholders (limited offering exemption), 58–59
Malpractice liability, 9, 33
Management
  basics, 19–21, 25, 36
  close corporations, 33
  LLCs, 13
  mismanagement, 37–38, 39, 42
  partnerships, 9, 10
Marriage and family therapists, 32
Married couples, 6–7
  buy-sell agreements for, 163
  divorces, 165
  how to take title to stock, 146, 147–148
  insurance for spouses/children, 89

joint stock ownership, 125–126, 130–131, 146, 147–148

limited offering exemption and, 60

Material disclosure. *See* Disclosure rules

Material financial interest. *See* Self-interested transactions

Medical benefits, 18, 89

Meeting minutes, 22

first directors' meeting, 113–129

Meetings

annual, 22, 33, 110

See also Directors' meetings; Shareholders' meetings

Minutes. *See* Meeting minutes

Mismanagement, 37–38, 39, 42

Mortgages, property transferred to corporation, 151

Mutual benefit nonprofits, 31

N

Names, 93–100

in articles of incorporation, 103

checking availability, 95–96

conflicts/rights issues, 94, 96

fictitious name registration, 7, 94, 100, 161–162

online resources, 93, 96, 99

personal, as corporate names, 95, 99

reserving, 96–97, 98

state requirements, 94–95

Name searches, 97, 99–100

Naturopaths, 32

Negligence, 42

No-advertising rule, limited offering exemption, 55

Nonprofit corporations, 2, 30, 31

Notice of meetings

directors' meetings, 121

waiver of notice, first directors' meeting, 114, 121, 129

Notice of Stock Transaction, 55–56, 136–143, 158

filing fee, 142, 143

form and instructions, 138–142

how to file, 136, 138, 143

Notice to Creditors of Bulk Sale, 144–146

Nurses, 32

O

Offering exemptions

federal, 63–66, 130, 137

state, 53, 54

See also Limited offering exemption

Officers, 19, 40–41

board resolution electing, 116, 122–123

close corporations, 33

compensation, 40–41, 116, 122–123

duties and authority, 40

immunity/indemnification, 38–39, 41, 104

as inside shareholders, 46–47

insurance for, 173

loans/guarantees for, 41

reliance on officer reports, 36

required positions, 42–43, 122

signatures on corporate documents, 158

See also specific offices

Offices of the corporation, 117, 123–124

One-person corporations, 42–43, 110, 122

Online resources

California Corporations Code, 30, 177

California Secretary of State, 93

California state website, 93

EIN application, 168

legal research, 30

online articles filing, 93

name searches/reservation, 93, 96, 99

Notice of Stock Transaction filing, 136, 138

SEC website, 67

Statement of Information filing, 161

Operating agreements, LLCs, 13

Optometrists, 32

Ordinary losses, 80–81. *See also* Losses

Organizational expenses, 118, 124–125. *See also* Start-up expenses

Organizational structure, 19–21

Osteopaths, 32

Out-of-state corporations, 24, 30

Out-of-state stock sales, 52

Owners
legal authority of, 10, 25
See also Investors; Shareholders

Ownership interest, profit/loss allocation and, 11, 17–18

Ownership transfers
gifts/inheritance, 147–148, 163, 165
restrictions on, 26, 27, 34, 65
See also Stock sales

P

Paper meetings, 49

Paperwork, 20, 22, 48–49
dissolution filings, 48
postincorporation paperwork, 161–166
See also Incorporation; Meeting minutes

Partnership agreements, 8, 10, 11

Partnerships, 8–12, 17
compared to other structures, 25–28
limited partnerships and RLLPs, 9, 13, 33
spousal partnerships, 6–7
taxes, 1, 6–7, 10, 17

Passive investors
corporate shareholders, 2, 19–20, 21
limited partners, 9
in LLCs, 13

Pass-through taxation, 15
LLCs, 12–13
See also S corporations

Patent and Trademark Office (PTO), 99, 100

Patents, 84

Payroll taxes, 15, 167, 168–169, 171–172

PDF forms, how to use, 183–184

Pension plans, 88–89

Performing artists, 73

Permits and licenses, 162, 172–173

Perpetual existence, 21–22, 31

Personal benefit. *See* Self-interested transactions

Personal holding companies (PHCs), 74

Personal income tax. *See* Income taxes, personal

Personal liability, 25
for debts of prior business after incorporation, 87–88
directors and officers, 37, 47, 104
general partners, 10
incorporators, 35
for malpractice, 9, 33
piercing the corporate veil, 15, 43, 48–49, 158
signatures on corporate documents and, 158
sole proprietors, 7–8
for taxes, 15
undercapitalization and, 43
See also Limited liability

Personal loan guarantees, 15, 44

Personal names, as corporate names, 95, 99

Personal service corporations, 32, 73, 80

Pharmacists, 32

PHCs (personal holding companies), 74

Physical therapists, 32

Physician's assistants, 32

Piercing the corporate veil, 15, 43, 48–49, 158

Podiatrists, 32

Postincorporation tasks, 161–166

Preincorporation activities, 35, 124–125

President, 40, 122

Principal executive office, 117, 123–124

Privately held profit corporations, 30–31

Private offerings
small offering exemption, 54
under federal exemptions, 63–67, 130, 137
See also Limited offering exemption

Probate, 7, 147, 148

Professional advice
reliance on, 36, 59
See also Lawyers; Tax advice

Professional advisors, for limited offering exemption, 59, 130, 135–136, 137

Professional corporations, 2, 9, 12, 30, 31–32

Professional partnerships, 33

    RLLPs, 9, 33

Professional services, 12

    malpractice liability, 9, 33

    See also Professional corporations; Professional partnerships

Profit corporations, 30–31, 32

Profit distributions

    by nonprofits, 31

    See also Dividends; Shareholder distributions

Profit/loss allocation

    close corporations, 33

    LLCs, 13, 17

    partnerships, 10, 11, 18

    S corporations, 17–18, 78–79

    special allocations, 17, 33, 78–79

Profits, retained/reinvested. *See* Retained earnings

Profit-sharing plans, 88–89

Promissory notes, 45

    for assets of existing business, 44, 85

    as payment for shares, 46, 127

    See also Loans

Promoters

    stock sales to, 57, 65

    See also Incorporators

Property

    as payment for shares, 46, 84, 85, 126, 127, 156

    real estate, 49, 86–87, 151

    See also Business assets; Corporate assets; Existing business assets

Property insurance, 173

Psychologists, 32

PTO (Patent and Trademark Office), 99, 100

Public offerings, 2, 53, 65

Punitive damages, directors' breaches of duty, 37

Q

Quorum requirements, directors' meetings, 110

R

Raising money, 2, 21, 26

    initial capitalization, 43–45

    See also Investors; Loans; Stock issuance

Real estate, 49, 86–87, 151

Receipts, for payments for shares, 151–157

    bill of sale for assets of prior business, 127, 151–153

    bill of sale for specific property, 156

    cash payments, 154

    debt cancellation, 155

    past services, 157

Recordkeeping, 48, 167

    corporate records book, 107–108, 129

    See also Meeting minutes; Paperwork

Registered limited liability partnerships (RLLPs), 9, 33

Regulation D exemptions, 58–59, 63–67, 137

Relatives of shareholders (limited offering exemption), 60

Release No. 33-4552 (SEC), 64, 65

Residency requirements, S corporations, 78

Retained earnings, 15–16, 23, 32, 71, 73, 75

    dividend payouts and, 46

    partnerships, 10

    personal service corporations, 32

    S corporations, 18

    sole proprietorships, 7

    unreasonable accumulations, 73

Retirement plans, 88–89

RLLPs (registered limited liability partnerships), 9, 33

Rule 504 (SEC), 67

Rule 505 (SEC), 67

Rule 506 (SEC), 64, 66

S

Salaries
   officers, 40–41, 116, 122–123
   See also Employees: compensation
Sales tax, 172–173
Schedule C, 6
Schedules K and K-1, 10, 13
SCOR (Small Corporate Offering Registration), 53
S corporations, 6, 16, 71, 74
   basics, 17–18, 75–79
   board resolution, 119, 125
   vs. LLCs, 76, 78–79
   making tax election, 76–77, 167
   pass-through of losses, 77, 78, 79
   status revocation/termination, 76–77
   tax return filing, 170
   tax year, 76, 80, 167
SEC. *See* Securities and Exchange Commission
Secretary of corporation, 42, 122, 129
Secretary of State, 93
   checking name availability, 95–96, 99
   contact information, Appendix B
   how to use forms, 183–184
   Statement of Information filing, 161
Section 351 exchanges, 44, 82–86
Section 1202 capital gains tax exclusion, 81–82
Section 1244 treatment, for stock losses, 80–81, 119, 125
Securities Act, 52, 63
Securities and Exchange Commission (SEC), 53, 63
   stock offering exemptions, 63–67
   website, 67
Securities laws, 27, 45, 52–53
   federal, 52, 53, 63–67, 130
   state, 52, 53
   See also Limited offering exemption
Security, for shareholder loans, 46
Self-employed health insurance deduction, 89
Self-employment taxes, 6, 77

Self-interested transactions
   directors, 36–37, 39
   incorporators, 35
   officers, 41
   shareholder approval, 37, 41
Seller's permit, 172–173
Service marks, 97, 99, 100. *See also* Trademarks
Services, as payment for shares
   future, 46, 127
   past, 45, 46, 84, 127, 128, 157
Shareholder distributions, 44, 46–47, 48. *See also* Dividends
Shareholder-employees. *See* Employees
Shareholder loans
   from corporation, 46, 127
   to corporation, 44–45, 79
Shareholder representation letters, 54, 129–136
Shareholders, 41–42
   actions requiring approval of, 37, 41, 47
   death/withdrawal of, 21–22, 25, 147–148, 163–164, 165
   lawsuits by, 37–38, 41–42
   limited liability protection, 1, 14–15, 41
   limited offering exemption suitability, 56–60, 130
   loans to corporation, 44–45, 79
   number of, 25
   passive investors, 2, 19–20, 21
   voting rights, 41
Shareholders' agreements, close corporations, 33–34
Shareholder's derivative lawsuits, 37–38, 42
Shareholders' meetings, 48–49
   annual, 22, 110
   bylaws provisions, 110, 111
   recordkeeping, 48–49
   special meetings, 183–185
   voting rules, 41
Shareholder suitability rules, limited offering exemption, 56–60, 130

Share price
  in buy-sell agreements, 164, 165–166
  initial, 127, 141, 142, 144, 150
Shares. *See* Stock entries
Signatures on corporate documents, 158
  articles of incorporation, 104
  checks, 118, 124
  minutes of first directors' meeting, 128, 129
  receipts for share payments, 153
  stock certificates, 150, 158
Small business corporations, 76
Small business stock, for Section 1202 purposes, 82
Small Corporate Offering Registration (SCOR), 53
Small corporations. *See* Closely held corporations
Small offering exemption, 54
Social Security tax, 16, 168. *See also* Payroll taxes;
  Self-employment taxes
Social workers, 32
Software, for incorporation, 3, 93
Sole proprietorships, 6–8
  compared to other structures, 25–28
  spousal businesses, 6–7
  taxes, 1, 6–7
Sophisticated shareholders (limited offering
  exemption), 58
Special allocations, 17, 33, 78–79
Speech-language pathologists, 32
Spousal partnerships, 6–7
Spousal sole proprietorships, 6–7
Spouses. *See* Married couples
Start-up expenses, 124–125. *See also*
  Organizational expenses
Start-up funding, 26. *See also* Capitalization;
  Raising money; Stock issuance
State Board of Equalization, 172–173
State law
  bulk sales law, 88
  California Corporations Code online, 30, 177
  LLC law, 13
  partnership law, 8, 10, 11

securities law, 52, 53, 54
  See also Limited offering exemption
Statement of Information, 161
State taxes
  basics, 70–71, 170–173
  corporate income (franchise) tax, 13, 22, 70, 71,
    79, 93, 170–171
  payroll taxes, 167, 171–172
  personal income tax, 70–71
  unemployment and disability insurance, 171–172
Stepped-up tax basis, 147–148
Stock
  authorized shares, 103, 127, 144
  joint ownership, 125–126, 130–131, 146,
    147–148, 163–164, 165
  multiple share classes, 2, 21, 76, 103
  tax basis in, 79, 83, 147–148
Stock bonuses/options, 1–2, 18, 21, 103
Stock certificates, 108, 143, 146–151
  board resolution, 117, 123
  distributing, 151, 158
  extras, 158
  filling out, 148, 150
  jointly-owned stock, 146, 147–148
  names on, 146
  sample, 149
Stock gifts, 148, 165
Stock issuance, 143–158
  after initial issuance, 54
  basics, 43, 45–46, 52, 127, 144
  board resolution authorizing, 120, 125–128
  bulk sales law compliance, 144–146
  for cancellation of indebtedness, 45, 46, 127,
    128, 155
  for cash, 22, 45, 126, 154
  disclosure rules, 56, 65, 130
  for existing business assets, 43, 82–88, 127–128,
    144–146, 151–153
  federal law/exemptions, 52, 53, 63–67, 130
  for future services, 46, 127

how to take title, 146–148

limited offering exemption, 30, 45, 53–63, 129

Notice of Stock Transaction, 136–143, 158

number of shares to authorize, 103, 127

out-of-state offerings, 52

for past services, 45, 46, 84, 127, 128, 157

for promissory note, 46, 127

for property, 46, 84, 85, 127, 156

public offerings, 2, 53, 65

receipts for payments, 127, 151–157

Section 351 exchanges, 44, 82–86

securities law compliance basics, 27, 52, 66–67

shareholder representation letters, 54, 129–136

transfer restrictions and, 65

See also Capitalization; Limited offering exemption; Stock certificates

Stock options/bonuses, 1–2, 18, 21, 103

Stock ownership plans, 79

Stock sales/transfers

buybacks by corporation, 20, 21, 165–166

buy-sell agreements, 163–166

restrictions on, 26, 27, 34, 65, 165

share valuation, 164, 165–166

taxation of stock gains/losses, 80–82

See also Stock issuance

T

Taxable gifts, 148

Tax advice, 3, 85, 177–178

Tax basis

in property transferred to corporation, 82–83, 85–86

stepped-up, 147–148

in stock, 79, 83, 147–148

Tax deadlines, IRS publication, 167

Tax debts, 15, 48, 87

Tax deductions

business loss deductibility, 17, 28, 77, 78, 79, 86

domestic production activities deduction, 72

employee compensation and benefits, 88–89

home office deduction, 8

organizational expenses, 124–125

stock losses, 80–81

Tax elections

approval of, 49

corporate tax election by partnerships/LLCs, 10, 12–13, 16, 74

S corporation tax election, 16, 17, 71, 76–77, 167

Taxes and taxation, 70–89

business termination and, 10, 18, 28

comparison chart, 27–28

corporate tax basics, 1, 15–18, 70–75, 167–173

double taxation, 15–16, 44, 70–71

estimated tax payments, 70

income splitting, 15–16, 71, 73, 74

and incorporation of existing business, 43, 82–87

LLC tax basics, 12–13

out-of-state corporations, 24

partnerships, 1, 6–7, 10

personal holding company penalty, 74

personal liability for business taxes, 15

retained earnings, 7, 10, 15–16, 32, 72, 73, 75

sales tax, 172–173

S corporations, 6, 16, 17, 71, 75–79

shareholder loans and, 44–45, 79

sole proprietorships, 1, 6–7

state corporate franchise tax, 13, 22, 70, 71, 79, 93, 170–171

See also Income taxes; Payroll taxes

Tax forms

federal, 167–170

first return and tax year, 123, 169–170

LLCs, 13

partnerships, 6–7, 10

sole proprietorships, 6–7

spousal businesses, 6–7

state, 170–173

See also IRS forms

Tax-free exchanges. *See* Section 351 exchanges
Tax rates
    corporate vs. individual, 75
    dividend income, 16, 44, 73
    federal corporate income tax, 16, 70, 71, 72, 75
    income splitting and, 15–16, 71, 73
    personal service corporations, 32, 73
    PHC income, 74
    professional corporations, 32
    state franchise tax, 70, 71
Tax resources, 167, 178
    professional advice, 3, 85, 177–178
Tax return preparation, 178
Tax returns. *See* Tax forms
Tax year, 76, 79, 80, 123, 167
    first tax year, 123, 169–170
Tenancy in common, 148
Termination/dissolution, 22, 47–48
    comparison chart, 25
    liquidation proceeds, 41
    nonprofits, 31
    paperwork, 48
    partnerships, 10, 11, 163
    of prior business, 162–163
    to reorganize as LLC, 17
    shareholder approval, 41, 47, 48
    sole proprietorships, 7
    tax issues, 18, 28, 77–78, 80–82
Therapists, 32
Third-party claims, 37, 38
35-shareholder rule, limited offering exemption, 60
Title to stock, 146–148
Tort liability, 12. *See also* Limited liability
Trademarks, 84
    corporate names and, 94, 97, 99–100
Trade names, 97, 99
Treasurer, 40, 122
Two-person corporations, 42–43

U

Undercapitalization, 43
Unemployment insurance, 171–172
Unemployment tax, 169
Uniform Partnership Act, 8
U.S. Patent and Trademark Office (PTO), 99, 100
Unlawful/unauthorized transactions, 15, 39

V

Valuation
    initial shares, 127, 141, 142, 144, 150
    of noncash payments for stock, 46, 127, 128
    share price in buy-sell agreements, 164, 165–166
Venture capital, 21
Veterinarians, 32
Vice president, 122
Voluntary dissolutions. *See* Termination/dissolution
Voting
    bank/investor voting rights, 2, 21
    directors' meetings, 110
    nonvoting share classes, 21
    quorum requirements, 110
    self-interested transactions, 36–37
    shareholder voting, 41

W

Wages. *See* Employees: compensation
Waiver of notice, first directors' meeting, 114, 121, 129
Withdrawal of owner. *See* Death/withdrawal of owner
Withholding certificates/taxes, 168, 171, 172
Workers' compensation insurance, 173

CATALOG

BUSINESS

	PRICE	CODE
Business Buyout Agreements (Book w/CD-ROM)	$49.99	BSAG
The CA Nonprofit Corporation Kit (Binder w/CD-ROM)	$69.99	CNP
California Workers' Comp: How to Take Charge When You're Injured on the Job	$34.99	WORK
The Complete Guide to Buying a Business (Book w/CD-ROM)	$24.99	BUYBU
The Complete Guide to Selling a Business (Book w/CD-ROM)	$24.99	SELBU
Consultant & Independent Contractor Agreements (Book w/CD-ROM)	$29.99	CICA
The Corporate Records Handbook (Book w/CD-ROM)	$69.99	CORMI
Create Your Own Employee Handbook (Book w/CD-ROM)	$49.99	EMHA
Dealing With Problem Employees	$44.99	PROBM
Deduct It! Lower Your Small Business Taxes	$34.99	DEDU
Effective Fundraising for Nonprofits	$24.99	EFFN
The Employer's Legal Handbook	$39.99	EMPL
Essential Guide to Federal Employment Laws	$39.99	FEMP
Form a Partnership (Book W/CD-ROM)	$39.99	PART
Form Your Own Limited Liability Company (Book w/CD-ROM)	$44.99	LIAB
Home Business Tax Deductions: Keep What You Earn	$34.99	DEHB
How to Form a Nonprofit Corporation (Book w/CD-ROM)—National Edition	$49.99	NNP
How to Form a Nonprofit Corporation in California (Book w/CD-ROM)	$49.99	NON
How to Form Your Own California Corporation (Binder w/CD-ROM)	$59.99	CACI
How to Form Your Own California Corporation (Book w/CD-ROM)	$34.99	CCOR
How to Write a Business Plan (Book w/CD-ROM)	$34.99	SBS
Incorporate Your Business (Book w/CD-ROM)	$49.99	NIBS
Investors in Your Backyard (Book w/CD-ROM)	$24.99	FINBUS
The Job Description Handbook	$29.99	JOB
Legal Guide for Starting & Running a Small Business	$34.99	RUNS
Legal Forms for Starting & Running a Small Business (Book w/CD-ROM)	$29.99	RUNSF
LLC or Corporation?	$24.99	CHENT
The Manager's Legal Handbook	$39.99	ELBA
Marketing Without Advertising	$20.00	MWAD
Music Law (Book w/CD-ROM)	$39.99	ML
Negotiate the Best Lease for Your Business	$24.99	LESP
Nolo's Guide to Social Security Disability (Book w/CD-ROM)	$29.99	QSS
Nolo's Quick LLC	$29.99	LLCQ
The Performance Appraisal Handbook	$29.99	PERF
The Small Business Start-up Kit (Book w/CD-ROM)	$24.99	SMBU
The Small Business Start-up Kit for California (Book w/CD-ROM)	$24.99	OPEN
Starting & Running a Successful Newsletter or Magazine	$29.99	MAG
Tax Deductions for Professionals	$34.99	DEPO
Tax Savvy for Small Business	$36.99	SAVVY
Whoops! I'm in Business	$19.99	WHOO
Working for Yourself: Law & Taxes for Independent Contractors, Freelancers & Consultants	$39.99	WAGE
Working With Independent Contractors (Book w/CD-ROM)	$29.99	HICI
Your Crafts Business: A Legal Guide (Book w/CD-ROM)	$26.99	VART
Your Limited Liability Company: An Operating Manual (Book w/CD-ROM)	$49.99	LOP
Your Rights in the Workplace	$29.99	YRW

CONSUMER

	PRICE	CODE
How to Win Your Personal Injury Claim	$29.99	PICL
Nolo's Encyclopedia of Everyday Law	$29.99	EVL
Nolo's Guide to California Law	$24.99	CLAW

Prices subject to change.

ORDER 24 HOURS A DAY @ www.nolo.com
Call 800-728-3555 • Mail or fax the order form in this book

	PRICE	CODE

ESTATE PLANNING & PROBATE

8 Ways to Avoid Probate	$19.99	PRAV
Estate Planning Basics	$21.99	ESPN
The Executor's Guide: Settling a Loved One's Estate or Trust	$34.99	EXEC
How to Probate an Estate in California	$49.99	PAE
Make Your Own Living Trust (Book w/CD-ROM)	$39.99	LITR
Nolo's Simple Will Book (Book w/CD-ROM)	$36.99	SWIL
Plan Your Estate	$44.99	NEST
Quick & Legal Will Book (Book w/CD-ROM)	$19.99	QUIC
Special Needs Trust: Protect Your Child's Financial Future (Book w/CD-ROM)	$34.99	SPNT

FAMILY MATTERS

Always Dad	$16.99	DIFA
Building a Parenting Agreement That Works	$24.99	CUST
The Complete IEP Guide	$34.99	IEP
Divorce & Money: How to Make the Best Financial Decisions During Divorce	$34.99	DIMO
Divorce Without Court	$29.99	DWCT
Do Your Own California Adoption: Nolo's Guide for Stepparents and Domestic Partners (Book w/CD-ROM)	$34.99	ADOP
Every Dog's Legal Guide: A Must-Have for Your Owner	$19.99	DOG
Get a Life: You Don't Need a Million to Retire Well	$24.99	LIFE
The Guardianship Book for California	$34.99	GB
A Legal Guide for Lesbian and Gay Couples	$34.99	LG
Living Together: A Legal Guide (Book w/CD-ROM)	$34.99	LTK
Nolo's IEP Guide: Learning Disabilities	$29.99	IELD
Parent Savvy	$19.99	PRNT
Prenuptial Agreements: How to Write a Fair & Lasting Contract (Book w/CD-ROM)	$34.99	PNUP
Work Less, Live More	$17.99	RECL

GOING TO COURT

Beat Your Ticket: Go To Court & Win! (National Edition)	$21.99	BEYT
The Criminal Law Handbook: Know Your Rights, Survive the System	$39.99	KYR
Everybody's Guide to Small Claims Court (National Edition)	$29.99	NSCC
Everybody's Guide to Small Claims Court in California	$29.99	CSCC
Fight Your Ticket & Win in California	$29.99	FYT
How to Change Your Name in California	$29.99	NAME
Nolo's Deposition Handbook	$29.99	DEP
Represent Yourself in Court: How to Prepare & Try a Winning Case	$39.99	RYC
Win Your Lawsuit: A Judge's Guide to Representing Yourself in California Superior Court	$29.99	SLWY

HOMEOWNERS, LANDLORDS & TENANTS

California Tenants' Rights	$27.99	CTEN
Deeds for California Real Estate	$24.99	DEED
Every Landlord's Legal Guide (National Edition, Book w/CD-ROM)	$44.99	ELLI
Every Landlord's Guide to Finding Great Tenants (Book w/CD-ROM)	$19.99	FIND
Every Landlord's Tax Deduction Guide	$34.99	DELL
Every Tenant's Legal Guide	$29.99	EVTEN
For Sale by Owner in California	$29.99	FSBO
How to Buy a House in California	$29.99	BHCA
The California Landlord's Law Book: Rights & Responsibilities (Book w/CD-ROM)	$44.99	LBRT
The California Landlord's Law Book: Evictions (Book w/CD-ROM)	$44.99	LBEV
Leases & Rental Agreements	$29.99	LEAR
Neighbor Law: Fences, Trees, Boundaries & Noise	$26.99	NEI
Renters' Rights (National Edition)	$24.99	RENT

IMMIGRATION

Becoming A U.S. Citizen: A Guide to the Law, Exam and Interview	$24.99	USCIT
Fiancé & Marriage Visas (Book w/CD-ROM)	$34.99	IMAR
How to Get a Green Card	$29.99	GRN

ORDER 24 HOURS A DAY @ www.nolo.com
Call 800-728-3555 • Mail or fax the order form in this book